PRAISE FOR
DOING WHAT JESUS DID

This is a great read! John and Sonja Decker understand what people need to know and understand about the Kingdom of God to be ministering people who can serve in the life-flow of Jesus Christ. In my opinion, every leader in today's church needs to read this book.

Jim Hayford, Sr., Senior Pastor
Eastside Foursquare Church, Bothell, Washington

Doing What Jesus Did is one of the most practical tools I have ever seen for equipping the saints. John and Sonja are anointed teachers who have shared their knowledge and insight with Christian leaders in city churches, rural congregations, and in meeting places in many foreign countries. Their wisdom is intensely practical and translates across all ethnic and social barriers. I highly recommend this book to men and women who want to base their ministry on a foundation that is scripturally solid and enduring.

Dr. Cliff Hanes, Vice President, International
Foursquare Churches, Los Angeles, California

What a treasure chest of practical guidelines and stories! Certainly 21st century Christianity is too much about theory and too little about practice. Theoretical, philosophical, doctrinal Christianity was meant to be a launching pad for powerful, personal, experiential Christianity. I hope every believer gets to discover for himself/herself the rich treasures in *Doing What Jesus Did.*

Ken Johnson, Senior Pastor
Westside Church, Bend, Oregon

PRAISE FOR
DOING WHAT JESUS DID

Doing What Jesus Did is a captivating book. It is biblical and balanced, simple and sound, informative and inspiring, practical and proven—an extremely valuable tool to equip the saints for the work of ministry in doing what Jesus did. John and Sonja Decker not only talk about "doing the stuff," they do it and show others how to do it—the works of Jesus, including miracles.

After more than thirty years of "doing the stuff" around the world, the Deckers are experienced practitioners and gifted trainers in leading others into supernatural ministry, both in the marketplace and the meeting place. They have discovered how to multiply ministry through the "training of trainers" who learn six essential and reproducible ministry strategies Jesus Himself modeled and taught His disciples—winning the lost, empowering for ministry, healing the sick, hearing God's voice, knowing the Spirit's leading, and casting out demons.

Doing What Jesus Did is the best way to communicate and demonstrate the Gospel "in all the world as a witness to all nations" as we anticipate the end of this age and the return of our Savior in power and great glory."

Dr. John L. Amstutz
Missions Trainer and Consultant
Foursquare Missions International
Fresno, California

DWJD

DOING WHAT JESUS DID

Ministering in the Power of the Holy Spirit

JOHN AND SONJA DECKER

Doing What Jesus Did

John and Sonja Decker

COPYRIGHT © **2003** by
Christ's Ambassadors International
P.O. Box 3631, Bend, Oregon 97707

ISBN 0-9728621-0-2

Printed in the United States of America

Contents

Preface

This book is an invitation to all Christians to learn how to move into the supernatural realm in which Jesus said we could enter. It means learning six essential ministry strategies that Jesus prescribes for effective discipleship. He said we would have to do what He did to get the same results that He did. We invite believers worldwide to join an expanding army of courageous ministers that are daring to believe for miraculous results. We are encouraging Christians to learn how to accomplish a series of personal ministry strategies that will help usher in the final ingathering of souls and Jesus Christ's second coming. The six ministry skills we will address are:

- Leading People to Christ

- Leading Christians into the Holy Spirit Baptism

- Learning How to Heal the Sick

- Hearing from God

- Healing the Sick by Revelation

- Dealing with Demons

Doing What Jesus Did

This book is intended to help Christians do what Jesus said they could do, including the miracles. We have framed our principles, insights, and recommendations around a large number of scripture passages. After every scripture reference there are suggestions of how to put God's Word into practice. We identify these as **DWJD** application points. These are intended to help us do what Jesus wants us to do. The authors have *italicized some words and phrases* to emphasize key points that should be examined carefully.

James 1:22-25
But be doers of the word, and not hearers only, deceiving yourselves. For if anyone is a hearer of the word and not a doer, he is like a man observing his natural face in a mirror; for he observes himself, goes away, and immediately forgets what kind of man he was. But he who looks into the perfect law of liberty and continues in it, and is not a forgetful hearer but a doer of the work, this one will be blessed in what he does. NKJV

DWJD

Every Christian's mission should be to put into practice what Scripture tells them to do. This Scripture says we will be blessed if we do what God's Word says. Our mission in this book is to encourage believers to not only hear the Word, but to *do it*.

John and Sonja Decker
Bend, Oregon

Acknowledgments

Thanks...

To our gracious God who has called all Christians to be like His Son Jesus Christ and to do the things He did.

To the International Church of the Foursquare Gospel, our wonderful church family, where people are loved, accepted and forgiven. We, with you, are contending for our supernatural heritage.

To Jim Hayford, Sr., Senior Pastor, Eastside Foursquare Church, Bothell, Washington, who has been a loving pastor and wise counselor over the years.

To Dr. John Amstutz, Missions Trainer and Consultant, Foursquare Missions International, who encouraged us to write *The Ambassadors Series* curriculum and this book. He took time to read every word of the manuscripts and to give us invaluable input.

To R. Larry Shelton, Th.D., Richard B. Parker Professor of Theology, George Fox Evangelical Seminary, Portland, Oregon, who has assured us that our theology and conclusions are sound and has encouraged us along the way.

To Greg and Karen Fry, our dear friends and co-laborers, who spent many hours of their busy schedules proofreading the manuscript and helping us laugh along the way. We treasure your friendship.

To the leadership of the Full Gospel Business Men's Fellowship International for unlimited opportunities to learn how to minister in the power and revelation of the Holy Spirit.

Introduction

WHO'S DOING IT?

Initiating a conversation about Jesus to pre-Christians is intimidating for most Christians in America. The thought of witnessing to friends, co-workers, or relatives about God produces fears of instant rejection, heated arguments, and being called a Bible-thumper. They say, "Who needs that? Forget it. Let the Pastor do it. That's what we pay him for."

We remember the first people we led to Christ. We experienced all the initial emotions of witnessing: fear of failure, stumbling over Scripture, and wishing we had better prepared our thoughts. What was amazing is how quickly the Holy Spirit took over in each occasion. The mere mention of having a personal relationship with a loving God caused Him to manifest in our midst. The rest of the conversations continued in a supernatural sort of way. Afterwards, joy and excitement flooded our hearts. We could only say, "God, You are so awesome!"

From those moments on we were hooked on doing what Jesus did. As we continued to share about the Lord and offer to pray for people, the more the Lord would manifest Himself. We started praying for the sick and God healed them! Our first attempts were pathetic, almost apologetic. But, we discovered that God could use amateurs. He could use untrained but willing disciples that would risk praying for people just to see what God would do.

Many who read this book have never done these things. Many people who profess Christ as their Savior want to, but lack the confidence. This is the main reason we wrote this book. It is our sincere prayer that Christian readers would at least consider learning how to do some of the things Jesus did that are presented in the following chapters. With some practical training that culminates in a series of positive experiences, today's Christians can become effective witnesses for Christ. They are then prepared to successfully fulfill their part of the Great Commission. It is our conviction that these last instructions given by Jesus Christ, recorded below, are for every person claiming to be a follower of Him.

Matthew 28:19-20
"Go therefore and make disciples of all the nations, baptizing them in the name of the Father and of the Son and of the Holy Spirit, teaching them to observe all things that I have commanded you; and lo, I am with you always, even to the end of the age." Amen. NKJV

DWJD

As we enter the end of the age, all Christians have been commissioned to go and make disciples. After we have learned the things Jesus commanded, we are to do them and teach others what we have learned.

The Apostles did it.
Many Christians believe this was just for the early apostles. Find the word "them" in the above passage. We believe this means "us." We are part of the "disciples of all the nations." We are a part of "them" that have been discipled since Jesus gave this command. He sent out the first generation of disciples to make more disciples. They obeyed His command. This has been going on since the first century and has continued with little interruption.

More disciples have been made in the last one hundred years than the previous nineteen hundred years. As we prepare for the final harvest, we need to incorporate strategies in which every believer can fully participate and help usher in the second coming of Jesus Christ.

It continues to happen.

Verifiable healings and miracles are happening today in many Christian denominations around the world. This is a well-established fact. The question we must attempt to answer is: Did Jesus truly intend for us to do the same things He did with the same results? There are passages in the Bible that support this controversial claim. They are: Matthew 10:1, 7-8; Luke 9:1-2, 6; and especially John 14:11-14.

John 14:11-14

"Believe me when I say that I am in the Father and the Father is in me; or at least believe on the evidence of *the miracles* themselves. I tell you the truth; anyone who has faith in me will do what I have been doing. He will do even greater things than these, because I am going to the Father. And I will do whatever you ask in my name, so that the Son may bring glory to the Father. You may ask me for anything in my name, and I will do it." NIV

DWJD

Jesus states that any willing believer in Him can do what He did, including the miracles. Jesus has authorized and empowered His disciples to do the things that He did.

Did Jesus really mean it? Did He authorize the twelve only? Has this promise passed away? Some professors, teachers, and pastors teach us that this Scripture applies to the early apostles and to a time long ago. How could Jesus promise this unless He intended it for all His disciples? Does this promise exclude us? Did He mean for us to actually do what He did? If so, how do we appropriate this promise? What do we need to know?

Go where it is happening.

Participating in authentic demonstrations of the Holy Spirit's power is the best remedy for unbelief. The reason miracles are more evident in Third World countries is simple. The Christians there are more prone to the supernatural. They are less sophisticated, and many have no other option than to believe for healing. John 14:11-14 is real to them and it comes to life when preached among these eager people. They expect miracles whenever they hear the Full Gospel preached in their towns and villages. Unlike those in the West, most believe what the Bible says, all of it.

Our doctor friend went to Thailand.
Believers desperately need to be discipled and mentored in this type of ministry. At our Ministry Training Centers (MTC), we teach a series of ministry skills as part of the weekly instruction. After thorough teaching and extensive practicing of the skills, students are ready to minister wherever they go. The following chapters outline these ministry skills.

One of our students, Dr. Carl Berner who is a surgeon, came to us and said, "I truly believe all of these accounts of miraculous, instantaneous healings and people being set free from demonic spirits because I not only hear it from you two, but I see Jesus doing it in the Bible. However, I have not seen that firsthand for myself, so my wife (she is a surgical nurse) and I want to go with you on your next trip to Thailand." They did go with us, along with other professionals and executives who were in that graduating class. They not only saw miracle healings, they saw them happen through their own hands.

The demon manifested.
Dr. Berner was waiting to see a bona fide deliverance, and that desire came to pass at a healing meeting in Chiang Mai. At one point during the ministry time, Dr. Berner came to John and urgently persuaded him to come see what was happening to a woman on the other side of the room. As John walked over and looked at the woman, he saw she was on the floor and in full demonic manifestation. He, of course, knew this only by the Holy Spirit's revelation gift of discerning of spirits.

Dr. Berner related that the woman's two caregivers had brought her forward for prayer for her bad heart. When the team began to pray for her, she had collapsed and seemed unconscious. Her caregivers thought she was having a heart attack. Dr. Berner immediately took her pulse and found it was steady and strong. From what he had learned in class, he suspected it was a demonic spirit, and that was why he had brought John to assess the situation.

It is humorous to think back on the scene. Dr. Berner who is six-foot-three-inches tall was in back of John and leaning forward so he would not miss a second of the ministry. John said later that he could feel Carl's whiskers on his cheek!

She had a grotesque look on her face.
This deliverance was pretty much like many others we have seen. John had the caregivers stand the woman up on her feet. Her eyes were rolling around, and she could not focus them. She had a grotesque look on her face and was making moaning sounds. John followed Jesus' example as recorded in the Gospels and addressed the evil demonic spirit by saying, "You spirit of infirmity, I command you to come out of this woman, in the name of Jesus!" After a few minutes the spirit was expelled, she literally came to herself, and a beautiful smile graced her face. She was set free and healed. It was wonderful. Dr. Berner had witnessed a spiritual deliverance "up close and personal." It is exciting to hear this wonderful man, this skilled surgeon, relate these supernatural experiences.

We must experience it.
Jesus Himself gave the authority by which we do these things for others. He proclaimed this promise to "anyone who has faith in me." That includes every Christian. There is no higher name or authority in the universe than the name of the Lord Jesus Christ. He said whatever we ask in His name, He would see that it would get done. He said He would place His stamp of authority on those things we do for the benefit of others when we do them in His name. The intent of this book is to convince Christians to believe what

14

Jesus says they can do. We also want believers to experience the life-changing presence of God working through them as they do what Jesus did.

The Main Premise of this Book

Jesus came to earth as a man.

We know that Adam and Eve and all mankind were stripped of the authority they originally had because of willful disobedience. Satan became the god of this world. However, God's plan of redemption centered in His Son, Jesus Christ, coming to earth, being born of a virgin. Even though Jesus was God in the flesh, He emptied Himself and became a man. Jesus, the last Adam, was all God and all man.

1 Corinthians 15:45
So it is written: "The first man Adam became a living being;" *the last Adam*, a life-giving spirit. NIV

Romans 8:3
For what the law was powerless to do in that it was weakened by the sinful nature, God did by sending his own Son *in the likeness of sinful man* to be a sin offering. NIV

Hebrews 4:15
For we do not have a high priest who is unable to sympathize with our weaknesses, but we have one *who has been tempted in every way*, just as we are—yet was without sin. NIV

Philippians 2:5-8
Your attitude should be the same as that of Christ Jesus: Who, being in very nature God, did not consider equality with God something to be grasped, but made himself nothing, taking the very nature of a servant, *being made in human likeness. And being found in appearance as a man*, he humbled himself and became obedient to death, even death on a cross! NIV

15

Jesus did everything on earth in human terms, in appearance as a man, filled with the mighty power of the Holy Spirit. Therefore, He can promise those who follow Him, who are filled with the same Holy Spirit, to be able to do what He did. In human terms, He is our perfect human example, the author and perfecter of our faith.

Jesus did everything as a man.
There are no recorded miracles in the first thirty years of Jesus' life. He began ministry after being baptized in the Holy Spirit. Jesus did everything as a man filled with the Holy Spirit. He ministered on this earth as God had created the first Adam to do. Only by being human could He become our Savior. He had to defeat Satan as a man obeying the Father in heaven by relying upon the power of the Holy Spirit. Jesus was the first perfect man since Adam. Thus, He was taking back the authority that Satan had stolen from the first Adam.

Jesus delegates His authority to the believer.
When Jesus died, was resurrected to eternal life, and was exalted into heaven, the plan of redemption was complete. He told His followers to go into all the world. He said we could now do what He did because His authority has been given to us, and He is with us. He told us to use His name and do what He did.

Matthew 28:18-20
Then Jesus came to them and said, *"All authority in heaven and on earth has been given to me. Therefore go and make disciples of all nations, baptizing them in the name of the Father and of the Son and of the Holy Spirit, and teaching them to obey everything I have commanded you. And surely I am with you always, to the very end of the age."* NIV

Ephesians 1:22-23
And God placed all things under his feet and appointed him to be head over everything *for the church,*
which is his body, the fullness of him who fills everything in every way. NIV

Jesus defeated death and hell and was given all authority in
heaven and on earth. Everything was placed under His feet
for the benefit of the church, which is His body on earth. He
delegated this authority to the church and commanded us to
go do what He did.

Now it is up to us, the church!
Ephesians chapter 1 says Jesus did everything for the benefit
of His body, the church. The church is to fulfill the Great
Commission by doing the same things Jesus did. He empowered us with the Holy Spirit so we can go into the entire world
and make disciples. His plan is to have us make disciples by
doing the things He did. The balance of this book illustrates a
series of ministry skills needed to help facilitate and fulfill the
Great Commission. We will discover what these skills are and
how we can do them.

How did Jesus do it?
Before we go any further we want to establish how Jesus
ministered to people, because we should do it the same way.

John 5:19-20
Then Jesus answered and said to them, "Most assuredly, I say to you, the Son can do nothing of Himself,
but *what He sees the Father do*; for whatever He does,
the Son also does in like manner. For the Father loves
the Son, and shows Him all things that He Himself
does; and He will show Him greater works than these,
that you may marvel." NKJV

When we learn how to hear from God by seeing what He wants done, we will be operating in the miraculous similar to how Jesus did. *We are convinced that the secret to Jesus' accomplishing perfect ministry of healing and setting people free was because He did everything by revelation.*

John 5:19-20 states that Jesus only did what He "saw" the Father doing. Close examination of this Scripture gives today's Christian the secret of how Jesus operated perfectly in all that He did during His earthly ministry. He did everything as the Father directed it.

What did Jesus see?
Any student of Greek who examines the words of this text, will come up with the same conclusion. For example: the word "sees" (*blepo*), in verse 19, is a very common but extremely important word the Gospel writer used to convey an active and continuous or repeated action in which Jesus engaged Himself with the Father. John was an eyewitness of how Jesus interacted with the Father on a daily basis. He also witnessed the results of this perfect kind of obedience. It must have amazed John to witness Jesus conducting ministry as He obeyed what He was "seeing" the Father reveal to Him.

All the words that He preached about the Kingdom, all the healings, all the actions, and all the miracles were a result of seeing and hearing from the Father for each and every occasion. Scholars agree that this passage confirms Jesus' total dependence on the Father. Jesus never acted independently apart from the Father's will and purpose. The Gospel of John emphasizes that Jesus Christ's work was to do the will of the Father, not as a slave, but as a Son. He was totally obedient to the divine purposes of the Father's complete revelation and will for all mankind.

The total mandate and will of the Father were present in Christ from the beginning of time. Furthermore, we want to call attention to how this manifested in Jesus' earthly ministry. John 5:19-20 strongly suggests that the will of the Father was implemented on a moment-by-moment basis through Jesus Christ. His words and actions were for the direct benefit of His followers to remember and record. As the Father revealed what He desired to be said and done, Jesus obeyed. His every action, word, and deed were in direct response to what the Father was revealing at the time.

Can we see the same things?
Jesus is the author and finisher of our faith. When our faith is based on the promises from His Word, coupled with divine revelation from the Holy Spirit, we begin to function just like Jesus. Jesus Christ introduced the supernatural gifts of the word of wisdom, word of knowledge, and discerning of spirits. He modeled the use of these gifts in His daily interactions with the disciples and anyone needing ministry. During prayer, the Father would reveal to Jesus what He wanted to accomplish for the day. As Jesus began the day, the Father would continue to reveal the specifics of what He wanted said and done. As Jesus saw what the Father wanted to do, He obeyed.

Jesus Christ shows His followers how to operate in the three gifts of revelation that Paul discusses in 1 Corinthians:

1 Corinthians 12:7-11
But the manifestation of the Spirit is given to each one for the profit of all: for to one is given *the word of wisdom* through the Spirit, to another *the word of knowledge* through the same Spirit, to another faith by the same Spirit, to another gifts of healings by the same Spirit, to another the working of miracles, to another prophecy, to another *discerning of spirits*, to another different kinds of tongues, to another the interpretation of tongues. But one and the same Spirit works all

these things, distributing to each one individually as He wills. NKJV

The Holy Spirit distributes the revelation gifts so we can minister to others in like manner as Jesus did.

The Holy Spirit wants us to see.
These revelations came in the form of words of wisdom, knowledge, and the discerning of spirits. Since we have the same gifts with us today, it is safe to say we can see the same kinds of things that Jesus saw with the Father. There will be no new revelations concerning the plan of salvation, redemption, Kingdom principles, or the written Word. But, there will be a host of specifics the Holy Spirit will reveal to us when we submit to His leadership and obey whatever He wants us to "see." To be effective in today's marketplace, we must learn how to minister in love, relying on the prompting and revelation of the Holy Spirit. Then we will be doing ministry just like Jesus did!

Doing what Jesus did requires that we grasp the ministry skill of attempting to obey what the Holy Spirit is revealing. To do ministry like Jesus did, we must learn not only how to hear God's voice, but to obey what He is revealing. A thorough discussion of operating by revelation knowledge will be given in chapters 5 and 6. It is exciting to know that God has a plan and purpose for every single believer. That plan is revealed in the Word of God and accentuated by occasional words directly from the Holy Spirit.

The Foundation for Doing What Jesus Did

What is the key that produces supernatural ministry?
Let us look at John 14:11-14 below. From this Scripture we will base our approach to ministry squarely on what Jesus said we could and should do. He said we could do what He did. He did not give us any specifics other than His reference

to miracles in verse 11. When we examine His track record and what He accomplished, we can only stand in awe. Then, He says we can do the same. What a revelation! When we couple John 5:19-20 with John 14:11-14, we begin to grasp how this can be accomplished.

John 14:11-14

"Believe me when I say that I am in the Father and the Father is in me; or at least *believe on the evidence of the miracles* themselves. I tell you the truth; anyone who has faith in me will do what I have been doing. He will do even greater things than these, because I am going to the Father. And I will do whatever you ask in my name, so that the Son may bring glory to the Father. You may ask me for anything in my name, and I will do it." NIV

We believe the secret for us to do what Jesus did requires that we believe and act on the promise that we can do what He did. If He said we could, then we can! This obviously involves a process of learning how to minister like Jesus did with reliance on the Holy Spirit and what He reveals.

What are the things Jesus said we could do?

If we dare to believe we can do the same works Jesus did, then let us take a look at some of the things He did. Let us examine the things that Jesus Christ authorized and commissioned His disciples to do as recorded in the Scriptures listed next. It seems that He clearly wants His followers to function in a series of ministry skills until His return. These ministry skills function for the benefit of anyone coming to the Lord for help, including the pre-Christian. When we function in healing and setting people free, this boldly demonstrates that Jesus Christ is Lord and is very much alive. This creates a prime opportunity for winning the lost to Him.

Matthew 10:1, 7-8

He called his twelve disciples to him and gave them authority to drive out evil spirits and to heal every disease and sickness. . . . "As you go, preach this message: 'The kingdom of heaven is near.' Heal the sick, raise the dead, cleanse those who have leprosy, and drive out demons. Freely you have received, freely give." NIV

Luke 10:8-9, 19-20

"When you enter a town and are welcomed, eat what is set before you. Heal the sick who are there and tell them, 'The kingdom of God is near you.'" . . . "I have given you authority to trample on snakes and scorpions and to overcome all the power of the enemy; nothing will harm you. However, do not rejoice that the spirits submit to you, but rejoice that your names are written in heaven." NIV

Matthew 28:18-20

Then Jesus came to them and said, "All authority in heaven and on earth has been given to me. Therefore go and make disciples of all nations, baptizing them in the name of the Father and of the Son and of the Holy Spirit, and teaching them to obey everything I have commanded you. And surely I am with you always, to the very end of the age." NIV

Acts 1:4-5, 8

On one occasion, while he was eating with them, he gave them this command: "Do not leave Jerusalem, but wait for the gift my Father promised, which you have heard me speak about. For John baptized with water, but in a few days *you will be* baptized with the Holy Spirit. . . . But you will receive power when the Holy Spirit comes on you; and you will be my witnesses in Jerusalem, and in all Judea and Samaria, and to the ends of the earth." NIV

The above series of Scriptures are powerful promises. They include many of the "things" Jesus did and then promised we could do also.

Here is a list of those things Jesus said we would do:
- Drive out evil spirits.
- Heal *every* disease and sickness.
- Preach the Full Gospel of the Kingdom.
- Heal the sick.
- Raise the dead.
- Cleanse those who have leprosy.
- Overcome all the power of Satan.
- Command spirits to submit to us.
- Go make disciples of all nations.
- Baptize these new disciples.
- Teach new disciples to obey everything Jesus commanded.
- Be baptized with the Holy Spirit.
- Receive the power of the Holy Spirit.
- Be His witness to the ends of the earth.

Can we do all of these things?

Yes! Jesus meant what He said. We may not accomplish the entire list. We may only experience a few of these things. However, we need to pay whatever price there is and start wherever we are. It may take some time, training, and a change of attitude. But it will be worth it. That is what this book is all about. We will focus on six things Jesus said we should be doing. We will call them "Ministry Skills." They are:

- Leading People to Christ.
- Leading Christians into the Holy Spirit Baptism.
- Learning How to Heal the Sick.
- Hearing from God.
- Healing the Sick by Revelation.
- Dealing with Demons.

The first step – Salvation!
We begin our strategies for the harvest in chapter 1 by discussing how to lead people to Christ. This is the first and most important mandate from our Lord Jesus Christ. He said, "Go and make disciples." This is a supernatural plan of salvation created by God Himself. Without the initial, supernatural rebirth of the human spirit all other strategies for the harvest cannot be understood or achieved.

Leading people into a supernatural salvation through the sacrificial blood of Jesus Christ cannot be understood with the rational mind. It can only be understood and experienced through the supernatural work of the Holy Spirit. The following is an attempt to explain the mystery of salvation through Jesus Christ.

Upon confessing our sins (true repentance) and accepting the Lord Jesus Christ into our lives as Savior, a mystical and spiritual impartation takes place (see Luke 13:5). The term "born again" truly best describes this awesome event (see John 3:3). Our spirits are touched, quickened by the Holy Spirit of God, and we receive God's life into our being. We are translated from the kingdom of darkness into His glorious kingdom of light (see Colossians 1:14). Wonders of wonders, we now begin to understand what the Bible says. We begin to receive revelation about spiritual realities.

Mysteriously, we, by faith, are brought into relationship with the triune Godhead. We are describing the interpersonal relationship with Jesus Christ as Savior, our Heavenly Father, and His Holy Spirit. It is our relationship with Christ that forms the basis for our salvation. God's Word tells us there is no other name whereby we are saved, and that no one can come to the Father except through Him. This relationship is the basis for all spiritual growth.

By fully responding to God's offer of the gift of salvation, we are entering into a covenant relationship with Him. This New Covenant (as contrasted to the Old Covenant that was sealed with the blood of animals) was sealed with His own blood and body. It is this tangible interpersonal relationship of Jesus Christ in us, the hope of glory that fuels our convictions and our desire to obey God's commands. It is the living presence of the Holy Spirit within and upon us that permeates our thoughts and influences our daily actions.

With that said, let us move on to chapter 1 and address the first ministry skill—Leading People to Christ.

Let's Practice

- James 1:22 says to DO what we have heard (read).
- Consider doing what is recommended in this chapter by referring to the "Let's Practice" in Appendix B, page 317-320.
- Do the Ministry Skill Assignment entitled, "Share What You Believe About Miracles."

Chapter One

Ministry Skill One

LEADING PEOPLE TO CHRIST

In this chapter, you will learn how to share your faith in a natural way by simply telling a thoughtful story of how you accepted Jesus Christ as your Savior and the change it has made in your life. No Bible-thumping, no Gospel tracts nor preaching are necessary.

Many of us can remember when we first became a Christian. We wanted to tell everyone what happened to us. We were so excited we did not care if we were politically correct. All we could talk about was God. "God did this. God did that. He did it for me and He can do it for you!" We allowed the Holy Spirit freedom to use us as a witness. The Lord placed a new urgency in our hearts to proclaim what God was doing. We were free of condemnation and guilt. We had been forgiven. We were on our way to heaven. It was all so wonderful we had to tell somebody! Ministry Skill 1 was already manifesting without our even thinking about it. We were obeying the "go" in Matthew 28 because we had become the "new creation" in 2 Corinthians 5.

Matthew 28:18-20
Then Jesus came to them and said, "All authority in heaven and on earth has been given to me. Therefore *go and make disciples* of all nations, baptizing them in the name of the Father and of the Son and of the Holy Spirit, and teaching them to obey everything I have commanded you. And surely I am with you always, to the very end of the age." NIV

2 Corinthians 5:17-20

Therefore, if anyone is in Christ, *he is a new creation;* the old has gone, the new has come! All this is from God, who reconciled us to himself through Christ and *gave us the ministry of reconciliation:* that God was reconciling the world to himself in Christ, not counting men's sins against them. And he has committed to us the message of reconciliation. *We are therefore Christ's ambassadors,* as though God were making his appeal through us. We implore you on Christ's behalf: Be reconciled to God. NIV

Jesus meant for His followers to reach out and make disciples wherever they can. All Christians have been given a ministry, that of reconciling their families, friends, and neighbors to Christ. We have been commissioned as ambassadors of reconciliation.

Every Christian is commissioned.

Every Christian has been commissioned to participate in the Great Commission as a witness for Christ. The part each of us plays depends on how God has gifted us. We are all gifted differently. A small percentage of Christians have a strong gift and desire for evangelism. The balance of the Body of Christ does not. But, this does not excuse any believer from becoming an effective witness. Jesus commissions every one of His followers to go and "make" disciples. This means they must find a way to participate in the "ministry of reconciliation." We must not ignore our responsibility to fulfill what God has given *every* believer to do.

Just tell what happened to you.

The first lesson of our six-volume curriculum entitled *The Ambassador Series* encourages student ministers to learn how to lead others into salvation. We devote from six to twelve weeks to enable them to master a personal testimony that can be used to accomplish this first and most basic ministry skill. With a little encouragement and a few guidelines, any willing disciple will be ready to respond to those who ask why we do what we do.

1 Peter 3:15
But in your hearts set apart Christ as Lord. Always be prepared to give an answer to everyone who asks you to give the reason for the hope that you have. But do this with gentleness and respect. NIV

DWJD

- Whenever anyone asks us to give the reason for the hope we have in Christ we must have a ready response.
- Our response should include a personal testimony of what Christ has done to give us this glorious hope.
- We should know how to end our witness with questions that will lead someone into salvation through Jesus Christ.

How the world will be evangelized.
We are convinced that true evangelism that produces lasting disciples is done on a one-on-one basis. By this we mean that Christians are trained how to effectively share their faith with pre-Christians and lead them into a personal encounter with the living Christ. They have been taught to "bring and include" the new convert in their church activities. They go with them to the class that is offered for new people (if there is one) and invite them to their home group. In other words, they accept some personal responsibility for seeing that the new believer is assimilated into the life of the church.

Not too long ago, a woman in our church who previously was a county commissioner came to me (Sonja) before church. She works with women ex-offenders who are coming out of jails and prisons and asked me to pray that the woman she had brought to church would accept the Lord. The woman was living a lesbian lifestyle. How fortunate we are to be part of a church that is so committed to the lost that we can feel safe to invite people who are not only lost but negatively predisposed toward Christians! That particular day our pastor, Ken Johnson, was talking about our not being a social hall for Christians but rather a rescue station for the lost and hurting and how we must treat them with the love and respect they deserve.

I saw my friend the next Wednesday, and she said her guest had loved the church, the message, and was joining a Bible study. It was not too long before this hurting woman gave her heart to the Lord and gave up her lesbian lifestyle.

That is how the world will be won—people who realize they have a responsibility to share the Good News with those they can reach and be committed to their becoming fully devoted disciples who in turn will reach others.

When we speak in churches on marketplace ministry, I (Sonja) often ask the congregation what would happen if they each led just one person to Christ and helped them to get plugged into the church during the coming year. The obvious answer, of course, is that the church would double in size. And if we discipled our new people to do the same, we would double again the following year. How simple!

Why Aren't We Doing It?

We will not take time to review the one hundred reasons why most of the churches in the West are not involved in effective evangelism. They just are not. Does this mean it is O.K. to ignore Christ's command to go and make new disciples? We think not. If you question any pastor, most have a desire to see evangelism take place in their church. But, they are searching for ways to incorporate it into the weekly routine of services. Some say, "I know evangelism is important; it's just not how we do church these days." We want to salute those pastors who are still brave enough to end their message with an invitation for visitors to receive Jesus Christ as their Savior.

Could it be we need a new paradigm? It would be nice if the majority of those who call themselves Christian had the knowledge and confidence to witness for Christ and could lead their friends and neighbors to Him. What a radical concept. According to 2 Peter, the Lord is patiently waiting for us to lead others to repentance.

2 Peter 3:9
The Lord is not slow in keeping his promise, as some understand slowness. He is patient with you, not wanting anyone to perish, but everyone to come to repentance. NIV

DWJD

- Since the Lord wants everyone to come to repentance, we should have a personal plan in mind to respond to those who ask us about our faith in Christ.
- Everyone we meet is a candidate to become a Christian. They just need someone to share the Good News with them.
- If every Christian were prepared to give a marketplace testimony with an invitation to receive Christ, the world could be won to Christ in a short period of time.

He was the most introverted person in the class.
We were doing a workshop in California for a large group of pastors and leaders. One of the men was an extremely introverted person. When he found out he would have to give a five-to-seven-minute marketplace testimony in front of the class, his face turned ashen! He rushed up to us at the break and told us he just could not do the practicum assignment. He had never been able to do such a thing, and he was not about to start now. We told him we could understand his consternation, but that it would be good for him. He did not agree, but he could tell we were not about

to make an exception. He then asked if he could be the last person to share. We did agree to that.

On Saturday it came his time to share with the class, and he was literally shaking from stage fright! With the carefully written out testimony in his hands, he began to speak. We were sure he was planning to just read it, but a wonderful thing happened. When he opened his mouth and spoke just a few words, the anointing of the Holy Spirit came upon him, and he was powerful! Those who knew him and his shy, introverted personality were amazed. When he finished, the class erupted in thundering applause and whistling. His story of how he came to Christ was exciting and interesting—no one knew his background. He even closed his testimony with the all-important invitation: "Now that is how I came to know Jesus Christ as my Savior. Would you like to have Him forgive all your sins, give you a clear conscience, and come into your life?" We all responded with a resounding "Yes!"

The Holy Spirit tapped him on the shoulder.
This great story does not end there. He went to work on Monday, and we received an e-mail on Tuesday. It said: "I went to work on Monday, and a fellow employee I knew was having a rough time came up to me. I had been praying for the man. He said that things had gotten so bad over the weekend that in desperation he had even picked up a Bible and began reading it. It was as if the Holy Spirit tapped me on the shoulder and said 'That's your cue.' I shared my testimony that I had written out, practiced and timed for hours before I gave it at class. I asked him the question, and guess what? He said yes, and I led him in the sinner's prayer I have heard a hundred times at church. Can you believe it? I led someone to the Lord! I would never, never have believed I could do such a thing! Thank you! Thank you! Thank you for making me take that step of faith. I will never be the same!"

31

It Happened to Me

I (John) vividly remember the events of early 1973. If the Campus Crusade for Christ leaders had not given witnessing tools to an engineering student named Dave, this book would not have been written. I could not witness as to how I came to know Christ. I could not teach anyone how to lead people to Christ. I might still be lost in my sin, unforgiven, and on my way to hell.

Dave was quiet and somewhat reserved. He was only nineteen. His parents attended the same church I did. He presented a booklet to me entitled, "The Four Spiritual Laws." My church did not preach that you must be born again. But, the booklet said you must. He would present me with the same booklet every other Sunday. Confused and quite irritated, I told him I did not appreciate his approach and to take his religion somewhere else. Each week Dave would smile, say hello, and with booklet in hand he would ask if I had any questions about what it said. Finally, to get him to go away I consented to listen to a tape he gave me.

For the first time in my life I heard the rest of the Gospel. God not only loved me, He had a plan for my life. If I allowed Jesus Christ to forgive me of my sin and asked Him to take control of my life, He would show me the plans that God had for me and would give me eternal life. All this from a thirty-minute cassette tape by a minister named Josh McDowell. The Holy Spirit was drawing me to Christ.

John 6:44

"No one can come to Me unless the Father who sent Me draws him; and I will raise him up on the last day." NASB

- The Father uses Christians to spread the Gospel in ways that draw the lost to Him.

- Your testimony, a tract, or a cassette tape can be used to "preach" the Gospel to those who do not know Christ.
- Faith to receive Christ comes by hearing the Word that will save them.

It happened in my living room.

The churches in my city launched a region-wide outreach program called "Key '73." Our church responded by arranging a series of home food-and-fellowship gatherings. I offered my home for one of the Sunday nights. Dave and some of his friends showed up. They began talking about how great it was to have a personal relationship with God and how He was directing their lives. They even talked about how they were absolutely assured where they would spend eternity. At the end of the evening they began to take prayer requests. When they asked me if they could pray for any of my concerns, I nervously indicated that I needed a few weeks to think over this "God stuff." I said I needed to make a decision about all this, but I needed some time to think about it.

They prayed out loud.

They prayed things like, "Thank you, Jesus, for being right here. Thank you, God, for seeing into John's heart. You know everything he is thinking right now. Help him to accept You as his Lord and Savior." All the prayers were so soft, personal, and non-condemning.

By the time it was my turn to pray, all I could do was cry. I said, "God, I quit. I'm so sorry. I didn't believe You arose from the dead. But, You did. You are alive. Take my life. Do what You have to do to me. Amen." I wept from way down deep inside me. I could not stop crying. Dave and everyone else came over and hugged me saying, "Welcome to the Kingdom, John. You've just been born again."

Dave had led me to Christ. The Holy Spirit had used Dave to introduce me to Christ in a way that caused me to want to accept Him as my personal Lord and Savior. God used a young engineering student who was willing to learn a few strategic phrases from a simple witnessing outline that placed me squarely in front of Jesus Christ. That is called effective marketplace witnessing.

It Needs to Be Simple

The Gospel is simple. We make it hard. Jesus' messages were very simple. He used language that everyone knew. The Holy Spirit unveiled the true message behind His stories. Only those to whom God gave understanding knew what He was saying. Religious people did not. The hardest people to witness to today are those who think they know God but do not have a personal relationship with Him. The best strategy for today is to keep it simple. It should be so simple that any believer can quickly learn how to become an effective witness. God does not need any more argumentative, self-styled theologians. He wants ordinary believers who can give a personal testimony that will touch the heart of their friends and co-workers.

Tell it like it is.

A short personal testimony of what God has done for you speaks more clearly than ten Bible verses fired off in rapid succession. Pre-Christians already know you are one. They do not want to hear a sanctimonious correction from your wealth of scriptural knowledge. They do want to hear about how God repaired your relationship with your spouse. Or how He helped you rise above your dysfunction and led you into wholeness. They want to hear how God healed you from an incurable disease. They want to hear how God works in a personal way. They will listen to things they can relate to and understand.

Dave only used one Scripture when he first began talking to me. I will never forget it. He used John 14:6 by saying, "John, I found out that there is only one sure way to God. I used to believe there were many ways to God. I found out that Jesus is the only true way to God."

John 14:6

Jesus answered, "I am the way and the truth and the life. No one comes to the Father except through me." NIV

Using this Scripture mixed into your testimony is a powerful way to proclaim an eternal truth that will lead others to Christ.

Then Dave said, "John, I had to go through Jesus to get to the Father! That sure made it simple when I discovered that." Then he would let me think about it. I was always nervous when he brought up the subject of a personal God. But, he always calmed my fears by personalizing the Gospel to his own life. He used his testimony to preach the Gospel to me. I did not figure out he was actually preaching until after I was born again. Dave did not think he was preaching either. He was just telling me what happened to him.

The best preaching.

The best way to preach is to tell your story of how you came to know Jesus Christ. Most everyone will listen to you, even family members. They already know you are peculiar. They want to know how you got that way. The trick is to know *when* to tell them. The Holy Spirit operates best when we share with sincerity and a loving attitude. We believe God will open multiple opportunities for witnessing if we pray for them. The best way to get over being too embarrassed or fearful is to ask the Holy Spirit to open opportunities for sharing our faith. Then when He does, we are confident that since He started it, we can be assured He will help us finish it. He is always there to help us say the right things.

Marketplace believers are ministers.

A marketplace believer is one who is equipped to share the Good News of the Lord Jesus Christ whenever there is an opportunity. We all have different "marketplaces"—where we work, where we shop, our neighborhoods—those places we frequent outside our homes. Whenever we share anything about God we are "ministering." Since the Bible does not make a distinction between clergy and laymen, that makes all Christians "ministers." In this book, we will use marketplace believers and marketplace ministers interchangeably.

Jesus was the consummate marketplace minister. As always, He is our perfect example. We see Him out and about—walking from one place to another. He comes upon a funeral procession of a widow's only son. His heart goes out to her, and He raises her son from the dead (see Luke 7:11-17).

In just two chapters, Matthew 8 and 9, we see Jesus healing a man with leprosy, healing the centurion's servant, setting demon-possessed men free, healing a paralytic, giving life back to a dead girl, healing a woman who had been bleeding for twelve years, healing two blind men and a mute. After all of this profound ministry, chapter 9 ends with the following passage stating that the workers are few.

Matthew 9:35-38
Jesus went through all the towns and villages, teaching in their synagogues, preaching the good news of the kingdom and healing every disease and sickness. When he saw the crowds, he had compassion on them, because they were harassed and helpless, like sheep without a shepherd. Then he said to his disciples, "The harvest is plentiful but the workers are few. Ask the Lord of the harvest, therefore, to send out workers into his harvest field." NIV

DWJD
We are to be those workers!

In Matthew 10, He calls the twelve disciples to Him and gives them authority to drive out evil spirits and to heal every disease and sickness. Jesus shows us what He wants us to do as we go about our lives. We can do this! What an exciting way to live! That is what we are talking about in this book.

The marketplace.

As we said previously, we define marketplace as anywhere outside our home where we interact with people. This includes where we work, where we play, our neighborhoods, and places we frequent. The ministry of reconciliation is played out wherever people are in touch with one another. This can be in your front yard, at your neighbor's barbecue, or in the produce section of the grocery store.

Marketplace Testimonies

Hold that plane!

We were returning from a ministry trip and our plane was late arriving in Portland, Oregon. As we ran to catch our connecting flight from Portland to Bend, Oregon where we live, we noticed the gate was closed. When we inquired, the agent told us to run to the gate and that she would call them. The plane was a prop commuter, the motors were running, and the door was closed. However, the door opened and the flight attendant yelled for us to wait a moment. The next thing we knew, two irritated stand-by passengers disembarked and we were told we could board the plane.

As we moved down the narrow aisle, I (Sonja) asked the Lord just what this was all about, and then my eyes fell on a young girl, perhaps twelve or thirteen, sitting in the seat next to where I was to sit. She was traveling alone, dressed in leathers and had lots of body piercing. I struck up a conversation over cookies I pulled out of my bag. Ten minutes into the flight I asked her what she believed about God. She thought for a moment and then said, "I think He is good." I met her where she was and told her she was exactly right. I then asked her if she knew that He loved her. The conversation moved along to the point that I felt led to ask her if she would like to know this God through His Son Jesus Christ so if something ever happened to her she would spend forever with this loving God. Then she told me how she had almost drowned the previous summer and how terrified she was at the time.

She prayed.

When I asked if she would like to pray and ask Jesus into her heart and to have Him forgive everything she had ever done that was wrong, she responded by bowing her head and folding her hands just like a little child. I was in tears as I led her in the sinner's prayer just moments before we landed. I gave her the name of a good church in her town and suggested she visit it on Sunday. She said she would. I put her name on my prayer list and often pray for her.

We believe the Lord will give us these opportunities if we are simply willing to be used, even if He has to detain an airplane to get us to the appointment on time! When we remain sensitive to opportunities for ministry, the Lord always opens fresh avenues for Kingdom business. Our daily prayer could be, "Lord, I'm open for business today. Let me know when You want me to do something." Being open for business means just being available to help someone. Needs are everywhere. When Jesus has a lot of "gift givers" working in the marketplace, it is easy for Him to give His gifts away to meet those needs. But He needs willing disciples that He can work through. That is where we come in. That is what Paul did in Acts 16.

Acts 16:13-15

On the Sabbath we went outside the city gate to the river, where we expected to find a place of prayer. We sat down and began to speak to the women who had gathered there. One of those listening was a woman named Lydia, a dealer in purple cloth from the city of

Thyatira, who was a worshiper of God. The Lord opened her heart to respond to Paul's message. When she and the members of her household were baptized, she invited us to her home. . . . NIV

DWJD

- Wherever people gather can be a place of witness.
- Our message must be relevant to those gathered, being sensitive to whoever may be listening.
- Lydia was a marketplace person dealing in purple cloth. It appears she and her household were the only ones who responded to Paul's testimony about Jesus.
- We, too, can be that kind of marketplace minister.

We have been given the ministry of reconciling a lost and dying world to Christ. It is a joint ministry as we work with the Holy Spirit. He gifts us to fulfill His mission. His mission is our ministry. He has a "business of blessing" going on. We are the delivery team. Wherever a need surfaces, there is a delivery person with a gift to bless and satisfy the need.

But, what if my mother is in hell?

Barb came to our neighborhood Bible study as a seeker. She was upfront about her skepticism of Christianity and its "exclusive claim of salvation." We welcomed her honest inquiries and lovingly answered her questions as best we could. After a few months, she said the only thing that was preventing her from accepting Christ as her personal Savior was the fact that her mother had died not knowing God, and that meant she would never have a chance to see her again. We asked the Lord for wisdom, and we were led to share the following with her:

- You cannot know for sure what was in your mother's heart. We look on the outside, but God looks in the heart.

- God in His foreknowledge knows everyone who is going to accept His gift of salvation.
- If your mother was going to accept salvation, she somehow did before her death. If she was not going to, she could have lived fifty more years and it would not have made a difference.
- What assurance do you have now of seeing your mother after death?
- God is totally just and merciful; therefore, you can trust Him in the matter.

This simple explanation answered her heart's cry, and she accepted the Lord Jesus Christ as her Savior. The transformation was remarkable as she was able to put the matter of her mother's eternal state squarely in the hands of this just and compassionate God she had come to know through a simple neighborhood Bible study.

Open for business.
One afternoon, I (John) was in a hurry to buy a witnessing Bible. There was only one other person in the Bible bookstore besides the clerk. I had some sales appointments within the hour so I had little time to browse. I became slightly irritated when this other person kept asking me which version of the Bible he should buy. I thought, "Why is he asking me? Doesn't he know I'm in a hurry? Why doesn't the clerk intervene here?" The Holy Spirit nudged me with, "Ask him if he knows Me?" I thought, "Oh Lord, I don't have time right now." Suddenly I remembered that I prayed that morning to be open for Kingdom business. I promised the Lord I would do whatever He told me.

Divine appointment.
Looking at my watch, I asked the man, "How well do you know the Author of that Bible?" He said, "What do you mean?" I said, "If you died today, would you be with Jesus Christ?" He said, "I don't know." I asked, "Would you like to know for sure?" He said, "Well, ah, yes." I heard the Lord say, "Kneel with him." I said, "Let's kneel right here and say

a little prayer. Would that be O.K.?" He said, "Sounds good to me." I led this man to Jesus Christ through a simple prayer, on our knees, in the middle of a bookstore. I had him tell the clerk what happened. Then I invited him to church as we were paying for our new Bibles. Afterwards, I made it to my appointments with time to spare. Being open for business does not mean carrying a big black Bible under your arm. It means being sensitive to any needs people have wherever you go.

The neighbor.
One day, I (John) was puttering around the yard when my pre-Christian neighbor came across the street to let me know his family was going on vacation. I offered to watch over their home and property. Even though we did not know each other very well, he was very appreciative and gave me instructions in case there was an emergency. Later, they were open to our invitation to attend a special musical outreach event at our church. We came to be very good friends. Their need pointed to one of God's gifts. They needed the gift of helps. We released it. They became open to the Gospel. We engaged in marketplace ministry as God's fellow workers.

2 Corinthians 6:1-2
As God's fellow workers we urge you not to receive God's grace in vain. For he says, "In the time of my favor I heard you, and in the day of salvation I helped you." I tell you, now is the time of God's favor, now is the day of salvation. NIV

God is always ready to save people. We should always be ready as His instruments to usher others into their day of salvation.

When is the Best Time?

There are little signs that let us know when an opportunity for witness is brewing. When you are in the presence of pre-Christians, there are obvious signs letting you know it is time to share a part of your story. Here are a few:

- Whenever the conversation naturally turns to any kind of spiritual subject.
- Whenever you hear them refer to God or Jesus but you are not sure they believe the way the Bible portrays them.
- Whenever they express a kind of problem they are having from which God previously rescued you. (Habits, substance abuse, family problems, sin, etc.)
- Whenever someone tells you they are facing a life threatening medical problem and you know someone (or yourself) that prayed and God brought them through O.K.
- Whenever they bring up a subject that you heard about in a sermon or a Christian book you recently read.
- Whenever the Holy Spirit says for you to do it.

The above list of signs can be defined as conversational "cues." These are a few from a hundred possibilities.

Cues from the Holy Spirit.

One of the easiest ways to naturally refocus a conversation on the Gospel is to wait for a natural cue from the one with whom you are talking. Sometimes these cues never materialize. You just wait until they do. They should happen naturally and are never forced. Many of these cues are obviously inspired by the Holy Spirit. For you to suddenly change the conversation to Jesus Christ for no reason causes a pre-Christian to put their guard up. If they go on the defensive, it becomes very difficult for them to hear your story. Let the Holy Spirit spontaneously do His job.

Sonja has become a master at capitalizing on conversational "cues" in the marketplace. It always amazes me to hear her quickly tap into a natural cue and redirect the conversation to the things of the Lord. One day her secretary came to work and asked her if she saw the New Age channeler on TV the previous night. As it turned out, Sonja had watched the program and seized the opportunity to dialogue about the supernatural of God as contrasted with the supernatural of Satan. The point she stressed was when the supernatural of God is manifesting through a Christian, the person is in control of his or her faculties. In the case of the channeler, by her own admission, "An entity possessed her and spoke through her." The secretary was amazed that the supernatural of Satan enslaves a person. On the other hand, the supernatural of God is used to heal them or set them free. Sonja eventually was able to lead her precious secretary to the Lord.

The story does not end there. Her secretary later invited the receptionist to a meeting where Sonja was speaking. When she gave the invitation for those who wanted to accept the Lord, the receptionist was the first to give her life to Christ. This was because Sonja naturally responded to a cue from a legitimate question about spiritual things. But, she did it with gentleness and respect in a non-threatening way. I believe this is what Peter was telling us to do.

1 Peter 3:15

But in your hearts set apart Christ as Lord. Always be prepared to give an answer to everyone who asks you to give the reason for the hope that you have. But do this with gentleness and respect. NIV

DWJD

- When we respond in a natural, non-threatening way, people will remain curious about our life in Christ.

- Gentleness and respect for people's feelings and having the understanding of spiritual things will open many opportunities to lead others to Christ.

What if they are ready now?

Once in a great while you may meet someone who is so ready to receive Christ that you just know it. If this happens, we recommend having two questions firmly in mind. During John's years with the Christian Broadcasting Network, these two questions were the pivotal difference between someone receiving Christ or not. We have since used this two-question approach in most witnessing situations. They are "yes" or "no" type questions. They work so well that we recommend them to anyone wanting a way to "cinch" the witness and have the person commit his or her life to Christ. It works like this:

DWJD

Ask: *"If you died today, would you be with Jesus?"*

Their response may be, "I hope so, or I don't know, or I don't think so."

Then ask: *"Would you like to know for sure?"*

Their response will be, "yes" or "no."

If they respond with a "yes," then you simply lead them in the following prayer:

"Jesus, I want to be with You when I die. Forgive me of everything I've done wrong. Come into my life. I repent of my sin. Become my Lord and my God. Amen."

Short and to the point.

In a fellowship gathering at church, one of our friends introduced us to their pre-Christian brother. During our short conversation, this man indicated he was "checking out God." Whenever a pre-Christian brings up "God," this is a bell-ringing cue from the Holy Spirit. I (John) simply said, "Do you mind if I ask you a question?" He said, "No." I said, "If you died tonight, would you be with Jesus Christ?" He said, "I really can't answer that." I said, "Would you like to know for sure?" He said, "Wouldn't everybody?" I said, "Say this prayer with me." I put my hand on his shoulder, bowed my head and began a simple prayer of repentance and asking the Lord to forgive him. He followed along with me word for word.

We both said "amen." He looked up at me and said, "That was powerful. Thank you." I asked him again, "If you died right now, would you be with Jesus?" He looked me in the eye, and with a big grin he said, "I believe I would!" I said, "I know you would, because you have just been born again." I gave him a firm handshake and told him he would never be the same. He thanked me again. Later, our friends that brought him told us they were amazed how easily we led him into salvation. We thanked them for preparing this man's way by praying for him. We knew he was ready. We were being marketplace ministers and just made sure the man had a bridge-burning encounter with Jesus Christ.

Is your hope showing?
Pre-Christians know who we are. It should be obvious. It is reflected in our actions and our conversation. Jesus said they would know us by the love we show each other. We do not have to preach to our co-workers. They already know what kind of person we are by how we treat them. A person can tell if we are sincere by watching us day-by-day. People are watching how we treat others at the office, at school, on the job, and at home. That is why Paul encouraged us to allow the fruit of the Spirit to flow through us. Then our actions will speak boldly of a person who has hope beyond the ordinary. When others see the fruit in action, a brilliant hope will radiate that only comes from an enthusiastic follower of Jesus Christ.

Hope opens the door.

Peter is right. We have a kind of hope that causes people to ask about it. 1 Peter 3:15 is a gem. It tells us what to do with the hope that we have. Hope opens the door for witnessing. People are drawn to those who have genuine hope. Hope that they can solve personal problems. Hope that they can overcome adverse societal pressures. Hope that they can believe in a God that leads them into personal restoration and peace. If we are this kind of person, people will eventually ask us about this hope and where they can get it too. That is when you say, "I'm glad you asked. Let me tell you about how I found hope for eternity!"

Little neighborhood cherubs.

At one point we lived in a beautiful new condo in a mostly adult complex. On Saturdays, I (Sonja) baked cookies and the aroma wafted through the air. One such day our doorbell rang and I opened it to find a beautiful little six-year-old girl standing there. She said, "Hi, my name is Gwendolyn, and I just wanted to thank you for making that wonderful smell." I chuckled as I smiled at the gorgeous little cherub with the dark long natural curls and replied, "My name is Sonja, and I would love to share our cookies with you if your mother says it is O.K." She hastily turned to leave and yelled back over her shoulder, "We just moved here; I know it will be O.K. with my mom." Sure enough, she momentarily returned, and I invited her in for cookies and milk.

We became fast friends, and every week she would show up with her new little friends she had met that week. Before too long it became apparent that none of these seven children were Christians or went to church. As they shared their lives with me each week, it was heartbreaking to hear about some of the events. One such story little Gwendolyn related was about her mommy and her boyfriend having a big fight and he moved out. But, not to worry, a new boyfriend had moved in the next day!

At Christmas time I shared the Christmas story with the children, and they loved it. Gwendolyn wanted to know if I would tell them a story each week. I said I would be happy to if their parents said it was O.K. I spoke with all the parents and told them I would just use the children's illustrated Bible, which I showed to them. They all agreed, and we began the New Year learning about Jesus. One by one I led each of those precious children—ages five to eleven—into a personal relationship with Jesus.

After a few months, Alan and Michelle's parents stopped me in the parking lot and thanked me for spending time with their children. They were amazed at the changes in them. I explained it was because they had come to know the Lord Jesus Christ in a personal way and He always brought positive change. They smiled and thanked me again.

By June, every one of those seven children had moved away. It was as if this was a God-ordained year in their precious lives where He could reach down into total dysfunction and capture the hearts of His precious ones.

To be effective marketplace ministers, we sometimes have to be non-traditional. These children's parents were not receptive to taking or even sending their children to church, but coming to our home in the neighborhood was fine. I often think about and pray for those little ones the Lord entrusted to me at that time.

Mastering Your Marketplace Testimony

Have you ever been at a loss for words when the subject of God came up? We all have. Most believers get tongue tied when they suddenly find themselves in the middle of a witnessing opportunity. One of our new students at MTC remarked, "I knew I was supposed to share my faith. But I felt so ill equipped. I thought if I did, I would screw it up so badly that the person might never come to the Lord. But, after a few weeks at MTC I felt confident to share my story with pre-Christians. To my utter amazement, the people I shared with wanted to accept Jesus Christ as their Lord and Savior!"

She had mastered her marketplace testimony. Mastering your testimony simply means telling a series of little stories about when Jesus Christ showed up in your life and how He made a difference. Everyone's story is different. That is what makes them so effective. Pre-Christian people are always curious about what makes Christians tick. They may seem skeptical and even hostile at times. But, they will seldom stop you in the middle of your story. If they do, the Holy Spirit may be telling you to save it for another time.

The Bible according to you.
It has been said that the only Bible the pre-Christian sees is you. How are they reading you? Are they reading you the way you want them to? Jesus said, "They will know you by the love you show to one another." He said, "A new command I give you: Love one another" (John 13:34). When we share how the grace of God has transformed us from who we were then to who we are now, people listen. Our stories reveal the incredible God of love who bestows grace, forgiveness, and restoration upon a broken and fractured race of people. Our stories release a fresh message of hope and the way out of the dead end of sin and debauchery. It is the Bible according to you. Pre-Christians not only need to hear it, they want to hear it.

A Story that Leads People to Christ

The recipe for a good story.
Mastering your marketplace testimony requires an understanding of why it is so powerful to the pre-Christian. Choosing parts of your personal history with Jesus Christ that will have high impact with others requires thought. Your hearers always welcome effective stories that pene-

trate personal hurts and needs in themselves. The recipe for a good testimony will include these ingredients:

- A short story of who you were and what you were experiencing before coming to Christ.
- The personal factors that finally caused you to look to God for help.
- The personal details surrounding the actual surrender and submission to God's will.
- A short story of who you have become and what you are now experiencing as a result of turning to God for help.
- An encouragement to those listening that they can experience the same results by submitting to Jesus Christ.

Keep it simple.

These ingredients may seem too simple. They can be said in less than five minutes. Many will argue that you must use a lot of Scripture to be effective. This may be true in some instances, but there will be ample opportunities to inject your favorite Scripture passage as you tell your story. Avoid using phrases like "the Bible says . . ." or "verse 9 of chapter 10 of Romans says . . ." Pre-Christians do not believe the Bible has any relevance to their lives. Simply paraphrase the truth from the Bible and insert it in your story. They will not know you are quoting the Bible. The Holy Spirit will use it to penetrate deep into their hearts and cause them to want to know Christ. Here are five things that make a powerful testimony:

1. Tell who you were.

Because we live in a negative world, people in America are used to hearing their friends talk about themselves in a negative way. It is part of our culture to stress the negative. We always refer to the next intersection as having a red light, not green. Polls often refer to the 25 percent that disagreed rather than the 75 percent that answered in the affirmative. When someone hears you sneeze, they most often respond with, "Are you catching a cold or is it an allergy?" The six o'clock news seldom reports on the good things that happened during the day. All we hear and see are fires, plane crashes, rape victims, murders, wars, and all categories of violence.

So, beginning your story with how messed up you used to be is a good way to get a pre-Christian's attention. They can relate to that. They have been there or may be experiencing the same circumstances. Everyone has periods in their lives when things do not work out. The negatives permeate our society. Bad things happen to good people. Even Christians are not shielded from accidents, abuse, and persecutions that invade our lives. We live in a fallen and decaying world. Bad things happen to everyone.

Incorporating the circumstance in our life that happened prior to our submitting to Christ should not be gloated about or referred to as something we want to revisit. We should not dwell on the gory details. They need to be presented as facts that describe what you were experiencing and what kind of person you were before encountering Jesus Christ. This is needed to emphasize that you were in a no-win situation and you needed help to escape. This sets the stage for the next phase of your story.

People like Sonja who accepted the Lord as a child may begin their testimony with a significant event in their life that caused them to turn to God with their whole heart. Perhaps it was a difficult marriage, bad health, death of a child, an accident, etc.

2. What caused you to look to God?

Most everyone can relate to times in their life when they ran out of ideas on how to fix their problems. It is vital to tell about those personal events and factors where you knew you were at a crossroads. You could stress the options of continuing like you were and where that would lead. You could also mention what your friends and family were suggesting for you to do. You could refer to specific people in your testimony that gave you input that eventually caused you to look to God for the answer. At this point in your story it is vital that you describe how you were feeling at the time. Now it is time to move to the next phase of your story.

3. What happened when you surrendered?

A pre-Christian needs to hear the specifics on how to surrender to Jesus Christ. Your story must include the personal details surrounding your submitting to God. This opens the door for your listeners to know how to submit to Jesus Christ. Take time to describe how you felt, what words you said to God, and the emotions you were experiencing at the time. This has high impact on anyone who hears your story. Do not lightly skip over this part. It is the pivotal point that causes another to either want to do what you did or dismiss the whole idea. Allow it to be a spontaneous description of your conversion and surrender to God's will for your life. By repeating the prayer you said to the Lord, you are showing the pre-Christian how to pray. It shows them how they can receive salvation like you did. You do not have to be dramatic. Just tell it like it happened.

4. Now what is happening?

Your story should conclude with what happened as a result of submitting yourself to God. This part should be in the positive. Even though we are all in process of becoming more like Jesus, no one has arrived. However, we are better than when we first began. So, tell a short story of who you are becoming and some of the good things that have happened since you made your decision to follow Christ. Relate what you are now experiencing as a result of turning to God. Tell how it has made a difference in your personal life, your work, or your relationship with others. Pre-Christians need to hear the personal benefits of giving their life to Jesus Christ, in very personal terms. This will help them decide to surrender their life to the Lord.

5. Give an opportunity for them to decide.

Always end your story with an encouragement for your hearers to do what you did. If you were sincere, truthful, and talking from the heart, your hearers will want to do something about what you said. If they need to get saved, ask them! If they need to rededicate their life to God, ask them! If they need to repent of their sin and get right with the Lord, ask them! By now the Holy Spirit is all over them, lovingly drawing them to Jesus. God has just used you to preach the Gospel in a way they can understand and grasp. Always end your story with a loving invitation for your hearers to submit their lives and situation to Jesus Christ. Always! God will give you the right words to say.

Always end your witness with a simple invitation, such as:

DWJD

"He did all this for me, and He will do it for you, too. Would you like to ask Jesus Christ into your life now? I will help you do it. Say these words with me to God:

'Jesus Christ, come into my life. I repent of all my sin. Forgive me for what I've said and done. I receive you as my Savior and Lord. Thank you for forgiving me. Amen.'"

Keep it simple. It can be longer or shorter. It all depends on the situation. The main thing is addressing the prayer to Jesus Christ and including repentance and forgiveness. Helping the person with what to pray relieves them of the embarrassment of not knowing what to say. Remember, they may only know what to say by what you have told them in your story. Make it as easy as you can for them to surrender their life to God. Keep it simple. Eyes open, eyes closed, standing, sitting, kneeling, hands clasped, hands at their side, it makes no difference. Whatever seems the most appropriate and natural, just do it. At this point God is in charge. Allow them space to have an authentic encounter with the Lord Jesus Christ.

Follow up.
It is critical for the person who just received Christ to immediately be told what to do next. This primary responsibility falls with the person who was the most instrumental in

their coming to the Lord. That could be you, the person who prayed the prayer with them, the evangelist who gave the altar call, or the pastor who gave the invitation. It is a tragedy that precious new babes in the Lord are allowed to leave God's altar of repentance without being told what to do next. The next steps are:

- Get water baptized to bury the old life.
- Get baptized in the Holy Spirit for power to resist sin and be an effective witness.
- Get a Bible and begin reading the New Testament daily.
- Get into a weekly Bible discipleship class for new believers and hang around those who have been walking with the Lord for a long time.
- Get into to a Spirit-filled, Bible-believing church every time they open the doors.

Leading People *Back* to Christ

Coming to Christ is one thing. Staying with Christ your whole life is another. There remains the tendency for us to wander away, some further than others. Jesus illustrates this in Matthew 18.

Matthew 18:12-13

"What do you think? If a man owns a hundred sheep, and one of them wanders away, will he not leave the ninety-nine on the hills and go to look for the one that wandered off? And if he finds it, I tell you the truth, he is happier about that one sheep than about the ninety-nine that did not wander off." NIV

Jesus' teaching clearly shows the value of the person who has wandered away. He goes to look for that person—sometimes through those of us who are willing to be used this way.

Seek those who are lost.

Over the years, I (Sonja) have been privileged to be used by the Lord to help people find their way back to Him. Following is an account of one such instance.

Why? Why?

I was working in a large office building that headquartered several companies. As I went up and down the elevators to and from my office, I would occasionally see a very attractive redheaded young woman get off the floor below mine. I felt the Holy Spirit prompting me to befriend her, but she was extremely aloof.

One day we were alone on the ride up. After greeting her, I asked her if she would like to have lunch some day. With a look of absolute consternation, she blurted out, "Why?" I was caught somewhat off guard by her response but recovered enough to say that I would just like to get to know her. Again, she adamantly responded with, "Why?" It was one of the most unusual responses I had ever had to a simple luncheon invitation. Again, I said I would just like to get acquainted. By then we were at her floor, she bounded out as she reluctantly said, "Well, I guess I could. How about Friday?" "That would be great," I replied. "I'll meet you in the lobby Friday at noon." With that, she scampered away like a frightened rabbit.

I was very perplexed.

I was certain the Lord was leading me to reach out to this young woman, but I admitted to Him that I was very perplexed. Friday came and we walked across the street to a hotel dining room. I picked it because it had an atmosphere that was conducive for conversation. I did a monologue for about twenty minutes. She simply would not engage in any dialogue.

Toward the end of our luncheon, she seemed to relax a bit. As we walked back to work, she finally disclosed the reason for her mysterious behavior. She said, "You really did just want to get acquainted, didn't you?" "Why, yes." I responded, "What in the world did you think I wanted to do?"

I broke into hilarious laughter.
She sheepishly related that she had heard I was a strong Christian, and she was backslidden. She was certain God had told me to get her aside and rebuke her and tell her she was headed straight for hell! As I stared at her in total disbelief, I broke into hilarious laughter—the kind where you almost wet your pants! She laughed too, laughed hard and long. That dirty liar, the deceiver, had once more been exposed!

That was the beginning of a lifelong friendship, not only with me, but also with all of my family—my husband, parents and grandparents. She began to attend my Saturday morning prayer meeting. I cannot remember the exact circumstances of when she came back to the Lord, it just happened over time. She is a very spiritual woman who is used mightily by the Lord.

They need someone to genuinely care about them.
Over the years I have led numerous hairdressers, neighbors, co-workers, and even church attendees back into relationship with Jesus. They simply needed someone to genuinely care about them and share just how much God loves them and is waiting for them to return. More often than not, I share the story of the ninety-nine sheep the Lord leaves to seek the lost one. Somehow that, more than anything, convinces them of God's personal love and concern for them. Of course the prodigal son story in Luke 15:11-31 is a great reference if they are having a "pig-pen" experience.

This is how it works.
Perhaps you are thinking, "Sure, Sonja, that's easy for you, but that is not my gift. I can't just extend myself to strangers that way. You see, I'm an introvert." Well I would respond by telling you that every Christian, yes *every* Christian, including you, can be used this way!

This is how it works: You discover how the Lord has gifted you. Perhaps it is mercy, encouragement, helps, service, hospitality, or any number of other gifts. We provide a gift assessment and teach on thirty gifts and talents of the Holy Spirit in our *Ambassador Series*. You simply tell the Lord you are willing to be used. He then takes you at your word and sets up an opportunity where you give your gift away.

Eventually, someone will comment or ask you why you did that or why are you that way. That is your cue to simply say that you are a Christian and you enjoy helping others. You might even say that you were not always this way, but Jesus has changed you. Do not overpower them, even if they act interested. Leave them wanting more, feeling safe. Too often a person shows a little interest, and we, in our zealousness, scare them or turn them off. If they are ready, they will keep coming around until they get back into relationship with the Lord. You can do it.

We may need more confidence.
If we lack confidence to be an effective minister in the marketplace, we should check how much the Holy Spirit has been allowed to work through us. Perhaps we need more of His power. The best way to gain more confidence is to ask God for more power to be an effective witness. When we ask Jesus for more power to witness, He will likely lead us to the Holy Spirit baptism. This spiritual baptism of power is the next step to becoming an effective marketplace minister. This is the next ministry skill that we will master in chapter 2.

Let's Practice
- James 1:22 says to *DO* what we have heard (read).
- Consider doing what is recommended in this chapter by referring to the "Let's Practice" in Appendix B, page 321.
- Do the Ministry Skill Assignment entitled, "Leading People to Christ."

Chapter Two

Ministry Skill Two

LEADING CHRISTIANS INTO THE HOLY SPIRIT BAPTISM

Jesus promised believers a wonderful spiritual experience. He called it "the gift of the Holy Spirit" and said they would receive power to become His witnesses and to do the works that He did. Once we have had this marvelous encounter with the Holy Spirit, we can then lead other Christians into the same experience.

The Holy Spirit baptism is a wonderful, biblical, empowering experience that is often the Christian's introduction to the supernatural power and realm of God. It certainly was mine! (Sonja)

Raised in an evangelical church where daddy was a deacon and mother sang in the choir, I came to faith in Jesus Christ so early I do not even remember exactly when. I had no trouble relating to God the Heavenly Father in large part due to my wonderful relationship with my earthly daddy. And Jesus Christ my Savior, my elder brother, was easily believed. I knew my sins were forgiven and if I died I would go to heaven. But, the Holy Ghost was some nebulous "It!" I did not know He was a person; much less did I know Him personally. However, that was all to change.

Twentieth century visitation.
During the twentieth century, the Holy Spirit of God, through a profound and life-changing supernatural experience, visited millions of Christians worldwide. These believers were longing

for a closer and more intimate relationship with God, and many were earnestly praying and seeking Him. In some cases the people were in desperate circumstances, even fearing for their very lives. Others were safe, affluent and possessed every material comfort a person could desire; yet, they too, were empty and devoid of spiritual reality. They lived in almost every country on the face of the earth and represented almost every ethnic group.

Hungry hearts.
It was as if the Holy Spirit swept over the face of the earth seeking those hungry hearts, and when He found them, He came upon them and they were transformed. There were no social, economic, ethnic, gender, or denominational barriers. I personally know of heads of state, ambassadors to the United Nations, physicists, pastors, teachers, lawyers, laborers, architects, surgeons, loggers, farmers, plumbers, students, ditch diggers, chief executive officers, 747 pilots, homemakers, actors and actresses, rock stars, priests, and nuns who have had this common experience.

We know from the Bible and historical fact that God has determined seasons and events that express His sovereign will and fulfill His eternal purposes. One such event was this outpouring of His Holy Spirit at this appointed time.

In his book entitled, *The Holiness-Pentecostal Tradition,* Vinson Synan discusses the stunning growth of the Pentecostal tradition at the end of the twentieth century. He says:

> "This could well be the major story of Christianity in the twentieth century. If what Peter Wagner says is true, that 'In all of human history, no other non-political, non-militaristic, voluntary human movement has grown as rapidly as the Pentecostal-charismatic movement in the last twenty-five years,' then Pentecostalism indeed deserves to be seen as a major Christian tradition alongside the Roman

Catholic, Orthodox, and Reformation Protestant traditions."

Back in the first century, A.D., John the Baptist named the experience by telling his contemporary believers that they were going to be baptized with the Holy Spirit.

Mark 1:7-8
And this was his (John's) message: "After me will come one more powerful than I, the thongs of whose sandals I am not worthy to stoop down and untie. I baptize you with water, but he will baptize you with the Holy Spirit." NIV

Jesus Christ is the One who baptizes with the Holy Spirit. All believers just need to ask Jesus for the gift of the Holy Spirit.

Sonja's Introduction to the Supernatural Power of God

When I was twenty-seven years old, I came to a point in my life where I began to cry out to God. I told Him that there had to be more to Him than I had experienced. I did not have enough power for myself, much less enough to help someone else. In my desperation, God met me in a most wonderful manner.

Cousin Fay is miraculously healed!
At this time, I had an older cousin who was dying from congestive heart failure and was confined to bed. We were expecting to hear of her death any day. Instead, my Grammy Hatcher informed me one day that my cousin had been miraculously healed. I was stunned, so I called cousin Fay and invited her over to my home to tell me what had happened. Honestly, she sounded like a different woman!

She came for a visit the next afternoon, and was I amazed to hear what had happened to her. As she lay in bed crying out to God to help her, suddenly her bedroom filled with the presence of God and she sat up and began to speak in a language she had never learned. She prayed and prayed in this new language so loudly that her husband came to look in on her. She said her church actually taught against this experience and she did not know anything about it, but her husband had been to a Pentecostal church when he was younger, and he knew what it was. He just smiled at her, closed the door, and left her with her Lord. The next day she was up and about, called her doctor for an appointment, and was not surprised to learn that her critically high blood pressure was normal and her heart was beating as it should!

Something stirred in me.

As I listened to my cousin, something stirred in me, a hunger for a relationship with God that would cause the supernatural to be evident in my life. Before she left that day, we knelt together and she prayed in English and then in the beautiful heavenly language the Lord had sovereignly given her. I could not deny the wonderful miracle healing that had happened in her life, yet I had serious reservations about the "speaking in tongues." By the way, she lived another twenty-five years in good health.

As one can imagine, everyone in the family was talking about what had happened to cousin Fay. My mother had an old book entitled, *The Gift of the Holy Spirit*, by John Stiles. I read the book but would stop and turn to the Scriptures in my Bible to make sure what I was reading was actually in my own Bible! Sure enough, they were there; I had just never read them with understanding before.

My church also taught against this experience.

Please remember, my church did not teach about the supernatural working of the Holy Spirit. In fact, they taught against it and warned me to stay away from such nonsense. This was a tremendous barrier for me to cross over. Yet as I read this book, I came to see that the Holy Spirit is a Person of the triune Godhead just as the Father and the Son are, and that I could have a personal relationship with Him. Further, I learned that I could know the Holy Spirit in a greater dimension as Teacher, Counselor, Comforter, and the One who would give me the ability to be an effective witness. Those were the very things my heart was longing for.

As previously mentioned, I did not have enough power for myself to live the Christian life, much less enough to help someone else. I had never led another person into a relationship with Jesus Christ. The most nervy thing I ever remember doing was inviting two girlfriends to visit my church, and they really only came because of the cute boy that was in my youth group. Talk about being powerless! I actually got embarrassed if a Christian began talking about Jesus in front of pre-Christians. I would think to myself, "Why don't they shut up? Can't they see they are embarrassing that person?" Later I came to realize that I would rather let that person go to hell than embarrass them!

Jesus baptized me with the Holy Spirit.
After I finished reading the book about the Holy Spirit, one Friday evening while home alone, I knelt beside my bed and prayed a very simple prayer that went something like this: "Lord Jesus, I understand that You are the One who baptizes with the Holy Spirit. I also understand that this is a free gift just like salvation, and it is mine for the asking. In receiving this gift I will come to know the Holy Spirit as Counselor, Teacher, Comforter and that He will give me the power to become an effective witness for You—something to give to others. I also would like to be able to pray more effectively, so I ask You for the ability to pray in languages I do not know. Thank you. By faith, right now, I receive your free gift and the next words I speak will not be English."

I took a deep breath, and began to speak nonsensical syllables that soon joined together into a fluent language. I prayed for a few minutes and then got up and walked down the hallway to the living room. On the way, I stopped at a mirror and looked at myself as I prayed. All of a sudden, I was half-way irritated as I said out loud, "Why, this is so easy, I could have done this as a child if only someone had told me!"

Would you do it over the telephone?

I went to the telephone and called Grammy Hatcher and told her I thought I had been baptized with the Holy Spirit. She rather cautiously asked me what made me think that, and I told her that I had asked Jesus for this gift and that I could speak in a language I had not learned. She asked me if I would do that over the telephone so she could hear me. Totally uninhibited, I began to speak in a beautiful language. Needless to say, she got very excited. I then learned that she had this experience when she was sixteen years old but had not talked to me about it because she knew my church taught against it. Now, it all made sense to me! As a child, I remembered hearing her singing little songs in another language. That is what this was! How amazing!

Are you taking super-vitamins?

I did not go around telling others about this wonderful experience, but within weeks my friends at my church began coming to me and asking what had happened to me. It was as if I was glowing with this new Presence. One friend asked me if I was taking super-vitamins! "No," I told them one by one, "I have had a wonderful life-changing experience with the Lord, and I would be happy to tell you about it over a cup of coffee sometime." One by one, I would share with them, and they would indicate their desire for this gift. We would pray, sometimes quietly sitting in a restaurant, and they would also receive. Because of the way I received, without any religious falderal, it was easy to lead them into the same simple, yet marvelous experience.

My transformation.

The transformation in my life was immediate and powerful. I went from someone who was embarrassed to share my faith with others to someone who is always looking for an opportunity to share. The precious Holy Spirit then became my

Teacher. He led me to read the Bible through time and again. I learned to use all of the Bible study aids, even an interlinear Greek-English New Testament. I also came into relationship with the Holy Spirit as Counselor and Comforter. He became my Friend who always exalted the Lord Jesus Christ.

In my studies I discovered that my friends and I were experiencing exactly the same things the apostles and disciples of Jesus experienced when they were baptized with the Holy Spirit. We will take a look at those experiences in a moment, but first I will give a brief teaching that has enabled me to share this controversial experience with literally thousands of believers.

The Holy Spirit Baptism
With – Within – Upon

The purpose of the Holy Spirit baptism is to be clothed with more power from heaven so we can be an effective witness for Jesus Christ. Prior to our asking for forgiveness and receiving the Lord as our Savior, the Holy Spirit was *with* us, drawing us to Christ. We received the Holy Spirit *in* us when we first believed, repented, and received Jesus Christ as Lord of our life. At that time, we were born again by the Holy Spirit. The baptism with the Holy Spirit is in addition to and separate from the initial new birth experience. The baptism with the Holy Spirit occurs when the Holy Spirit comes *upon* a believer who asks Jesus Christ for this gift of the Holy Spirit that was promised by the Father.

The following Scriptures clearly reveal this distinction of having the Holy Spirit with, within or upon us.

John 14:16-17
"And I will ask the Father, and he will give you another Counselor to be with you forever—the Spirit of truth. The world cannot accept him, because it neither sees him nor knows him. But you know him, for he lives *with* you and will be *in* you." NIV

Acts 8:15-17

When they arrived, they prayed for them that they might receive the Holy Spirit, because the Holy Spirit had not yet come *upon* any of them; they had simply been baptized into the name of the Lord Jesus. Then Peter and John placed their hands on them, and they received the Holy Spirit. NIV

Acts 10:44-46

While Peter was still speaking these words, the Holy Spirit came *on* all who heard the message. The circumcised believers who had come with Peter were astonished that the gift of the Holy Spirit had been poured out even *on* the Gentiles. For they heard them speaking in tongues and praising God. NIV

Acts 19:5-6

On hearing this, they were baptized into the name of the Lord Jesus. When Paul placed his hands on them, the Holy Spirit came *on* them, and they spoke in tongues and prophesied. NIV

DWJD

- We see that the Holy Spirit is *with* us, drawing us to the Savior prior to our salvation.
- When we came to the point of surrender and asked Jesus Christ to forgive us of our sins and to come into our lives, the Holy Spirit came *within* us, quickened our spirits, and made us alive unto God. We were born of the Spirit, born from above. We became God's son or daughter. If we died, we would go to heaven.
- However, the Scriptures very clearly demonstrate that there is a subsequent experience with the Holy Spirit where He comes *upon* us and baptizes us with power. That is what we and millions of other believers have personally experienced.

The Holy Spirit in the Book of Acts

We are now going to take a little sojourn through the first twelve chapters of the book of Acts and see for ourselves how the Holy Spirit came upon the apostles, disciples, Jews, Gentiles, men and women. We will look at the experiences they had and hopefully be able to see ourselves on those pages. We should be having the very same life-changing, supernatural encounters they had in the first century A.D.

We will see what the Father, the Lord Jesus Christ, John the Baptist, and the apostles Peter and Paul had to say about this life-changing gift. Keep the following words in mind as you read: *with, within, upon, on, gift, filled, power, and baptized with the Holy Spirit.* It is exciting to observe the activity of the Holy Spirit in the birth of the New Testament Church.

The Father's promise.

Luke 24:49

"I am going to send you what my Father has promised; but stay in the city until you have been clothed with *power* from on high." NIV

DWJD

Jesus said the Father promises we will be clothed with power. The Holy Spirit baptism is for power to witness.

Jesus instructed His disciples to wait for the Father's promise. They had no idea what to expect, but wait they did. On the day of Pentecost the promise came.

Jesus is the One who baptizes with the Holy Spirit.
We begin with John the Baptist's message as recorded in the first chapter of the gospel of Mark.

Mark 1:7-8

And this was his message: "After me will come one more powerful than I, the thongs of whose sandals I

65

am not worthy to stoop down and untie. I baptize you with water, but he will baptize you with the Holy Spirit." NIV

In this passage, John distinguished between the water baptism he was administering and the baptizing with the Holy Spirit that Jesus would do.

Jesus instructed His disciples to wait for the gift.

The following Scripture records a command Jesus gave His followers:

Acts 1:4-5

On one occasion, while he was eating with them, he gave them this *command*: "Do not leave Jerusalem, but wait for the *gift* my Father promised, which you have heard me speak about. For John baptized with water, but in a few days *you will be baptized with the Holy Spirit.*" NIV

Jesus gave us a command, not a suggestion, to wait for the gift of the Holy Spirit. This means we should be baptized in the Holy Spirit so we can become an effective witness.

Jesus said His disciples would receive power.

Acts 1:8

"But you will receive *power* when the Holy Spirit comes *on* you; and you will be my witnesses in Jerusalem, and in all Judea and Samaria, and to the ends of the earth." NIV

Jesus said the purpose for the Holy Spirit baptism is for power to be an effective witness.

Jesus' word comes to pass on Pentecost.

We know these Scriptures were fulfilled as documented in Acts chapter 2. The Holy Spirit came on Pentecost.

Acts 2:1-4

When the day of Pentecost came, they were all together in one place. Suddenly a sound like the blowing of a violent wind came from heaven and filled the whole house where they were sitting. They saw what seemed to be tongues of fire that separated and came to rest *on* each of them. All of them were *filled with the Holy Spirit and began to speak in other tongues as the Spirit enabled them.* NIV

The Holy Spirit came just as the Father and Jesus had promised. These believers caused quite a commotion with this supernatural empowering that enabled them to speak in languages they had not learned. We can do the same.

They were declaring the wonders of God, and the God-fearing Jews from every nation under heaven were bewildered and inquired of them what this meant. A large crowd gathered. Peter stood up, raised his voice, and addressed them with an anointed, masterful message. He referenced the prophet Joel by saying in part:

Acts 2:17-18

"'In the last days, God says, I will pour out my Spirit on all people. Your sons and daughters will prophesy, your young men will see visions; your old men will dream dreams. Even on my servants, both men and women, I will pour out my Spirit in those days, and they will prophesy." NIV

After Peter finished speaking, the latter part of Acts 2 records the people's response:

Acts 2:37-41
When the people heard this, they were cut to the heart and said to Peter and the other apostles, "Brothers, what shall we do?" Peter replied, "Repent and be baptized, every one of you, in the name of Jesus Christ for the forgiveness of your sins. And you will receive the *gift of the Holy Spirit.* The promise is for you and your children and for all who are far off— for all whom the Lord our God will call." With many other words he warned them; and he pleaded with them, "Save yourselves from this corrupt generation." Those who accepted his message were baptized, and about three thousand were added to their number that day. NIV

DWJD

The Holy Spirit is *upon* us so that we may continue the task of reconciling the world to God through Jesus Christ.

This promise is for us today.
I am so glad the Holy Spirit had Peter's words recorded so we could know for certain that this promise is for us today. We can see with certainty that the gift of the Holy Spirit we received is the same gift the first believers received—and with the same results. My friends and I had received that same gift of the Holy Spirit and were beginning to experience the supernatural things of God. This was the dimension that was missing in our lives. Yes, we knew Jesus Christ as Savior, but we were absolutely powerless. All that changed when we received the gift of the Holy Spirit after we repented and were baptized for the forgiveness of our sins.

New Testament Church Birthed in the Supernatural

The New Testament church was birthed in this marvelous supernatural outpouring of the promised Holy Spirit. But it did not stop there. Tremendous healings, deliverances and miracles were taking place, and God was adding believers to the church every day.

The crippled beggar is healed.

As we read through the book of Acts, we are captivated by the dynamic of the power of the Holy Spirit. In chapter 3, Peter heals the crippled beggar, and again, a crowd gathers and he preaches another message urging them to repent and turn to the resurrected Jesus Christ for the forgiveness of sins. Many who heard the message believed, and the number of men grew to about five thousand. *What had happened to Peter who, prior to being baptized in the Holy Spirit, was in hiding for fear of the Jewish leaders?*

By what power?

Peter and John were put in jail overnight. The next day the rulers, elders, and teachers of the law met in Jerusalem. They had Peter and John brought before them and began to question them: "By what *power* or what name did you do this?"

It is the name of Jesus Christ of Nazareth.

Peter, *filled with the Holy Spirit*, again preaches yet another time. He says, "It is by the name of Jesus Christ of Nazareth, whom you crucified but whom God raised from the dead, that this man stands before you healed. Salvation is found in no one else, for there is no other name under heaven given to men by which we must be saved" (Acts 4:10, 12).

Acts 4:13-14

When they saw the courage of Peter and John and realized that they were unschooled, ordinary men, they were astonished and they took note that these men had been with Jesus. But since they could see the man who had been healed standing there with them, there was nothing they could say. NIV

DWJD

When we experience miracles as we minister, the skeptics have nothing they can say. It is the power of the Holy Spirit that captivates the pre-Christian.

This notable miracle could not be denied, so the leaders threatened Peter and John about speaking no longer to anyone in this name, but did not punish them because they said, "Everybody living in Jerusalem knows they have done an outstanding miracle, and we cannot deny it" (Acts 4:16). All the people were praising God for what had happened. For the man who was miraculously healed was over forty years old (see Acts 4:21-22).

Astounding power.
The unleashing of power through the Holy Spirit baptism was astounding! The unschooled fishermen from Galilee who had been with Jesus were turning their world upside down. It is the same today. Uneducated (and educated) people who come into personal relationship with Jesus Christ and are baptized with His Holy Spirit also turn their worlds upside down! This has happened through the centuries with countless millions of people and is happening today around the world.

I (Sonja) began to see the miraculous manifest.
I personally had this power come into my life. As I began to study about the supernatural healing recorded in the book of Acts, faith for healing began to rise up within me. As I began to venture out to pray for people, I began to see the miraculous manifest through my own hands.

Corporate executive healed.
One time a corporate executive with whom I worked was scheduled to give an important presentation. He came to me and asked me to pray for him because he had such a bad migraine headache he could hardly see. One of the other vice

presidents overheard him ask me and asked if he could observe how this worked. I told him that would be fine and suggested the three of us simply walk away from the group like
we were having a discussion. As we did, I simply reached up,
put my hand on the executive's head and commanded the
pain to leave in the name of Jesus. He was instantly healed,
and the other man was astounded. He said he had heard
about this type of healing, but that was the first time he had
observed such a thing. I then explained about the desire of
the Lord to heal and the power of the Holy Spirit, being extremely careful to give the credit and glory to the Lord Jesus
Christ. As a vice president of that company, the Lord gave me
numerous opportunities to pray for the sick in a very natural
way that demonstrated His goodness. The executive I prayed
for soon became a Christian.

Place of prayer shaken.
Peter and John returned to the believers who were gathered
and reported all that happened to them, and then they all
raised their voices together in prayer to God. After they
prayed, the place where they were meeting was shaken. And
they were all filled with the Holy Spirit and spoke the Word of
God boldly (see Acts 4:23-24, 31).

How long has it been, if ever, since the meeting place where
you pray has been shaken? The power of God was being released in their midst, and it is our firm conviction that He
wants to do the same today! We have had experiences in pre-
service prayer times where it was so powerful that if you
opened the door, the power emitting from those assembled
would almost knock you to your knees.

Revelation gifts begin to operate.
As we move on to chapter 5 in Acts, we see the revelation
gifts of the Holy Spirit being manifested through the apostles
in a frightening and awesome way concerning a husband and
wife named Ananias and Sapphira. They lied to the apostles
about a gift they gave to the church and both were struck
dead for "testing the Spirit of the Lord." Because of this, great

fear seized the whole church and all who heard about these events.

Apostles heal many.

Acts 5:12-16

The apostles performed many miraculous signs and wonders among the people. And all the believers used to meet together in Solomon's Colonnade. No one else dared join them, even though they were highly regarded by the people. Nevertheless, more and more men and women believed in the Lord and were added to their number. As a result, people brought the sick into the streets and laid them on beds and mats so that at least Peter's shadow might fall on some of them as he passed by. Crowds gathered also from the towns around Jerusalem, bringing their sick and those tormented by evil spirits, and all of them were healed. NIV

The believers were now doing what Jesus did and with the same results! This remains true today. Believers filled with the Holy Spirit are healing the sick.

The encounter they had with the Holy Spirit on the day of Pentecost had obviously transformed them into powerful servants of the living Christ!

It is still true today.

We have experienced this same power manifested through us for preaching, healing, and deliverances. Specific examples are given in later chapters of this book.

Angels open prison doors.

The apostles are jailed for causing such an uproar in Jerusalem, an angel frees them, and yet another opportunity is provided for Peter and the other apostles to preach Jesus. The ruling Jews of the Sanhedrin had them flogged, again ordered them not to speak in the name of Jesus, and let them go. They left rejoicing because they had been counted worthy of suffering disgrace for the Name (see Acts 5:18-19, 40-41).

Stephen martyred.

Now Stephen, a man full of God's grace and power, did great wonders and miraculous signs among the people. The men who opposed him could not stand up against his wisdom or the Spirit by whom he spoke. However, they conspired against Stephen with false accusations and had him brought before the Sanhedrin. After he preached a wonderful and convicting message, they dragged him out of Jerusalem and stoned him to death. Saul of Taurus was watching and giving approval of his death.

The Church Persecuted and Scattered

On the day Stephen was martyred a great persecution broke out against the church at Jerusalem, and all except the apostles were scattered through Judea and Samaria.

Philip in Samaria.

Acts 8:4-8

Those who had been scattered preached the Word wherever they went. Philip went down to a city in Samaria and proclaimed the Christ there. When the crowds heard Philip and saw the miraculous signs he did, they all paid close attention to what he said. With shrieks, evil spirits came out of many, and many paralytics and cripples were healed. So there was great joy in that city. NIV

When we allow the Holy Spirit to minister through us, He will cause evil spirits to come out, healings to manifest, and miraculous signs to happen.

Simon the sorcerer.

Acts 8:9-13

Now for some time a man named Simon had practiced sorcery in the city and amazed all the people of Samaria. He boasted that he was someone great, and all the people, both high and low, gave him their attention and exclaimed, "This man is the divine power known as the Great Power." They followed him because he had amazed them for a long time with his magic. But when they believed Philip as he preached the good news of the kingdom of God and the name of Jesus Christ, they were baptized, both men and women. Simon himself believed and was baptized. And he followed Philip everywhere, astonished by the great signs and miracles he saw. NIV

As we obey the leading of the Holy Spirit, we will experience the same things that happened to Philip. We must be full of the Holy Spirit for "great signs and miracles" to manifest.

Apostles visit Samaria.

Acts 8:14-19

When the apostles in Jerusalem heard that Samaria had accepted the word of God, they sent Peter and John to them. When they arrived, they prayed for them that they might receive the Holy Spirit, because the Holy Spirit had not yet come *upon* any of them; they had simply been baptized into the name of the Lord Jesus. Then Peter and John placed their hands on them, and they *received the Holy Spirit.* When Simon saw that the Spirit was given at the laying on of the apostles' hands, he offered them money and said, "Give me also this ability so that everyone on whom I lay my hands may receive the Holy Spirit." NIV

- Laying on of hands is a scriptural pattern for those already baptized in the Holy Spirit to minister this experience to others.
- The people who were being baptized in the Holy Spirit were believers that had already been baptized in water.

The Holy Spirit baptism is for the converted.

This is an excellent example of the subsequent work of the Holy Spirit *after* repentance, salvation, and water baptism. We know Philip would never have baptized people who were not born again by the Holy Spirit through faith in the Lord Jesus Christ. But, *"the Holy Spirit had not yet come upon any of them; they had simply been baptized into the name of the Lord Jesus"* (Acts 8:16). Yet when Peter and John placed their hands on them, they received the Holy Spirit. Simon the Sorcerer "saw that the Spirit was given at the laying on of the apostles' hands." He even offered them money if they would give him that ability. Of course he was sternly rebuked (see Acts 8:18-23).

Aeneas and Dorcas.

Peter was traveling about the country empowered by the Holy Spirit and doing the miraculous. Two notable miracles, the healing of Aeneas and the raising of Dorcas from the dead, resulted in many people coming to the Lord in Lydda, Sharon, and Joppa.

Acts 9:32-35

As Peter traveled about the country, he went to visit the saints in Lydda. There he found a man named Aeneas, a paralytic who had been bedridden for eight years. "Aeneas," Peter said to him, "Jesus Christ heals you. Get up and take care of your mat." Immediately Aeneas got up. All those who lived in Lydda and Sharon saw him and turned to the Lord. NIV

Holy Spirit baptized believers should be available to heal the sick wherever they go. In this passage, the Lord used healing to quickly evangelize the communities of Lydda and Sharon.

It happened to us in Thailand.

We must remember that one of the main purposes of the miraculous is to draw pre-Christians to the saving knowledge of the Lord Jesus Christ. We experienced this in a refugee camp in northern Thailand. Our hosts were Christians, and almost their entire camp had become Christians. The children were well behaved, and we could sense the peace of the Lord. The camp was clean and there was order.

Our host had arranged for us to visit another camp that was totally pre-Christian. What a contrast! The children were like little wild savages, clawing at us as they were begging. Several of the women approached the men in our group to see if they were interested in sex for money. It was quite an environment in which to preach the Gospel.

We boldly declared that our God would heal the sick.

John was led to have the music played loudly to draw a crowd. He then preached a simple message about the God we serve and how powerful He is. Next, he boldly declared that our God would heal those that were sick to show them that He loved them. Immediately, a man that was obviously well known came forward. He had suffered with terrible back pain for quite some time. After prayer, he was healed and it caused quite a stir among the hundred or so people watching. Afterwards, John gave an altar call for salvation and people responded. This was unheard of since the camps usually respond only when the tribal chief indicates it is the thing to do. However, some responded for salvation because of what they had observed. The chief invited our host to come back the next week because he wanted to explore Christianity further.

Cornelius calls for Peter in Acts 10.

At Caesarea there was a Gentile man named Cornelius. He was a centurion in the Roman army. He and all his family were devout and God-fearing. He gave generously to those in need and prayed to God regularly. One day he had a vision wherein an angel of God spoke with him and told him to send men to Joppa to bring back a man named Simon who was called Peter. The angel even told him the exact home where Peter was staying.

The next day as the messengers were approaching the city, Peter was given a vision about not calling anything impure that God has made clean. While he was pondering the meaning of the vision, the Spirit told him three men were coming, and he was to go with them to Caesarea. The next day he went with the men to Cornelius' home and upon arrival explained that even though they were Gentiles, God had shown him he was not to call any man impure or unclean. Peter then began to preach a powerful message about Jesus of Nazareth.

The Holy Spirit comes on the Gentiles.

Acts 10:44-48

While Peter was still speaking these words, the Holy Spirit came on all who heard the message. The circumcised believers who had come with Peter were astonished that the gift of the Holy Spirit had been poured out even on the Gentiles. For they heard them speaking in tongues and praising God. Then Peter said, "Can anyone keep these people from being baptized with water? They have received the Holy Spirit just as we have." So he ordered that they be baptized in the name of Jesus Christ. Then they asked Peter to stay with them for a few days. NIV

Speaking in tongues (spiritual language) and praising God is a definite pattern in Scripture that accompanies the Holy Spirit baptism. The same should be expected whenever the Holy Spirit comes *upon* those who believe.

Peter explains his actions.

Acts 11:1-4

The apostles and the brothers throughout Judea heard that the Gentiles also had received the word of God. So when Peter went up to Jerusalem, the circumcised believers criticized him and said, "You went into the house of uncircumcised men and ate with them." Peter began and explained everything to them precisely as it had happened. NIV

Acts 11:15-18

"As I began to speak, the Holy Spirit came on them as he had come on us at the beginning. Then I remembered what the Lord had said: 'John baptized with water, but you will be baptized with the Holy Spirit.' So if God gave them the same gift as he gave us, who believed in the Lord Jesus Christ, who was I to think that I could oppose God?" When they heard this, they had no further objections and praised God, saying, "So then, God has granted even the Gentiles repentance unto life." NIV

The Holy Spirit baptism convinced Peter, the apostles, and other Jewish believers that Gentiles were acceptable to God.

It is for today!

Here we have recorded that the Holy Spirit was poured out on Gentile men and women. It was fulfilling Acts 2:37-39 where Peter said the *gift of the Holy Spirit* was for them and their children and all who are far off—*for all whom the Lord our God will call.* This clearly demonstrates that this wonderful gift is also for us today as we are "all who are far off—for all whom the Lord our God will call."

Saul's conversion and ministry.

After Saul's encounter with the living Christ on the road to Damascus and the godly Ananias obeys the Lord's instructions given to him in a vision, he at once began to preach in the synagogues that Jesus is the Son of God.

Some years later, Paul was on a missionary journey that took him to Ephesus. There he found some disciples and asked them, "Did you receive the Holy Spirit when you believed?"

Acts 19:1-7

While Apollos was at Corinth, Paul took the road through the interior and arrived at Ephesus. There he found some disciples and asked them, *"Did you receive the Holy Spirit when you believed?"* They answered, "No, we have not even heard that there is a Holy Spirit." So Paul asked, "Then what baptism did you receive?" "John's baptism," they replied. Paul said, "John's baptism was a baptism of repentance. He told the people to believe in the one coming after him, that is, in Jesus." On hearing this, they were baptized into the name of the Lord Jesus. When Paul placed his hands on them, the Holy Spirit came on them, and *they spoke in tongues and prophesied.* There were about twelve men in all. NIV

DWJD

Here is recorded yet another instance, years after Pentecost, where the same pattern is followed. Once believers have the proper understanding for receiving the Holy Spirit, hands are laid on them, they receive the gift of the Holy Spirit, and then release a spiritual language or prophesy.

Paul prays in tongues.

It is clear that the baptism with the Holy Spirit was a foundational truth and experience in the New Testament Church. The great apostle Paul obviously enjoyed this experience himself because he told the Corinthians later that he prayed in tongues more than all of them (see 1 Corinthians 14:18).

Sonja experienced the same things they did!

The apostles had been with the Lord for three and one-half years. He had personally mentored them. After His resurrection, but before His ascension, He had breathed on them and they had been born again. I, too, had been born again. Yet, they were full of fear and ineffective, just like I was.

Jesus instructed them to wait for the promise of the Father, for the *gift* of the Holy Spirit, to be endued with power from on high. On the day of Pentecost, the Holy Spirit came *upon* them in such a powerful and supernatural way that they were never the same. They evangelized the then-known world and most were martyred for their faith. What transformed them? It was the Holy Spirit of God who baptized and clothed them with His power. That is exactly what happened to me. I have never been the same!

What Happens When We Ask?

Jesus Christ gives the Holy Spirit to those who ask.

Luke 11:10-13

"For *everyone* who asks, receives; and he who seeks, finds; and to him who knocks, it will be opened. Now suppose one of you fathers is asked by his son for a fish; he will not give him a snake instead of a fish, will he? Or if he is asked for an egg, he will not give him a scorpion, will he? If you then, being evil, know how to give good gifts to your children, *how much more will your heavenly Father give the Holy Spirit to those who ask Him?*" NASB

We receive the gift of the Holy Spirit the moment we ask, just like when we asked for salvation.

How to ask.

If you have not had the experience before and would like to receive the gift of the Holy Spirit, you can pray this simple prayer:

Jesus, baptize me in the Holy Spirit. Fill me with Your power so I can be a better witness for You. Thank You, Lord. I have received. Help me now to release my spiritual language. Amen.

Expect the Holy Spirit to come upon you and give you faith to speak words that are foreign to you. He gives the words, you do the speaking.

Biblical Reasons for Speaking in Tongues

1 Corinthians 14:5

I would like every one of you to speak in tongues, but I would rather have you prophesy. He who prophesies is greater than one who speaks in tongues, unless he interprets, so that the church may be edified. NIV

Paul encouraged everyone to speak in tongues and prophesy.

1 Corinthians 14:4

He who speaks in a tongue edifies himself; but he who prophesies edifies the church. NIV

Jude 20

But you, dear friends, build yourselves up in your most holy faith and pray in the Holy Spirit. NIV

Praying and worshiping in tongues edifies the believer spiritually and builds up the inner spirit.

1 Corinthians 14:14-15

For if I pray in a tongue, *my spirit prays*, but my mind is unfruitful. So what shall I do? *I will pray with my spirit*, but I will also pray with my mind; *I will sing with my spirit*, but I will also sing with my mind. NIV

Praying and worshiping in tongues allows us to enter the realm of the supernatural. We are communicating with the Lord in the natural and supernatural dimensions.

1 Corinthians 14:26

What then shall we say, brothers? When you come together, everyone has a hymn, or a word of instruction, a *revelation*, *a tongue* or *an interpretation*. All of these must be done for the strengthening of the church. NIV

Praying in tongues allows us to hear words of instruction from the Holy Spirit, receive revelation from Him, and may give us the interpretation of what the Holy Spirit is saying.

How Important is Speaking in Tongues?

You probably know by now that we feel that the Holy Spirit baptism and speaking in tongues are essential if we are going to do what Jesus did. The core issue is about power, supernatural power—*dunamis* dynamite power—given by the Holy Spirit. The vehicle God has chosen for the imparting of this power is the Holy Spirit baptism. The accompanying supernatural occurrence of speaking in tongues is His idea, not ours.

No thanks, Jesus.

How important is speaking in tongues? Let us ask you this: If Jesus says to you, "I have a gift for you. It is going to empower you and make you an effective Christian. You can be a powerful witness for Me and become a candidate to be used in supernatural gifts to minister to others. Do you want the gift?" How will you respond? Who in their right mind would say, "No thanks, Jesus. I don't want Your gift. I'm satisfied with things just the way they are."

They need additional prayer.

One of the reasons we contend for those who have not released their spiritual languages is because it is most often their initiation into the supernatural realm of God. We have observed this over and over. People have prayed, asked for the gift of the Holy Spirit, but have not released their language. Because they asked, the Holy Spirit has come *upon* them, they know *something* happened, but they know there is more.

Everyone who asks receives.

We read in Luke 11:10-13 that everyone who asks receives, and that the Heavenly Father gives the Holy Spirit to those who ask Him. However, for whatever reason, if people do not release their spiritual language right at that moment, often a barrier is erected, and they need additional ministry. When we give them a clear, biblical teaching and pray against the barriers, almost 100 percent receive their language. Once that happens, they begin to move in the supernatural dimensions of God.

Many, many people have had this happen to them.

We do not have space to record the numbers of people we know who have had the experience we just described. One is our friend, Jim Hayford, Sr., Senior Pastor of Eastside Foursquare Church, Bothell, Washington, who has spoken into our life and ministry in tremendously significant ways. When we first asked him about our understanding of people getting baptized in the Holy Spirit and releasing their language at a later time, he smiled and related the following testimony regarding his receiving the baptism of the Holy Spirit.

Pastor Jim Hayford, Sr.

When I was fifteen years old, I visited my brother Jack and his wife Anna in Indiana where they were pastoring a small church. During the course of that summer I attended two Foursquare summer camps my brother was directing. An emphasis was made on the ministry of the Holy Spirit. This summer with my brother was my first personal experience with Pentecostal teaching or practice. Believe me when I say, it was "quite an eye-opener!"

It was at the closing of a morning class on "The Baptism of the Holy Spirit" in the big sawdust-floored tabernacle at Spencer Lake, Wisconsin that I felt compelled to respond to the invitation to "receive the baptism." I know that my young heart was convinced that I needed more of the power of God in my life and so I went forward for prayer. A number of well-meaning people prayed with me that morning for a considerable period of time hoping that I would speak in tongues and give them "evidence" of my Holy Spirit baptism.

I remember walking out of that auditorium with two distinct and equally strong impressions. First, I knew God had met me in a profound way that I could not explain—and I knew I was "different" because of it. Second, I felt self-conscious of the fact that I had somehow disappointed my prayer partners because I had not spoken in tongues. Regardless of my feelings or impressions, I am convinced that I rode away from that youth camp the next day having experienced the promise of the Lord Jesus that "...out of your innermost being shall flow a river of living water..." (John 7:38 KJV)

My recollection of that following year of my life involved an entirely new dimension of boldness in my Christian testimony. I remember that the Bible came alive to me. I found myself regularly reading it with true interest and spiritual hunger rather than just as required by my parents. My leadership ability became apparent at my church and was recognized by adults and kids alike.

I attribute this remarkable surge of spiritual and personal growth in my life to what happened to me at that altar back in Wisconsin the summer before. I believe—even though I did not speak in tongues that historic morning—that I most definitely was baptized in the Holy Spirit. The release of spiritual strength and witness in my life was the direct result and "evidence," if you please, of that experience.

A seed of doubt was most definitely planted in my young mind and developing theological construct after walking away from the altar without a prayer language. I did question (to myself) if I was "Spirit-filled." I sometimes did wonder if I had somehow "flunked" a God-test by not speaking in tongues as prompted. What could I do? I remember praying and asking the Lord to: "Give me the gift of tongues in His way and in His time...I was open."

It was fourteen months later sitting in the back row of the Foursquare Church in Corning, California on another summer day where a friend of our family was pastoring that I first spoke in tongues. Much to my own surprise I found myself speaking quietly in a language I had not learned while I sat all alone and was actually focusing my prayers at the time on a small group of young people who were at the front of the church being prayed for by the pastor about some other issue. Hot tears ran down my face as I acknowledged that the Lord had indeed answered my prayers about receiving the gift of tongues. This expression of God's grace has been part of my life every day since.

Years later as a pastor and student of Scripture I would learn that the baptism of the Holy Spirit and the gifts of the Holy Spirit are not to be confused with one another. While the gift of tongues is obviously important to every believer as indicated by its sovereign occurrence at Pentecost, this gift is not synonymous with one's baptism. They can be concurrent or they can be separate. I believe that all of the gifts flow out of the baptism experience...some sooner than later.

I thank God for the development of the gifts of the Holy Spirit, beginning with the gift of tongues that occurred a full year after my Holy Spirit baptism. Many other spiritual gifts have developed over the years into a useful and edifying part of my life and ministry. I hope this testimony will be encouraging and helpful to others like myself who have struggled with the issue of not speaking in tongues "when they were supposed to."

Relationship with the Holy Spirit.
Our personal relationship with the Holy Spirit is the key issue. Are we in intimate communion with Him? It is through this personal interchange with Him that His gifts begin to flow through us. Gifts without relationship, love, and biblical foundation can be deceiving.

The gift is given when we ask in faith.
We know that classical Pentecostal theology states that you are not baptized in the Holy Spirit until you speak in tongues. However, we believe that the gift is given when we ask in faith believing—just like salvation. Then we can speak in a spiritual language if we understand that we can and if we want

86

to. Because ministers do not always give a thorough scriptural basis for receiving, people often respond with misunderstandings and, therefore, end up with a less-than-satisfactory experience. If the teaching is nebulous, the experience is likely to be nebulous as well.

That is scary to me.

We ask people who come to us for prayer for this gift if they thoroughly understand what they are asking for. On numerous occasions, when asked if they want to release their spiritual language when the Holy Spirit comes upon them, they have responded, "Oh, no! I don't want to do that. That's scary to me." We then open the Scriptures to them and make sure they fully understand the supernatural nature of the experience. Once they see it in the Bible, they then can make an informed decision. If we had prayed before interviewing them, we would have been trying to lead them where they did not want to go. Many people have had horrible experiences because of expectations put upon them by uninformed or insensitive ministers.

We respect your opinions.

We know many Pentecostals will disagree with our thesis that believers are baptized in the Holy Spirit when they ask in faith for the gift. If they are unable to release their spiritual language at that very moment, they often do as soon as they get alone and quiet before the Lord. Or, they may need further instructions and encouragement before they break the barrier and begin speaking. We will never argue about this subject. We respect the rights of others' opinions and respectfully ask they would do the same.

Being Continually Filled with the Spirit

After we are baptized with the Holy Spirit, we are then admonished to be *filled* with the Holy Spirit. This experience produces power to live an effective Christian life characterized by joy.

Ephesians 5:18-19
Do not get drunk on wine, which leads to debauchery. Instead, be *filled* with the Spirit. Speak to one another with psalms, hymns and spiritual songs. Sing and make music in your heart to the Lord. NIV

DWJD

We are baptized in the Holy Spirit once. We are then to be filled with the Holy Spirit on a daily basis.

This is not a once-for-all experience. Rather, it is one we should consciously contend for on a daily basis. One of the primary ways to stay filled is to pray in your spiritual language (tongues) by the enabling of the Holy Spirit. Other ways include: daily reading, studying, and meditating in the Bible; journaling; fellowshipping with believers; and participating in a small group with other Christians.

Singing spiritual songs.
As stated in Ephesians 5:19, when we are filled with the Spirit we can sing spiritual songs. These often come in the form of unpremeditated worship in our spiritual language. We may sing the Spirit-inspired words to a known melody or a brand new one—depending on how the precious Holy Spirit leads us. This adds a supernatural dimension to private and corporate worship and is a truly beautiful experience.

Misunderstandings

The baptism with the Holy Spirit has brought much confusion to the Body of Christ—primarily because of a lack of proper teaching. It has now been experienced by millions of believers worldwide in all Christian denominations, yet there are still those who deny its authenticity. Here are some of the primary reasons:

- It is not necessarily a sign of spirituality; it is a gift for the believer, no matter how young they are in the Lord. A brand new believer can have this experience. Without a proper biblical foundation, some immature believers have inferred to other Christians they were "more spiritual" because they "spoke in tongues." Wrong, wrong, wrong! There are many very spiritual Christians who have not had this experience. However, if they desire more of the Holy Spirit in their lives, this gift is for them also. They already have salvation, but this experience is about supernatural power to more effectively live the Christian life and better understand the supernatural realm.

- Many people equate this experience to only "speaking in tongues." As wonderful as that experience is (speaking in languages one has not learned—glossolalia), it is only a small part of the total experience. As we have seen, the experience is about supernatural power, edification, and many other dimensions of the Holy Spirit. It is often the introduction of the believer to the supernatural of God and provides insight into the supernatural of Satan as well.

- We must always bear in mind that this experience is about our personal relationship with our Lord Jesus Christ and the Holy Spirit. It is out of this relationship that the gifts and power of the Holy Spirit are released for the benefit of others.

- We know of very few Christians who are comfortable dealing with demonized people if they have not been baptized with the Holy Spirit. To set these unfortunate souls free, one must be operating in the supernatural gifts of discerning of spirits, words of wisdom and words of knowledge. We continue to see numerous people set free, but it is always by the working of the Holy Spirit through us, showing us the source of the demonic activity.

- Many people ask why a person would want to speak in a language they have never learned. That is certainly a fair question. The primary reason is the ability to allow the Holy Spirit to pray through us according to the perfect will of God. After we have prayed with our understanding, we often feel inadequate. Sometimes we do not even know how to pray. It is at those times that the Holy Spirit enables us to pray in an unknown language. Something happens in the spiritual dimension because the very Spirit of God has interceded on our behalf!

- Many people confuse the experience of being baptized with the Holy Spirit and praying in tongues (that is for all believers) with the gifts of "speaking in different kinds of tongues" and "interpretation of tongues" that are discussed by Paul in 1 Corinthians 12:7-11.

- The speaking in tongues that all believers can experience is a devotional prayer dimension that Paul refers to 1 Corinthians 14:2. "For anyone who speaks in a tongue does not speak to men but to God. Indeed, no one understands him; he utters mysteries with his spirit." Paul even thanks God that he "speaks in tongues" more than all of them.

- The gifts discussed in the 1 Corinthians 12 passage are for the messages from God to the church. In other words, when believers pray in tongues, it is the Holy Spirit praying through the believer to God and according to His perfect will. When a message is given to the congregation via a person speaking in tongues, it is from God to the assembled people. That, of course, would need to be interpreted so the people could know what God was saying. One is the Holy Spirit praying and interceding through the person to God; the other is God speaking to the congregation through the person, and that must be interpreted.

How to Lead a Believer into the
Baptism with the Holy Spirit

- Determine if the person is born again. This experience is only for believers.

- Determine their motive. If it is simply to speak in tongues, make sure they have a scriptural understanding before you proceed; i.e., supernatural power.

- Explain that this gift is a free gift just like salvation. You receive the gift the moment you ask in faith believing, just like salvation.

- Hindrances: Incomplete or wrong teaching, unforgiveness, or occult practices can hinder a person. If there seems to be a hindrance, give them a scriptural understanding and lead them in a prayer of repentance about these matters before proceeding.

- Explain exactly what you are going to do. Tell them, "We will examine Scripture, pray to receive the Holy Spirit, and release a spiritual language."

- Instruct the person to pray (or lead them in a prayer) that asks the Lord Jesus Christ for the gift of the Holy Spirit and the ability to pray in languages they have not learned.

- Reassure them that they will receive the moment they ask. Do not rush them. Give them "grace and space."

- Instruct the person to take a deep breath and allow the Holy Spirit to give them the words. The best description is that it may sound like a baby learning to talk with non-sensical syllables. Jesus asks us to become like little children and speak words of praise to the Heavenly Father. We simply speak the words the Holy Spirit prompts. What it sounds like is up to Him. Many people think they are

91

"just making it up." We like to continue praying and encouraging them until they are speaking fluently. When the language is flowing out of them so fast that they know they cannot be making it up, the reality of the supernatural nature of this wonderful experience dawns on them.

- Put your hand lightly on the person's shoulder and pray softly in your own prayer language. Do not push; give the person a few moments to respond to the Holy Spirit. Gently encourage them to not be afraid nor care what it sounds like. They will begin speaking, and you simply keep encouraging them and validating their experience.

- Finally, encourage them to pray in their new language as often as possible, to not get "religious" about it. Pray riding in the car, taking walks, or any other activity that lends itself to prayer.

- Summary of speaking in tongues from 1 Corinthians 14:

  It is a real language.

  You are speaking to God.

  You are speaking spiritual secrets.

  You are being personally built up and edified.

  Your spirit is praying.

  You are giving thanks well.

Becoming Marketplace Ministers

Because of the controversial nature of this gift, we have attempted to give a brief but fairly comprehensive teaching about the experience. Hopefully, it will be helpful in answering questions as you step out and begin to share this wonderful gift with those in your marketplace.

How this works in the marketplace.

One day I (Sonja) was sitting in my office when a secretary from another building stopped by to chat. Knowing I was a Christian, she asked me what I thought about that "speaking in tongues stuff." I responded by telling her that I happened to have had that experience. She was stunned, exclaimed her disbelief that I would do such a thing, and hurriedly exited.

I did not see her for a few days but had to laugh to myself when my company's reorganization was announced the next week, and that she was going to be working with me. I am sure Lois thought I would be all over her, trying to convince her to "speak in those awful tongues." However, as a corporate executive for many years, I have learned some "marketplace savvy." That is, let them come to me with a question, share a little, then change the subject. Always leave them wanting more. Pretty soon they begin to feel safe and will inquire more and more.

That was the way I handled this situation when Lois asked me about this subject. I gave my brief testimony of how I was baptized with the Holy Spirit and what had happened since. I then changed the subject. This went on for a couple of weeks until one morning she burst into my office and said, "I must be baptized with the Holy Spirit today! I can't wait any longer!" True to my convictions of not being too eager, I said, "That is great, but you will have to wait until lunch time. We cannot do that on company time."

Hamburgers and the Holy Spirit.

She anxiously waited for the noon hour. I had called a friend who worked in another building close by and asked her to pick up hamburgers, fries, and cokes and come for lunch. I had previously led her into this wonderful experience, and she was thrilled to be able to help pray with someone else to be baptized with the Holy Spirit.

After we finished lunch in the conference room, we simply laid our hands on Lois, led her in a simple prayer, and she immediately received a beautiful and fluent spiritual language. It was such a privilege to see my co-worker have the same astounding life changes that I had experienced after receiving this power encounter. She went on to become one of the most dynamic marketplace ministers I know. She and her husband own a large real estate agency, and she is a powerful witness in her community.

This is one of many, many such marketplace experiences I had while in corporate America. Now most of my encounters are on airplanes, in hair salons, and with my neighbors.

Ministering one-on-one.

Leading an individual believer into the Holy Spirit baptism is easy because you can answer their questions and calm their fears while assuring them this gift is theirs for the asking. As the above illustration demonstrates, when the seeker is properly prepared, we just lay our hands on them and pray a simple prayer, and they receive!

Ministering to small groups.

Both of us have had multitudes of opportunities to lead small groups of believers into this wonderful, life-changing experience. We always have the people who are responding to our invitation come forward so we can make eye contact with each person. If there are more than twenty, it is helpful to move to another room if possible.

I (Sonja) was recently ministering at a women's retreat. When I gave the altar call for the Holy Spirit baptism, the women flooded the front of the room where we were meeting. There was no stage, so I was trying to determine how I could make eye contact with each of the women. Spontaneously, one of the women grabbed a chair; I climbed on it, and led over twenty women into the baptism with the release of their languages. The picture in our newsletter makes me appear to be about seven feet tall in the midst of the women!

When people respond to our invitation, we explain exactly what we are going to do:

- We will pray for you.
- We will lead you in a prayer in which you will ask Jesus to baptize you with His Holy Spirit.
- We will lay hands on you while we are praying in our spiritual language.
- The Holy Spirit will come upon you, and you can begin speaking in your spiritual language.

The vast majority of those seeking, receive and release a spiritual language on the spot, and we tell them they may leave when they have received that for which they came. By doing this, we know with whom to keep praying and ministering. If people have previously asked for the gift and did not have a satisfactory experience (such as not releasing their language), they usually have some type of a mental blockage. Oftentimes they are expecting the Holy Spirit to do the speaking. We explain that the Holy Spirit gives the words, but we must do the speaking. We address these mental blockages, and usually they are released into a beautiful spiritual language. We will address this more fully at the end of this chapter.

If you are teaching on the Holy Spirit baptism and plan to give people an opportunity to respond, then ask the Holy Spirit to show you ahead of time the type of response you can expect. He has shown us on a multitude of occasions that hundreds would respond. That would allow us to discuss logistics beforehand with the pastor so we could be assured every person would have a good experience. By thoroughly teaching on the subject and having people respond on the basis of the Word and not some hyped-up emotional appeal, it is easy for them to receive.

Ministering to large groups.

It requires some planning to lead large groups of fifty or more into the Holy Spirit baptism. We recommend meeting with those in charge of the service or outreach meeting well before the actual start of the meeting. Everyone needs to know ahead of time how the altar call will be done and how many are expected to respond. The pastor or leader in charge of the service, the main speakers, the worship team, the worship leader, and all of the altar workers need to be in agreement. Always plan for a maximum response whether it materializes or not. Everyone needs to know what is expected of him or her once the altar call begins. Here are a few tips on how to avoid chaos and try to guarantee that each person responding will have a satisfactory experience with the Holy Spirit:

- Train each altar worker how to lead Christians in the Holy Spirit baptism with a graceful way that ensures the release of a new spiritual language (speaking in tongues).
- Teach each worker how to gather a little group of three-to-five from the larger group and lead them through the process of receiving the Holy Spirit baptism. Give each a "Prayer Team" name badge. If a hundred respond, twenty to twenty-five altar workers would be advisable.
- The altar call: Have them come forward to the front of the auditorium. Next, tell them to proceed to a designated room or part of the auditorium that is well away from the sound of the concluding worship music. Or, do not begin the concluding music until after the group has received instructions and has prayed to receive the Holy Spirit baptism.

- Once the large group has responded and gathered together, designate one person (normally the speaker) to explain exactly what is going to happen and what they are going to do.
- Invite those seeking ministry to join up with an altar worker in groups of three-to-five.
- Once gathered in little groups, the speaker would have everyone pray out loud inviting the Holy Spirit to come upon him or her and baptize them in the Holy Spirit.
- The altar workers would then pray and work with each person in their group until everyone has had a satisfactory release of their spiritual language.

Training is the key.
The biggest hindrance to ministering the Holy Spirit baptism in large groups is the lack of qualified altar workers. We recommend conducting a training workshop prior to the meeting to ensure a quality experience for each individual. We continually have people coming to us expressing negative experiences where they were part of a large crowd being instructed to all speak in tongues at once. It may have been satisfactory for the main speaker, but it results in a sizable number who need personal, one-on-one ministry to release their new language in an authentic and personal way.

Federal Way, Washington, USA.
We were privileged to talk to a large sanctuary full of eager Christians at Northwest Church in Federal Way, Washington. It was a special meeting dedicated to the Person of the Holy Spirit and the reasons we need His power for a more effective witness. Sonja received a word from the Holy Spirit that there would be an unusually large response. The altar call resulted in two hundred Christians coming forward for empowerment. Sonja separated one hundred and twenty of those confessing they had previously asked for this but had never released a satisfactory spiritual language. She took them into a separate meeting room. John remained with the eighty who had never asked for the gift of the Holy Spirit. We prayed and laid hands

on each of them. We took adequate time to fully explain what was to happen when they prayed for this free gift. To our knowledge, all but one released beautiful spiritual languages, personally confirming that they had been Holy Spirit baptized. Even with a sizable number of home group leaders helping us, it took an extra two hours for us to personally confirm that each one released an authentic spiritual language. It was a very exciting time. The pastor thanked us more than once and said, "The way you guys do it is unique and it surely saves a lot of time and effort for the one ministering."

Bangkok, Thailand.
I (John) was invited to be one of the daytime speakers at the three-day "Power Evangelism" conference near downtown Bangkok, Thailand. I spoke on why we need the power of the Holy Spirit to live a victorious Christian life. The daytime attendance was three thousand and over five thousand at night. The reason we stress having a lot of trained altar workers was clearly revealed at this conference. Speaking through an excellent interpreter, I preached with everything I could muster. I was speaking from a gigantic raised stage at the end of one of the largest auditoriums I have ever seen. The Holy Spirit was gracious and motivated three hundred to respond to the altar call for the baptism with the Holy Spirit.

Now what?
I quickly realized I needed help. How could I ensure that all three hundred would receive the power and speak in an unknown tongue? I did not know Thai and they did not speak English. My interpreter just shrugged his shoulders, indicating he did not know either. The Holy Spirit came to my rescue. He said, "Call on the Thais that do speak in tongues to come listen to their fellow believers speak in unknown tongues." I immediately invited about fifty Spirit baptized Thais to merge into the crowd down front. I told them to listen carefully to each person as they spoke and worshiped in tongues. When they confirmed a new spiritual language being

released in each person, they were to signal me with a "thumbs-up." What a joy to see the workers going from one seeker to another carefully listening for an unknown language.

It only took about fifteen minutes to confirm that all but a few had released a genuine spiritual language. The conference leaders came to me later and remarked they had never seen this done before. I had to say I had not either! We were all praising the Lord for such an awesome move of God. In addition to the three hundred who were baptized in the Holy Spirit, an additional five hundred people gave their lives to Jesus Christ by the end of the conference.

Let's do it right.

We have many more stories where we have led scores of hungry Christians into the baptism of power. Because we have been doing this for a long time, we forget there is a whole new generation of Christians that have not heard that there is a Holy Spirit baptism. In America today there are pastors who call themselves "Spirit-filled," yet they do not feel confident in leading the members of their congregation into the Holy Spirit baptism.

From our perspective as ordained international evangelists primarily ministering to Pentecostal pastors and leaders, we feel something is missing. Where did they get their training? What kind of training have they received since leaving seminary? We feel the Holy Spirit baptism should be high on the list of personal priorities for all disciples attending a Spirit-filled church. It is the only way for our new believers to have any chance of survival in witnessing to the hostile, twisted, and demonic world outside the church walls. So, let us do it right! Let us become truly Spirit-filled in such a way that we can turn around and lead our fellow believers into the same power-filled experience we have received.

Praying for a Satisfactory Experience

We are always sensitive toward those Christians who have previously prayed for the gift of the Holy Spirit, but did not have a satisfactory experience. There are usually twice as many of these people who respond to our altar calls as those seeking the gift for the first time. After ministering to countless numbers of people for over thirty-five years, we have come to the following conclusions:

- The teaching on this subject has been more experiential than scriptural.
- The believers did not realize that the gift of the Holy Spirit baptism is theirs for the asking and they received the moment they asked in faith.
- There often is too much loud, emotion-based ministry, and newcomers become overwhelmed.
- If they did not release a spiritual language, they feel there was something wrong with them; therefore, God was withholding His gift from them.

Once a person has an unsatisfactory experience, a mental barrier goes up. They may continue to respond for ministry time and again. When they fail to release a spiritual language, the barrier becomes reinforced with each negative experience. This always revolves around releasing their spiritual language.

God is not withholding His gift from them.
I (Sonja) usually begin ministering to these people by saying that God is not withholding His gift of the Holy Spirit and a spiritual language from them. Further, I tell them He gave them the gift when they first asked in faith. I ask them if they have seen a change in the power of God in their lives. More often than not, they say they have seen a change, more power manifesting through them, but they know there is more. By then, many of them (men and women) have tears in their

eyes. They have felt like something was wrong with them, and I dispel that notion.

Hindrances are dealt with.
Next, we explore what the hindrances might be; e.g., previous teaching against speaking in tongues, unforgiveness, or occult practices. A few of the people may have these issues, and we simply have them pray a prayer of repentance, renouncing the sinful behavior. When they do this, that barrier is broken from their lives. Most often, however, the reason they have not released their prayer language is that they simply do not know how to yield to the Holy Spirit. We can see the Holy Spirit all over them, wanting to give them their language, but they just cannot let go and begin speaking.

Sydney, Australia.
We were ministering in a large church in Sydney, Australia. John was praying for the sick on one side of the church, and I (Sonja) was praying for believers to be baptized in the Holy Spirit on the other side. Over thirty people had received and released their spiritual language. As we finished, I noticed an older man who had been standing off to the side carefully watching me minister. He came to me and told me he had been seeking the Holy Spirit baptism for over twenty-five years! He said he had requested every visiting high-powered evangelist to pray for him, but so far he just could not speak in tongues.

Are you afraid you will look and sound foolish?
I breathed a little prayer and asked for wisdom. A word of knowledge came to me, and I shared it with him by asking this question: "Are you afraid you will look and sound foolish and be embarrassed?" With a shocked look on his face, he said that had been a tormenting fear all those years. I proceeded to minister to him by reminding him that Jesus said unless we become like little children we would not see the Kingdom of God. I then asked him if he would be willing to let

101

go of his ego and his fear of looking foolish. Would he simply trust Jesus to give him a good gift?

He released a beautiful spiritual language.
With tears in his eyes, he nodded his head and prayed a humble, simple prayer asking the Lord to forgive him for his lack of childlike trust. I then laid hands on him, and he began to speak fluently in a beautiful spiritual language. He was thrilled and said, "Well, little lady, you did what the high-powered evangelists could not. Praise God!"

Home group ministry.
This next example happened in our small group that meets in our home each week. It is always interesting to see how the Holy Spirit arranges a certain mix of folks for a certain purpose. I (Sonja) am always extra curious when only a couple of people show up. Inevitably, He has a special need He is going to address.

This particular evening only Greg and Karen Fry came. It was highly unusual—the other dozen folks that normally attend were unable to attend for various reasons. Since it was just the four of us, we asked the Frys if there was anything special they wanted to pray about. Greg immediately responded by saying he wanted a greater release in his spiritual prayer language. He had received a few words, and had been prayed for multiple times, but with no satisfactory results. In fact, he was fairly discouraged about the whole situation.

Shortly, the Holy Spirit was gushing forth from him.
We said, "Well, let's just relax and begin to worship the Lord," which we did. After ten to fifteen minutes, we all became extremely joyful, even laughing. In this precious environment, the Holy Spirit came upon Greg and he began to speak and laugh at the same time. Shortly, the Holy Spirit was gushing forth from him like "streams of living water." It was the breaking down of a dam of resistance, and our dear friend has never been the same. A year later, he and Karen joined

102

us in the ministry. He flows freely in teaching, and they both operate in prophetic prayer and healing gifts. Thank You, Lord!

When working with people who are seeking a release of their spiritual prayer language, be respectful of their feelings, and ask the Lord to give you the key to the blockage.

I broke its power off of them.

Another time, I (Sonja) was teaching a group of people about the Holy Spirit baptism. Most of them had prayed for the gift before, but had not released their spiritual language. I prayed for them as a group, taking authority in Jesus' name over the previous wrong teaching they had received. I broke its power off of them and loosed them into the fullness of this wonderful experience. After I had prayed, I led them in a prayer, and they all released their spiritual language.

He had been raised as a Jehovah's Witness.

At the coffee break, a man came to me with a wonderful testimony. He had sought the Holy Spirit baptism for a number of years, but could never release his language. However, when I prayed and broke the power of the wrong teaching off of his life, he said it was as if "something actually broke off of me"—he felt it leave. He then explained he had been raised as a Jehovah's Witness, and he was sure that was what left him and allowed him to fully receive God's Gift.

We can all do this.

By sharing these examples, we hope you will be convinced of how easy this ministry really is. It can be done one-on-one or with a large number of Christians. All that is needed are the power and presence of the Holy Spirit as we minister. The same power and presence are needed as we learn how to heal the sick. This is the next ministry skill we will learn in chapter 3.

Let's Practice

- James 1:22 says to *DO* what we have heard (read).
- Consider doing what is recommended in this chapter by referring to the "Let's Practice" in Appendix B, page 322-323.
- Do the Ministry Skill Assignment entitled, "Leading Christians into the Holy Spirit Baptism."

Chapter Three

Ministry Skill Three

LEARNING HOW TO HEAL THE SICK

Jesus told us that He wanted us to do the things that He did—including healing the sick. There has been much misunderstanding within Christianity regarding this truth. In this chapter, we will carefully review what the Bible has to say about healing and learn how we, too, can be used to heal the sick.

I (John) became a Christian in March of 1973 and became a member of the Seattle Chapter of the Full Gospel Business Men's Fellowship International (FGBMFI) two months later. I watched in amazement as members of this para-church organization prayed for anyone needing healing. In astonishment I saw people get healed. The men would pray with such conviction that I assumed they were sent directly from God. Some of the healings were obvious. Not all were healed, but those who were healed got my attention. I thought these men had special powers from God. I had no idea where or how they received these special powers. So, I made it a priority to be up front where all this was happening. Christianity was new to me. I wanted to experience everything that was going on. I wanted to see how they did it. This began my journey of learning how to heal the sick.

Jesus heals the sick.
One-third of Jesus' earthly ministry was healing the sick. In Matthew 9 and 10 below, Jesus taught, He preached, and He healed the sick. If we are to do what Jesus did, healing the sick will also be a part of our ministry.

After demonstrating to His disciples how to do it, Jesus immediately gave His followers the power and authority to also heal the sick. Healing the sick is a vital part of the Lord's evangelistic strategy to win the world to Himself. Healing grabs the attention of the pre-Christian, softening their hearts to hear the way of salvation. It is a sign to them that the message the person is preaching while healing the sick is on behalf of God. It demonstrates that the Lord is working with them as an authentic ambassador of Jesus Christ.

Matthew 9:35
And Jesus went about all the cities and villages, teaching in their synagogues, preaching the gospel of the kingdom, and healing every sickness and every disease among the people. NKJV

Matthew 10:1
And when He had called His twelve disciples to Him, He gave them power over unclean spirits, to cast them out, and to heal all kinds of sickness and all kinds of disease. NKJV

As a disciple of Jesus Christ we have been authorized and empowered by Him to heal all kinds of sickness and all kinds of disease.

John's history.
We will start learning how to heal the sick by giving some early snapshots of how I came to believe in divine healing and how I began praying for the sick. My snapshots will allow you, the reader, to compare your own experiences that may coincide with mine. Your episodes may be more or less frequent. The Lord's desire is to have us arrive at the same destination, to firmly believe that Jesus Christ is still healing the sick today.

A growth of faith.

For me it all started within months of my becoming a Christian early in 1973. As the years progressed, I noticed a natural progression of faith as I witnessed God healing the sick. There were two stages of my coming to a full understanding about divine healing: *surprise encounters* and then *discovering the authentic.* Chapter 5 will thoroughly discuss the final stages where we minister healing by reliance on the Holy Spirit and His revelation gifts. In both stages, a compassionate, supernatural God progressively manifests Himself as a God who is willing to heal us. This is clearly illustrated in the following passages:

> **Mark 1:40-42** Matthew 8:2-3 Luke 5:12-13
> Then a leper came to Him, imploring Him, kneeling down to Him and saying to Him, "If You are willing, You can make me clean." And Jesus, moved with compassion, put out His hand and touched him, and said to him, "*I am willing*; be cleansed." As soon as He had spoken, immediately the leprosy left him, and he was cleansed. NKJV

DWJD

- The above Scriptures reveal God's will concerning healing. His will is plainly revealed in these three passages. They all say the same thing: He is willing to heal us!

- He is willing not only to heal leprosy, He is willing to heal *all* manner of sickness and disease. Jesus has revealed His eternal compassion and mercy to heal the sick.

- Most believe that God is able to do anything He wants. These passages proclaim that God is not only able, He is also willing to heal those who come to Him in faith.

- Therefore, we can preach with confidence that divine healing is now available through the mighty name of Jesus Christ.

- Sick people (like this leper) who are serious and determined to get healed, demonstrate the kind of faith that will set the stage for healing.
- The timing of when the healing will actually manifest is always left in the hands of the Lord. Even though He is willing to heal now, the full, physical manifestation may be instant or may take hours, days, or weeks.
- Nowhere in Scripture can we find a passage that permits us to demand an instant healing. That is foolish presumption. Because Jesus is willing, healing starts the moment we start praying for the sick.
- Our confession remains: "God is willing to heal you now. Your healing starts today. We will continue to thank Him until the physical manifestation comes to pass."
- Only God knows those sicknesses that will end in death (see John 11:4). This is why we need revelation knowledge from the Lord about how to pray in these kinds of situations. We contend for healing until the Lord reveals otherwise.

Surprise Encounters

My first attempt.

I (John) will never forget the very first time I prayed for a person needing healing. He was an old man with a damaged knee. He and I attended a luncheon meeting of the FGBMFI in north Seattle. The speaker for the meeting was a fiery faith-filled businessman who announced to everyone that God wanted to heal anyone who would come to the front for prayer. I was seated on the first row and was excited that I could watch what was going to happen. By the time the old man limped to the front for prayer, all the chapter officers were busy praying for the sick. Assuming that I was one of the "ministers," he turned to me and rolled up his pant leg. He showed me a painful bandaged knee, and asked me to pray for him. Not wanting to disappoint him, I said, "Yes, sir. We will. I'll go get somebody."

He must have been hard of hearing. He took a firm grip on my sleeve to steady himself and said, "Please! I want you to pray for me!" I turned once more to those who knew what to do. They all waved me away, firmly indicating that I was interrupting their healing ministry. So, I sat the old man down in my chair. I quickly looked around and observed what the other men were doing and saying. I looked back at the mangled knee and said, "Oh God, help me. Do something here, please." Then I heard one of the men behind me boldly say, "In the name of Jesus!" I promptly added, "Oh, that's right, God, please do it in the name of Jesus. Amen."

I did not know what to believe.
I was afraid to open my eyes. I did not know what to do next. So, with my hand still on his knee, I kept my eyes closed and silently hoped I could exit gracefully. I felt him stand up. Then I heard him shout, "I'm healed! I'm healed!" I opened my eyes and was stunned that he was jumping up and down exclaiming that God had just healed him. I said, "You are? Are you sure?" Again, he did not hear me. With no limp, he confidently marched back to his seat and testified to his friends that God had just healed his knee.

I left the meeting in a state of awe. I had no idea how that old man got healed. It sure was not because of me. I did not have a clue of how to do it. All I knew was that Jesus Christ had set up a situation where people could get healed. The old man simply needed someone to help him release his faith. I was a reluctant participant in what Jesus had set in motion two thousand years ago. It was the old man's faith that healed him. Not mine. The woman in the following Scriptures illustrates the principle of this kind of unwavering faith in Jesus Christ as the source of divine healing.

> **Luke 8:43-48** Matthew 9:20-22 Mark 5:25-34
> A woman was there who had been subject to bleeding for twelve years, but no one could heal her. She came up behind him and touched the edge of his cloak, and immediately her bleeding stopped. "Who

109

touched me?" Jesus asked. When they all denied it, Peter said, "Master, the people are crowding and pressing against you." But Jesus said, "Someone touched me; I know that power has gone out from me." Then the woman, seeing that she could not go unnoticed, came trembling and fell at his feet. In the presence of all the people, she told why she had touched him and how she had been instantly healed. Then he said to her, "Daughter, your faith has healed you. Go in peace." NIV

- There will be times when those we pray for will be exercising a high degree of faith toward God for healing. Any kind of physical contact with another believer will cause them to release their faith and receive an immediate healing.
- In these cases our faith is superfluous. We simply make physical contact, agree with what they believe will happen, and then watch God do the rest.
- Note: Jesus did not initiate the healing. Power transferred from Jesus to the woman when *she* touched Him, not vice versa.
- Everyone was crowding into Jesus, yet He only acknowledged one person touching Him with pure faith. Her faith was based totally on the divine presence of a healing Lord who is willing to heal anyone whose hope is found in Jesus Christ.

My quest begins.

That was the beginning of my quest to find out how God operates through His people. Over the months and years of participating in rallies, conventions, and meetings with the FGBMFI, watching ordinary businessmen exercise their faith in Jesus Christ, my faith for the miraculous steadily increased. Each week I would hear the leadership say, "Anyone filled with the mighty power of the Holy Spirit can do what

Jesus did!" Slowly my understanding about Kingdom principles changed. One day I finally convinced myself, "If they can do it, so can I!" So I hesitantly began praying for the sick just like the other men were doing. If they could do what it says in the Bible, then so could I!

Do what Jesus says you can do.

Eventually I came to believe Jesus Christ Himself was the source of divine healing power. These men simply believed the healing promises in the Bible proclaimed both in the Old and New Testaments. I began to believe what these men said and did. They said things like, "The Bible declares that believers can do what Jesus says they can do, one of which is praying for the sick and believing the sick will be healed." I would hear them quote Scripture, and then I would see them doing what it said. Sometimes healing would manifest, sometimes not. But I saw enough results that I eventually believed what the Bible was saying to them: "Just do what the Word says and you will get results!"

I began to do it.

At first I began to assist the men in praying for others. I would simply join in by laying hands on the person and saying "amen" to whatever they prayed. I got used to hearing certain words and phrases they would use. The more I would do this, the more confidence I had that something was going to happen. Not by how I prayed, but how they prayed. Faith comes by hearing and I think faith for healing was beginning to manifest in my mind. Eventually I began to think I could try it for myself. My thinking was similar to the disciples in Luke 17. I needed the Lord to increase my faith.

Luke 17:5-6

And the apostles said to the Lord, "Increase our faith." So the Lord said, "If you have faith as a mustard seed, you can say to this mulberry tree, 'Be pulled up by the roots and be planted in the sea,' and it would obey you." NKJV

Faith is increased by reason of constant use. Taking Jesus at His Word by continuing to pray for the sick over and over again will eventually cause faith to increase. We will experience success if we continue to pray for the sick.

Luncheons and dinner meetings.

The first breakfast meetings I went to were held at a hotel ballroom in Seattle's University District in the spring of 1973. To me these were spectacular. We were packed in like sardines with great expectation of whatever God wanted to do. The praise and worship were electrifying. It was there I learned how to sing in my spiritual language by hearing and watching others doing it. The presence of the Lord was strongly manifesting. So many came that they were forced to move to the largest hotel ballroom in downtown Seattle. It was there I began praying with conviction for the sick. I did not see too much happen, but I continued to minister to the sick like the other men I had been watching the past months. If you were to be a part of this group, it was understood that you would boldly pray for the sick at every meeting.

The Word changed my thinking.

By mid-1974, I had read through the Old Testament once and the New Testament a couple of times. I began to concentrate on the promises of Jesus and what He said we should be doing. I underlined the Scriptures that were being preached to me by various speakers at FGBMFI and other faith-filled preachers. Some I heard in person, others I listened to on tape. They all were saying the same thing: "You can do what Jesus says you can do." I purposed to associate with faith-filled businessmen that believed and were practicing this. I began to understand how faith comes as stated in Romans 10:17. My faith was increasing as I witnessed the spoken Word of God produce healing as it was incorporated in their prayers over people.

Romans 10:17

So then faith comes by hearing, and hearing by the word of God. NKJV

- Faith for doing the miraculous increases as we meditate on what Jesus said we could do.
- It will also increase when we act on what He says we can do and begin praying for people to receive what He promises.
- It will also grow when we continue to associate with those who are operating in the supernatural and boldly praying for the sick.

The man called Miracle.

One of these businessmen was coincidentally named Ken Miracle. Ken was about ten years older than I and had come to Christ quite a few years earlier. He encouraged me to "practice the Word." I followed his lead and did as he did. It began to work. He kept saying, "The Word works. Just act like it's so." He, and others like him, kept reinforcing what I was reading and highlighting in Scripture.

I teamed up with Ken and began ministering with him. We would pray for anyone who needed healing. I began to see evidence of what he was talking about. Pains were leaving people as we prayed. Some people never received anything, others did. Headaches would leave, casts from broken bones would come off early, sore backs would become normal, and sinuses would clear up. Some of the healings would take awhile. Other healings were instant. Nothing too spectacular, but to me as a newcomer, they were all miraculous. Ken even went to the local hospital looking for someone to pray for. The nurses found out what he was doing and firmly insisted he leave. He did, but not before the doctors recorded a series of "unexplainable" miracles. Ken and his devotion to biblical truth changed my thinking. I finally did what Jesus said I could do. I boldly began to pray for the sick.

Jesus prayed twice.

We tend to give up too soon when learning how to heal the sick. When we examine Mark 8:22-26 below, we see Jesus praying at least twice before the blind man could clearly see. Jesus worked with the man until his sight was totally restored. This is an excellent lesson for those desiring to pray for the sick. If it took two prayers for Jesus to see results, we can expect to offer two or more prayers before we see results. There will be times when we pray multiple prayers over a period of time before the healing finally manifests.

Mark 8:22-26

Then He came to Bethsaida; and they brought a blind man to Him, and begged Him to touch him. So He took the blind man by the hand and led him out of the town. And when He had spit on his eyes and put His hands on him, He asked him if he saw anything. And he looked up and said, "I see men like trees, walking." After that He put His hands on his eyes *again* and made him look up. And he was restored and saw everyone clearly. Then He sent him away to his house, saying, "Neither go into the town, nor tell anyone in the town." NKJV

Jesus shows us some important ministry techniques to ensure success in healing the sick:

- Lead the person away from doubt and unbelief.
- Listen to and follow the Holy Spirit's instructions. If the Holy Spirit says, "Spit and lay on of hands," do it.
- Ask them what is happening as you continue praying for them. Jesus asked him if he saw anything. We should do the same.

- JESUS PRAYED A SECOND TIME! If it does not work on the first prayer, pray again. Offer to keep praying for the person until the Holy Spirit says you are through.
- Caution those you pray for to avoid an atmosphere of unbelief. Instruct the person to continue thanking God for their healing until the medical community has confirmed it.

They asked me to share my testimony.

In 1975, I was invited to speak at my first FGBMFI dinner meeting in Mount Vernon, Washington. I earnestly prayed that God would use me like the other men. After sharing my story of how I became a Christian and was baptized in the Holy Spirit, the Lord granted me the privilege of praying with two men that gave their life to Christ. I also prayed for some men who needed healing. One was healed from pain. The others left without acknowledging any change. That was the beginning of speaking and ministering at FGBMFI chapter meetings all over the Northwest USA and Canada. I gained years and years of practical ministry experience for which I am very thankful. I was privileged to be one of their speakers for over twenty-five years. Sonja and I were very grateful when the Seattle Chapter inducted us into the "Hall of Faith" in the fall of 1998.

Another surprise.

FGBMFI luncheons became the spiritual shot-in-the-arm for many men in Seattle. I remember one in 1976 in north Seattle where I arrived spiritually drained. I had not read the Word in a week. I had not prayed. I had not done anything to bolster my faith. I showed up to get blessed, not to be a blessing. Toward the end of the meeting I saw a man I had never met. When I looked at him, the Holy Spirit said, "He has pain in his back. Go to him. I will heal him." God's voice manifests spontaneously, sometimes when you are not expecting it. This happened to Peter.

Acts 10:19-20
While Peter was still thinking about the vision, *the Spirit said to him,* "Simon, three men are looking for you. So get up and go downstairs. Do not hesitate to go with them, for I have sent them." NIV

Whenever we hear words in our minds that are out of the ordinary and come as a "jolt," it is most likely the Holy Spirit urging us to do something. Obey!

So, I did what God said. I went to him and delivered what I had heard. He said, "You are right. My back is killing me." I laid my hands on where it hurt and said, "Pain, leave in the name of Jesus Christ." The pain left immediately. He became a believer in miracles and a "regular" at Full Gospel functions from then on. When you think God cannot use you because of a negative circumstance, this is precisely when He is likely to take command of the situation and surprise you. God works best when we acknowledge total dependence on Him.

Hang around those who are doing it.
During the early years, I was invited to accompany some key Full Gospel individuals on speaking engagements that accelerated my learning curve for operating in the supernatural of God. The first was Don Ostrom, the president of the Seattle Chapter. He became a mentor to many men over the years. On one particular trip to a Bremerton, Washington chapter meeting, he encouraged me to be sensitive to the Holy Spirit and do whatever God led me to do. It was that night I first prophesied in a public meeting. He critiqued me with some positive advice and gave me some pointers for the next time I was up to bat. It is nice to get good feedback from those who precede us in the ministry. That is how we learn to do things right. The early disciples received feedback from Jesus in the following passage.

Matthew 17:19-21

Then the disciples came to Jesus privately and said, "Why could we not drive it (the demon) out?" And He said to them, "Because of the littleness of your faith; for truly I say to you, if you have faith the size of a mustard seed, you will say to this mountain, 'Move from here to there,' and it will move; and nothing will be impossible to you." ["But this kind does not go out except by prayer and fasting."] NASB

DWJD

When learning how to heal the sick, watch how your mentor does it. Jesus' disciples were quick to ask Jesus why their attempts to drive out a demon did not work. Jesus used the situation to teach them a more sure way to do ministry. He told them it had to do with the littleness of their faith and that prayer and fasting should be employed.

Look for mentors.

Another early mentor was Steve Lightle, a completed Jew who sold out to Jesus about five years before I did. He eventually became the European Coordinator for FGBMFI and lived in Brussels, Belgium for a number of years. He was a great speaker, using funny testimonies about himself along with miracle stories. He did not like to travel alone and invited others to accompany him. He asked me to go with him to a Kent, Washington men's meeting. It was a turning point in my life. He had a prophecy for me that confirmed my calling and future in the ministry. It has come to pass just as he prophesied.

Grab a toe and pray.

It was Steve who called a person back to life whose heart had stopped beating. It happened outside a Full Gospel convention in a downtown Seattle hotel lobby. I witnessed the whole episode. The lady passed out and fell to the lobby floor. A call to 9-1-1 immediately brought an aid truck. They hooked up the heart monitor revealing an absence of a heartbeat. Steve maneuvered close to the feet of the lady. I will never forget how he took authority over the situation. The only place he could "lay on of hands" was by grabbing the lady's big toe sticking out from the medic's blanket. He just boldly grabbed her toe and commanded life back into her body. It worked! The monitor immediately started beeping. The paramedics were relieved the machine registered a heartbeat where there was none before. Most would classify the event as a miracle, close to a "raising of the dead." Steve considered it as such, even though they had not declared her clinically dead. Either way, it demonstrates the power of speaking life-giving words that release the healing power of God, similar to what Peter experienced in Acts 9.

Acts 9:40-41

Peter sent them all out of the room; then he got down on his knees and prayed. Turning toward *the dead woman*, he said, "Tabitha, get up." She opened her eyes, and seeing Peter she sat up. Then he gave her his hand and lifted her up . . . . NIV

DWJD

- Jesus mentored Peter. Peter had seen Jesus raise the dead. When it came time for Peter to do it, he knew what to do. Like Jesus, Peter first prayed, and we assume he received instructions from the Father of what to do (see John 5:19). Then, he addressed the dead person by name and commanded her to get up.

- Peter had seen Jesus take Jairus' daughter by the hand. So, he did it just like Jesus, his mentor. Peter gave her his hand and lifted her up.

- Because Peter obeyed what the Holy Spirit wanted to do, it removed all doubt and disbelief from him so he could do it just like Jesus had taught him, and a miracle transpired.

- Because Peter was obedient, the Lord was glorified. Acts 9:42 states, "This became known all over Joppa, and many people believed in the Lord." NIV

Steve was the kind of mentor that helped shape my early ministry skills. He was good at improvising ministry techniques that few would dare try. He believed in a creative God that would honor anyone who would operate spontaneously according to the whole counsel of the Bible. I still believe this today and minister with the same attitude. One thing I learned from Steve was to always give God all the glory and credit for the many victories that are achieved in ministry.

They got what they believed for.
FGBMFI chapter officers always prayed that God would do the miraculous at every meeting. They would invite speakers that had personal testimonies that included exciting moves of God. They concentrated on ordinary businessmen that encountered a miracle-working God. The businessmen would give their testimonies of how God had changed their lives. They would always say, "God is no respecter of persons. If He did it for me, He will do it for you." This resulted in some very exciting meetings. It would cause astonishment to the skeptics, similar to the next Scripture passage.

Acts 4:13-14
When they (the high priests) saw the courage of Peter and John and realized that they were unschooled, ordinary men, they were astonished and they took note that these men had been with Jesus. But since they could see the man who had been healed standing there with them, there was nothing they could say. NIV

Whenever we give testimony of an authentic healing, it closes the mouth of the skeptics and produces an atmosphere of faith toward God. Always be open for opportunities to share what God has done, especially when He heals you or someone you know.

The FGBMFI meetings produced an atmosphere of faith and expectancy. By the end of the main speaker's message, they would announce to those assembled that the Holy Spirit was invited to do anything He wanted. The speaker would always invite people to receive Christ. Many would give their lives to Christ. Then they would invite others to receive the Holy Spirit baptism and be prayed over for healing. That is when most of the miracles took place. They got what they believed for. The leaders depended on God to finish the meetings. The FGBMFI leaders were notorious for allowing the meetings to go way too long. We never cared about the time because there was so much going on. These meetings were similar to Paul's, described in the next passage.

Acts 20:7-12

. . . . Paul, ready to depart the next day, spoke to them and continued his message until midnight. There were many lamps in the upper room where they were gathered together. And in a window sat a certain young man named Eutychus, who was sinking into a deep sleep. He was overcome by sleep; and as Paul continued speaking, he fell down from the third story and was taken up dead. But Paul went down, fell on him, and embracing him said, "Do not trouble yourselves, for his life is in him." Now when he had come up, had broken bread and eaten, and talked a long while, even till daybreak, he departed. And they brought the young man in alive, and they were not a little comforted. NKJV

DWJD

Jesus still wants to heal the sick even when our meetings go on until midnight. In this case, a miracle happened in the middle of the night when everyone was tired and worn out. God never sleeps. We can be sure that Eutychus was glad the meeting did not dismiss until after Paul had raised him from the dead.

Keep believing in spite of the circumstances.

In 1978, after a particularly exciting FGBMFI meeting in Bellingham, Washington, a client of mine who had heard me speak asked me to go pray for his ailing mother in a Seattle hospital. Still basking in the faith of the meeting I said, "I'd love to pray for her. I believe she will be healed!" On my return to Seattle, I went to her bedside and found her in a coma. That did not matter to me. I had learned not to trust in circumstances. I was to release my faith and believe that God would perform a miracle. I boldly anointed her with oil and prayed the prayer of faith. When I returned the next day, her room was empty. I began to rejoice for what God had done. She must have been healed. My joy quickly turned to bewilderment when the nurse informed me she had died during the night. I sat in the car and asked God what had happened. I thought I heard Him say, "You don't know what I know. Just obey Me and keep doing what I tell you." That was a big lesson to learn. My job was to obey the Lord and His Word, pray, and leave the final results up to a merciful God.

Eternity awaits everyone.

When Christians die, they immediately enter into the glorious destination promised by the Lord Jesus Christ, eternity with Him! From the perspective of eternity, dying for the Christian is the consummation of the promise of eternal life where there is no more death, mourning, crying, or pain. Our responsibility is to pray for those who are asking for prayer, including those who may be dying. Our goal should be to lead them into relationship with Jesus Christ before they die. Everyone should be given the choice of entering into the glorious promise of eternal life.

Start with something easy.

In learning how to heal the sick, we sometimes have to start with something that does not seem to require much faith. Headaches, high fevers, pains in the neck, or sore backs may be easier to tackle than praying for someone dying of terminal cancer. All healing is easy for God. However, for the Christian who has never prayed for the sick, start with something similar to the next passage.

Luke 4:38-39   Matthew 8:14-15   Mark 1:29-31
Luke 4:38-39: Now (Jesus) arose from the synagogue and entered Simon's house. But Simon's wife's mother was sick with a high fever, and they made request of Him concerning her. So He stood over her and rebuked the fever, and it left her. (Mark 1:31: and took her by the hand) and immediately she arose and served them. NKJV

DWJD

This is a great example of how many Christians begin healing the sick. Do it just like Jesus did:
- Respond to any request of people needing healing by going to where the sick person is.
- Take charge of the situation by going directly to the sick person.
- Rebuke the fever, sickness, or pain by speaking to the problem area in the name of Jesus Christ.
- Act on the prayer you just prayed by encouraging the person to do something they could not do because of the sickness or pain. Example: Take them by the hand, have them stand up, and continue their daily routines.
- Keep expecting the fever, sickness, or pain to leave the person at any moment. Eventually, their healing will manifest.

The crooked elbow.
During that same year, I had a surprise encounter that I will never forget. About 2:00 p.m. one wintry afternoon I got a call from the president of the Kelowna, B.C., Canada FGBMFI Chapter. He was requesting that I find a way to get from Seattle to Kelowna by 7:00 p.m. to speak at their evening meeting. They could not find a suitable speaker from

Canada and were calling at the last moment because they were desperate for a dinner speaker. The scheduled speaker neglected to inform them of a conflict of dates and had to cancel the day before. After a series of miracles, Larry Day, the president of the Bellevue Chapter, checked out a Cessna 210 from his flight club at Boeing Field. He was a good pilot, and we got to the meeting just as they were finishing praise and worship. We stepped onto the platform just in time to be introduced. It was a sold-out house because of the reputation of the scheduled speaker. God had something He wanted to do and He wanted us in on it.

Larry gave a short but riveting testimony about Jesus healing the sick. Then I spoke about similar healings. This resulted in about a dozen people receiving Christ and three healing lines were formed. Lines formed in front of Larry, the chapter officers, and myself. One by one, we began to pray for the sick and hurting. The one healing miracle I will never forget was a young woman who had fallen as a child and had broken her arm at the elbow. She could not straighten her arm. It was permanently crooked. She asked me to pray for her arm. Like Paul in Acts 14, I looked directly at her and saw something in the Spirit.

Acts 14:8-10
In Lystra there sat a man crippled in his feet, who was lame from birth and had never walked. He listened to Paul as he was speaking. Paul looked directly at him, *saw that he had faith to be healed* and called out, "Stand up on your feet!" At that, the man jumped up and began to walk. NIV

DWJD

- Whenever we are preaching, teaching, or testifying about the Lord's desire to heal people, we must be very sensitive to those listening.
- Because of the Word's ability to penetrate people's hearts, faith will rise up in those in need of healing.

123

- The Holy Spirit is strongly at work when the Word is preached. Pause and allow Him to speak regarding anyone who may need healing.
- As you look at the people around you, the Holy Spirit may cause you to "see" the ones who have faith to be healed.
- We "see" through the eyes of the Holy Spirit when He says to us, "That one, over there . . . call out to him to stand up on his feet!"
- When the Holy Spirit initiates the ministry, they are always healed.

I saw that she had faith to be healed.

I said to her, "Do you believe God will straighten your arm when we pray?" Without hesitation she looked into my eyes with such faith I knew a miracle was about to happen. She firmly said, "Yes, I do!" I quickly agreed with her. I said, "In Jesus' name, arm, be made straight!" She, her mother, and I began to marvel as God slowly straightened her arm to match the other one. We heard a gentle snapping sound as the arm came into normal position. She joyously began to cry. Her mother began to weep. Tears came to my eyes. Up until that time, I had never witnessed such a profound healing miracle. This was a case where her faith made her whole. It was similar to what Jesus did in Mark 3.

Mark 3:1-6 Matthew 12:9-14 Luke 6:6-11

And He entered the synagogue again, and a man was there who had a withered hand. So they watched Him closely, whether He would heal him on the Sabbath, so that they might accuse Him. And He said to the man who had the withered hand, "Step forward." Then He said to them, "Is it lawful on the Sabbath to do good or to do evil, to save life or to kill?" But they kept silent. And when He had looked around at them with anger, being grieved by the hardness of their hearts, He said to the man, "Stretch out your hand." And he stretched it out, and his hand was restored as whole as the other. Then the Pharisees went out and immediately plotted with the Herodians against Him, how they might destroy Him. NKJV

There may be occasions when the Holy Spirit urges us to pray for the sick in front of religious leaders who do not believe in healing. We must obey God rather than man when it comes to divine healing. God would have us to heal the sick instead of arguing whether divine healing is appropriate in church or not.

I saw in her eyes that she had faith to be made well. That is when I said with a loud voice, "Arm, be made straight!" I had no revelation of what God wanted to do for her until she revealed her unwavering faith by her confession as she looked through me to Jesus Christ as her Healer.

Discovering the Authentic

As I (John) continued to grow in my faith and understanding, God continued to confirm His Word with signs and wonders. By the late 1970s and early 1980s I began to discover the importance of operating by revelation knowledge. This seems to be the missing ingredient that eludes most ministers seeking to operate in God's supernatural arena. Jesus promises to speak to all believers who seek a deep personal relationship with Him. This became evident when I realized healing miracles were more frequent when I obeyed God's voice and did what He revealed.

I began to closely examine the methods others employed as they prayed for the sick. Some seemed to operate by revelation, others did not. I noticed peculiarities in style and mannerisms that were sometimes suspect. It was as if they were relying more on what worked in the past than on what

God wanted to do at the moment. I needed to take Paul's advice to the Thessalonians.

1 Thessalonians 5:19-21
Do not quench the Spirit; do not despise prophetic utterances. But *examine everything carefully*; hold fast to that which is good. NASB

Luke 9:49-50
Now John answered and said, "Master, we saw someone casting out demons in Your name, and we forbade him because he does not follow with us." But Jesus said to him, "Do not forbid him, for he who is not against us is on our side." NKJV

DWJD

- Jesus grants more grace toward us than we do to each other. Just because a minister displays an unusual style in healing the sick, we need not discount him because he is unorthodox.
- Jesus reminds us to examine the fruit of their presentation. Are people genuinely healed? Do they give God all the credit? Are people being saved? We shall know them by their fruit.
- Remain on the side of Jesus by following His examples from the written Word.

Upon careful examination, I discerned that those acting on what God was revealing at the moment were reaping authentic and lasting healing miracles in those to whom they ministered. Those acting in their own faith or on past experience were having results, but not nearly to the same degree as those operating by revelation. This became a firm reality when I became involved in doing the "circuits."

Doing the "circuits."

By 1980, I was invited to speak at more and more of the FGBMFI chapters in the Western USA and Canada. Because of a career change, I was available to speak for multiple chapters over three to five days in one trip. We called those meetings a "circuit." As I look back, I realize they invited me more on my availability than on reputation as a great speaker. In any case, one of the more memorable "circuits" I was privileged to do was in northeastern Washington State.

I kept a journal of what happened.

I was invited to speak at three different chapters: one located in Sandpoint, Idaho; one in Colville, Washington; and another in Newport, Washington. Each held their meetings in the same week (Tuesday, Thursday, and Saturday evenings). The reason this trip is memorable is because it was the only trip in all those years where I kept a journal of what happened. If you do not keep a journal, you quickly forget all the marvelous things God does. Here is a recap of some of the memorable events. The agenda was always the same: a buffet dinner, strong worship, a few short testimonies, then the main speaker gave his testimony and had an altar call for salvation, Holy Spirit baptism, and healing. I followed this format at each meeting.

Tuesday evening at Sandpoint, Idaho was a relaxed time of ministry. Two men got saved, one couple was baptized in the Holy Spirit, and God removed head, neck, back, and ear pains from five people. When I read the following Scriptures, I could almost envision the story.

Luke 6:17-19   Matthew 4:24-25   Mark 3:7-12
He went down with them and stood on a level place. A large crowd of his disciples was there and a great number of people from all over Judea, from Jerusalem, and from the coast of Tyre and Sidon, who had come to hear him and to be healed of their diseases.

Those troubled by evil spirits were cured, and the people all tried to touch him, because power was coming from him and healing them all. NIV

DWJD

- Whenever we are asked to go and speak about the wonderful things God is doing, we must petition the Lord and plead for His anointing to manifest in the meeting place. Without the strong presence of the Lord, nothing much will happen.
- Multitudes came to Jesus, expecting great things to happen because of the news that He was healing the sick. Healing miracles are the best advertisement for causing crowds to show up.
- The power spoken of here is the tangible presence of the Lord in full manifestation. When this begins to happen, move quickly and minister to as many people as possible, keeping in the flow of revelation from the Holy Spirit.
- Be aware of people with religious spirits announcing that you are special. Avoid allowing people to "puff you up" by praising you for what is happening.
- Respond by having everyone lift their hands and voices in praise and thanksgiving, glorifying the Lord Jesus Christ for what He is doing.

Thursday night at Colville was the meeting I will never forget. I had prayed hard that God would somehow use me for His purposes. I was not disappointed. As I was in the middle of my testimony, the Lord began to interrupt my thoughts with pictures, words, and a strong pull toward certain individuals. At the end of my testimony, the Holy Spirit brought to my remembrance each person He wanted to minister to. I took the bold step to obey, even though I was not sure what would happen. The first leading was so strong I was compelled to obey.

Holy Spirit radar.

As I scanned the group of about eighty people, the Holy Spirit directed my attention to a middle-aged man and He said to me, "He is not saved. Go to him and ask him if he wants to become a Christian." I obeyed. Both he and his wife said, "We both want to." I grasped their hands, and we prayed the sinner's prayer right at their table. Afterwards, with tears and smiles, they giggled through the rest of the meeting. A teenage boy also gave his heart to the Lord.

The little white dog.

There was a hush of expectancy, and the fear of the Lord fell upon everyone in the room. All eyes were on me. The gift of faith came upon me. The Holy Spirit showed me a picture of a woman with a cane and a little white dog on a leash. With the picture came the words, "I will heal her when she comes for prayer." I repeated this to the crowd. An elderly lady with a cane stood up and her husband helped her slowly come to the front. She could hardly stand by herself and told me she had incurable angina of the throat and a weak heart. She could barely function anymore. But, she believed God wanted to heal her. I agreed with her as I laid my hand on her shoulder. A surge of power went through her and she immediately raised her hands, dropped her cane, and began walking back and forth, loudly praising and magnifying God for instantly healing her.

Healed collarbone.

A man came forward with his arm in a sling. He said he had fallen and broken his collarbone. He could not raise his arm. I asked, "When will God heal you?" He said, "Right now!" I laid my hands on the broken side and said, "I agree. In Jesus' name, receive your healing!" He immediately lifted his arm, removed the sling, and walked away completely healed.

Severed nerve repaired.

A young man stood in front of me and said an illness had left him completely deaf in his right ear. The doctor said the nerve seemed to be severed and there was nothing more he could do. As he was talking to me, the Holy Spirit created a picture in my mind. I saw myself spitting on my finger, placing it in his right ear, and commanding hearing to return. I did exactly as I saw in the Spirit. He was somewhat startled when he discovered he could hear perfectly in both ears.

The little girl on a swing.

A young woman and her husband came to me and wanted prayer for their relationship. They said they were having great difficulties being intimate. I had no idea how to pray for them. So I asked, "Would you mind if I exercised my prayer language? Sometimes the Holy Spirit tells me how to pray." They did not mind. I began to pray in tongues as I had my hands on their shoulders. The Lord showed me a picture of a happy little girl on a swing. I also saw a dark adult male figure come up behind her, taking her off the swing, and aggressively carrying her away behind some bushes. I heard the words, "Her stepfather molested her. Command the unclean spirit to depart." I repeated this to the woman. She began to cry uncontrollably as I disclosed what the Lord had showed me. When I commanded the unclean spirit to depart she immediately began to smile, rejoice, and praised God that that "ugly" feeling was no longer in her. I later saw them leaving the meeting happily embracing each other with big smiles on their faces.

Saturday night at the Newport, Washington FGBMFI meeting, three people gave their lives to Christ. A man came with severe pain in both shoulders. In one prayer he was healed and then filled with the Holy Spirit. He walked away praising God in a new prayer language. Two women and a young man were also healed of pain in their bodies. Everyone went home from these meetings praising God for demonstrating His presence in signs and wonders.

These meetings, though spectacular, were representative of how God would manifest Himself by saving, healing, and filling people with the Holy Spirit. I look back now and re-call that the intensity of God's presence depended greatly on the degree of intercession and then obeying what we were seeing in the Spirit. I had moved from being surprised to expecting God to move in an authentic way. Similar to the account in John 5, people would gather their sick friends and family members and go to wherever healing was happening. Ultimately, they would discover that Jesus Christ is the source for all healing.

John 5:2-9

Now there is in Jerusalem by the sheep gate a pool, which is called in Hebrew Bethesda, having five por-ticoes. In these lay a multitude of those who were sick, blind, lame, and withered, [waiting for the mov-ing of the waters; for an angel of the Lord went down at certain seasons into the pool and stirred up the water; whoever then first, after the stirring up of the water, stepped in was made well from whatever dis-ease with which he was afflicted.] A man was there who had been ill for thirty-eight years. When Jesus saw him lying there, and knew that he had already been a long time in that condition, He said to him, "Do you wish to get well?" The sick man answered Him, "Sir, I have no man to put me into the pool when the water is stirred up, but while I am coming, another steps down before me." Jesus said to him, "Get up, pick up your pallet and walk." Immediately the man became well, and picked up his pallet and began to walk. NASB

DWJD

- Before praying for a person with a long, chronic illness, interview them to determine if they still have faith that God will heal them.
- Remain sensitive to what the Holy Spirit wants to do. Obey whatever He says.

- Ask them what Jesus asked the man, "Do you wish to get well?"
- Listen for any kind of response that has faith in it.
- Finally, ask *when* they want God to heal them. When you hear "Now," immediately agree with them that God is starting the healing process and will continue to restore them to health according to God's timetable.
- God will sometimes heal them immediately. Always leave the results up to God.

Do only what God says.

As I discovered the authentic, I learned a critical lesson every evangelist should know. Never get ahead of the Holy Spirit during public ministry. I was invited to speak at an Aberdeen, Washington monthly chapter meeting. I invited another evangelist to accompany me. We felt somewhat smug and a bit proud having our friend Larry fly us to Aberdeen in a Cessna from the Boeing Flight Club. Perhaps that was the mistake that resulted in what happened next. In my discovering the authentic, God was about to make an obvious distinction between ministering in presumption and operating by His leading.

Just before I was to speak, my evangelist friend called my attention to a man in a wheelchair. He said, "I feel like we are to minister healing to that man and get him out of that wheelchair." I thought it would really be great for that to happen. So, I made opportunity for him to be wheeled to the front so we could minister to him. We both commanded him to get up and walk. He could not get up, so we tried to pull him up and make his legs work. He finally fell, fortunately back into his wheelchair. We tried to save the meeting by singing a few more choruses. It did not help. The meeting was over. We left embarrassed, refusing the normal honorarium. Not too much was said on the flight home.

We learn by making mistakes.

Listen to God's instructions for ministry, not others'! Do only what the Holy Spirit tells you to do. What seems right may not be in God's timetable. If you have no direct revelation of what to do, always ask the person in the wheelchair what they believe God is willing to do. Then agree in prayer at their level of faith. If they want God to remove a headache, that is as far as you go. When God wants us to command them to rise up and walk, He will tell us how and when. The Holy Spirit does not honor religious zeal that is birthed in the flesh. Jesus illustrates this in the following passage by asking the blind men what they wanted Him to do for them.

Matthew 20:29-34 Luke 18:35-43

Matthew 20:29-34: Now as they went out of Jericho, a great multitude followed Him. And behold, two blind men sitting by the road, when they heard that Jesus was passing by, cried out, saying, "Have mercy on us, O Lord, Son of David!" Then the multitude warned them that they should be quiet; but they cried out all the more, saying, "Have mercy on us, O Lord, Son of David!" So Jesus stood still and called them, and said, "What do you want Me to do for you?" They said to Him, "Lord, that our eyes may be opened." So Jesus had compassion and touched their eyes. (Luke 18:42: Then Jesus said to him, "Receive your sight, your faith has made you well.") And immediately their eyes received sight, and they followed Him. NKJV

DWJD

- The Holy Spirit initiated healing of the blind by revelation.
- Notice: Jesus asked him, "What do you want Me to do for you?" Jesus already knew what the Father wanted to do, but He was testing the person's faith for healing. We should do the same. At times, it may seem obvious what needs to be done.
- Other times, we should ask what they believe God will do for them. We should not attempt to go beyond what a person believes God will do.

- Jesus touched their eyes. When appropriate, we too, should lay our hands on the part of the body needing healing, using discretion, of course.
- In Luke 18:35-43, Jesus *spoke* the answer to the problem. "Receive your sight! Your faith has made you well!" We should do the same.
- "Moved with compassion." When someone comes earnestly seeking healing with all of his or her heart, we will also be moved with compassion.
- The men immediately regained their sight. The timing is always up to the Lord, not us. We always pray as if it IS going to happen. We should not be surprised if the healing takes awhile to manifest.

My first mission trip.

In 1979 God caused a businessman to pay for my plane ticket to Seoul, Korea. I was to be part of a four-man team representing the American FGBMFI at the annual Asian Christian Layman's Conference. My roommate was an old prayer warrior from Seattle, Gil Bean. Two evangelists from California rounded out the team. An Israeli, Slomo Isaac, from Jerusalem was one of the main speakers. During his sermon, the Lord called me to the "nations." As he looked at me I was transfixed, only able to hear him say, "You will be going into all the world!" I heard the voice of the Lord authoritatively speaking through this man I had never met. I was riveted to my seat, wondering what this meant. I quickly wrote these words on a napkin that I keep in my prophetic word journal to this day.

They had lined up speaking engagements for all of us. Gil and I had two. The first was a Sunday morning service in a large Presbyterian church. The second Sunday was a service at a Pentecostal church of about two hundred. What a contrast. They both preach Jesus Christ as Savior, but the Pentecostal church expected God to move supernaturally in every service. I did not know that, even though I was advertised as the main speaker for that morning.

The unexpected happened.

I prepared a nice three-point sermon on the grace and love of God. Gil prayed that the Holy Spirit would have His way no matter what. I did my best through the Korean interpreter, but it seemed they were expecting something more. The members sat on the floor while the pastors sat in big chairs on the stage. As I finished, they were very polite and seemed to like what I said. Then, something unexpected happened. The senior pastor gave some kind of invitation for people to come forward. The whole church stood up, took two steps and began to crowd toward the stage.

Gil waved me over to center stage and whispered, "They just told me this was advertised as a healing service. You and I are now supposed to heal the sick." "What?" I said. Gil said, "Did you bring your oil?" I said, "All I have is this little felt pad thing on my key chain." He said, "Forget the oil. It's too late now." I said, "How do I know what to pray for?" Gil said, "You can't understand them, and they don't know what you are praying either. But God knows. So, start praying in tongues and go down the line patting each on the head. I'll start on this end. You start on the other. Let's go!"

We could not pray fast enough.

They did not do it this way in America. Thank God for Gil's years of experience with Asians. I quickly went to the right, Gil to the left. They were like a bunch of hungry baby birds when momma bird shows up with the food. They were tightly crowding together, pushing their way up the altar steps, until I found myself up against the wall with the Korean flag draped across my face. We could not pray for them fast enough. When I did, they fell under the power of God, causing an obstacle course for the next wave needing healing. It was the most bizarre healing meeting I had ever attended—and I was supposed to be in charge!

I tried using my little felt oil pad, but it ran out in about five minutes. They did not care. There was such an atmosphere of faith that no matter how we prayed, they knew God was going to heal them. All we had to do was touch them or allow them to touch us. We were experiencing what Jesus did in Mark 3.

Mark 3:9-10
Because of the crowd he told his disciples to have a small boat ready for him, to keep the people from crowding him. For he had healed many, so that those with diseases were pushing forward to touch him. NIV

DWJD

- Large crowds can cause problems. Have a plan and use others for crowd control.
- Always give all the honor and praise to the Lord for healing the sick.
- Avoid anyone who wants to "puff you up" by praising you for what happened.
- The Bible says, "Man is tested by the praise he receives." (Proverbs 27:21) NIV

Intercession was the key.
We were still praying for the sick when the leaders took us by the arm and ushered us out the side door for our drive to lunch. We were informed at lunch that the whole church had been fasting and praying for an outpouring of God's healing power for this meeting. No wonder we experienced what we did. It was because of intercessory prayer! This was something the Koreans have been doing for decades. Unlike the Americans, they knew how to break down any barriers of unbelief and usher in the presence and favor of God. We just happened to be participants in their reward. The price had already been paid—on their knees.

Christ's Ambassadors International

In 1979, the Lord gave me the vision for what Sonja and I are now doing. During an intense time of prayer, the Lord caused me to see a brilliant sunset over the Olympic Mountains west of Seattle, Washington. In the sun's rays, I saw the words, "Christ's Ambassadors."

2 Corinthians 5:20
Therefore, we are ambassadors for Christ, as though God were making an appeal through us; we beg you on behalf of Christ, be reconciled to God. NASB

We are ambassadors for Christ with delegated authority and power to do what Jesus did. He sealed our ambassadorship with His blood.

A maker of Timothies.
As I was transfixed in the vision, the Lord said, "You will be training ambassadors for Me, and they will be going into all the world. Prepare yourself for the task." That vision was confirmed over and over again as I attended various prayer meetings and FGBMFI conferences. The same prophetic word became commonplace in our life. "You will be a maker of Timothies. You will affect nations. You are called to prepare the saints for the work of the ministry. You will do this together as a team." We continue to rejoice and thank the Lord for all these confirming words over the many years. Today, we know for sure that we are in the middle of God's will. We purpose to stay there.

Sonja and I held B.S. degrees in Business Administration. But, at the time of the initial vision, neither of us had a formal theological education. We read every book we could find about the supernatural power of God. We felt an urgency to be better grounded in the Word. I enrolled in Bible school by correspondence, earning a diploma in a little over a year. The next few years I attended every Christian ministry seminar, church seminar, conference, crusade, and FGBMFI function within driving distance of Seattle. Healing the sick usually was a part of these conferences.

Later, both Sonja and I attended seminary at Regent College graduate school, Vancouver, B.C., Canada, at the encouragement of Dr. Larry Shelton, former Dean of the School of Religion at Seattle Pacific University, Seattle. At the same time, we became very active ministering in our local church. Sonja taught the new believer's class, and I became a staff pastor and taught various classes, all pertaining to equipping believers for ministry. We both ministered weekly in the upfront prayer ministry at our church.

We began ministering in other churches in the Seattle area and eventually the Northwest USA. We participated in major evangelistic events that came to town. Often, we directed the prayer and ministry teams for these visiting ministries. Healing was the major ministry focus for most of these meetings. We continued to witness miracle after miracle. We no longer were surprised when God healed the sick. We were discovering the authentic move of God and expected Him to continue healing the sick. People who came for healing had a high expectation similar to the centurion in the next passage.

Luke 7:1-10 Matthew 8:5-13 John 4:46-53
Now when He concluded all His sayings in the hearing of the people, He entered Capernaum. And a certain centurion's servant, who was dear to him, was sick and ready to die. So when he heard about Jesus, he sent elders of the Jews to Him, pleading with Him to come and heal his servant. And when they came to Jesus, they begged Him earnestly, saying that the one for whom He should do this was deserving, "for he loves our nation, and has built us a synagogue." Then Jesus went with them. And when He was already not far from the house, the centurion sent friends to Him, saying to Him, "Lord, do not trouble Yourself, for I am not worthy that You should enter under my roof. Therefore I did not even think myself worthy to come to You. But say the word, and

my servant will be healed. For I also am a man placed under authority, having soldiers under me. And I say to one, 'Go,' and he goes; and to another, 'Come,' and he comes; and to my servant, 'Do this,' and he does it." When Jesus heard these things, He marveled at him, and turned around and said to the crowd that followed Him, "I say to you, I have not found such *great faith*, not even in Israel!" And those who were sent, returning to the house, found the servant well who had been sick. NKJV

DWJD

- Whenever we meet someone with great faith in Jesus Christ as their Healer, it becomes much easier to agree with them for healing. Their eyes are on Christ and not us.

- If we only do what we see the Father doing (just like Jesus), then we will see the manifestation of what He wants done. We go ahead and "speak the word only" and it will be done.

- If the Father says, "Go, come, do that, do this . . ." and you obey, then your commands are backed up by the power and authority of God Himself! You can be sure the words and commands will be fulfilled. That is operating in *GREAT FAITH*. You then are operating in the gift of faith that comes with obeying what the Father is saying via the Holy Spirit.

Experience convinced us.

By the mid-1980s, our belief in a healing God was firm. We witnessed so many authentic healings we could no longer deny the fundamental truth that God is willing to heal anyone coming to Him in faith. By then, we could discern the genuine from the contrived. We respected people's unwavering faith in a God that heals. But, to be authentic, we encouraged those convinced of a healing that was "in process," to get confirmation from the medical community.

Upon returning with a good report, everyone could rejoice in a bona fide miracle. This is illustrated in Luke 17.

Luke 17:12-19

Then as He entered a certain village, there met Him ten men who were lepers, who stood afar off. And they lifted up their voices and said, "Jesus, Master, have mercy on us!" So when He saw them, He said to them, "Go, show yourselves to the priests." And so it was that as they went, they were cleansed. And one of them, when he saw that he was healed, returned, and with a loud voice glorified God, and fell down on his face at His feet, giving Him thanks. And he was a Samaritan. So Jesus answered and said, "Were there not ten cleansed? But where are the nine? Were there not any found who returned to give glory to God except this foreigner?" And He said to him, "Arise, go your way. Your faith has made you well." NKJV

DWJD

- People with incurable diseases are no different to God than people with headaches. All healing is easy for God.
- Faith in Jesus as their Healer is the key. The lepers demonstrated faith by crying out to Jesus for healing. They earnestly sought Jesus to heal them.
- As they obeyed what Jesus commanded, to "go," they were purified/cleansed as they *went*. Strict obedience to what the Holy Spirit reveals is necessary.
- One came back giving thanks and glorifying God. Because of this, he was 100 percent healed (not just cleansed).
- Jesus said to the one, "Your *faith* has made you well." Continually giving thanks to God completes a healing that is in process.

God gets the credit.

Moving from surprise encounters to authentic manifestations of God's healing power was a process that took over ten years. We observed all kinds of healings. Some were questionable and some were obvious. Some were routine and some were spectacular. Regardless of who was ministering or how they prayed, we learned one vital truth. We are very careful to always point to an awesome God who receives all the credit and glory. We receive no acclaim on how we or anyone else achieved the various healings. Prolonged intercessions with fasting may have played a part. However, the ultimate reason for the healing lies in a compassionate God who is willing to heal those who rely on His Word, His mercy, and His grace.

We went fishing.

Some years ago, a pilot friend from church mentioned we could rent a plane and fly to a remote British Columbia lake to do some trophy fishing. I (John) love to fly fish and persuaded my theologian, professor friend, Dr. Larry Shelton, to share expenses and come along. We loaded our gear into a Cessna 170RG and began our journey from Snohomish, Washington bound for a remote fishing lodge on Bear Lake, Northern B.C., Canada. Once airborne, Larry reminded the pilot to stay at about five thousand feet because he suffered from congestive heart failure. Any higher altitude would cause breathing problems, putting undue pressure on his weakened heart. It was a relief to finally locate the lake after flying for over an hour without seeing any roads or signs of civilization. We buzzed the lodge twice, assuming they knew who we were. They were to pick us up at the airstrip.

We landed on the rough, gravel strip alongside an abandoned railroad track about two miles from the lodge. We waited and waited. Finally, we decided to carry all of our bags and fishing gear down the old tracks in the general direction of the lodge. We had trudged for about half a mile when Larry suddenly dropped all of his gear, sat on a bag, out of breath, saying, "I can't go any further. You guys go on and come back and get me." He did not mention it, but we knew it was his heart. We agreed to come back with help.

The maintenance man from the lodge found us. He was with two native Canadian boys, all riding on all-terrain vehicles. We went back and got Larry and proceeded to the lodge. The couple that ran the lodge said, "How come you didn't radio us when you arrived?" The pilot said, "They told us to buzz you and you'd come get us." They said, "Every plane that comes by buzzes us. Why didn't you call us on the radio?" The pilot apologized to everyone and said we were thankful to finally be there. Larry said, "Especially me. I couldn't take another step. I'm tired."

Call for a helicopter.
Two days later Larry had a heart attack. It happened early in the morning as we were getting ready for a major fishing expedition to a remote river. Larry did not come to breakfast. I went to his bedroom and saw him sprawled on his bunk looking very weak and pale. He said, "John, it's my heart. I won't be going fishing today. In fact, if I don't get any better, I don't know if I'll make it or not." Here we were, hundreds of miles from nowhere. If we tried to get him back to the plane, it would kill him. Using the lodge radio, the host called the nearest hospital, 150 miles away. Upon learning the symptoms, the doctor said, "You need to get him here immediately. He is having a heart attack." We finally got a response from a logging company helicopter, the only aircraft in the area that could be at the lodge within an hour. He was on his way.

Larry was not looking good. Suddenly, the Holy Spirit said, "John, you know what to do. Pray for him!" I laid my hands on Larry and began commanding the spirit of death to leave, his heart to function normally, and healing and health to return to him. I even prayed that God would give him a new heart. This was my friend. I was not going to stand around and let him die. His wife, Vangie, would want to know that we did all we could to save him. She would not think much of any of us if we had not at least prayed for him before he died.

I said a loud "amen" and then we waited. The chopper came in about forty-five minutes. I do not remember if it was the Holy Spirit or my idea, but I began taking pictures of the whole event. I snapped some of Larry on the bunk, some more of the men carrying him up a hill on a chair to the chopper, and then loading in. I even took one of him looking very shaky as he lifted off. My reasoning had something to do with being able to tell the complete story to Vangie should the worst happen.

Take the short cut!

On the way to the only hospital within 150 miles, the pilot asked Larry if he wanted to go straight over the mountains with altitudes exceeding ten thousand feet or go around them, taking another forty-five minutes. Larry said, "Go up and over. I don't know how much time I have left." They arrived safely and rolled Larry into the emergency room over three hours after his heart attack. The doctor on duty just happened to be a heart specialist. Working very quickly, they stabilized him in about two hours. Later, the doctor calmly said, "Larry, the damage to your heart was severe. There is no way you could have lasted as long as you did. Any other person in the same circumstances would have died enroute. You are a very lucky man." Larry said, "I had a Christian friend who prayed for me. That's how I made it!" God did give him a new heart three years later, when he received a heart transplant!

Healing those who are deaf and mute.

It may seem hard at first to minister to those that are deaf, mute, or both. We discovered that the source of some of these difficulties is spiritual rather than physical. The key is allowing the Holy Spirit to reveal which it is. When there is a spirit involved, we have learned to pray in similar fashion to how Jesus did in the next passage.

Mark 7:32-37

Then they brought to Him one who was deaf and had an impediment in his speech, and they begged Him to put His hand on him. And He took him aside from

143

the multitude, and put His fingers in his ears, and He spat and touched his tongue. Then, looking up to heaven, He sighed, and said to him, "Ephphatha," that is, "Be opened." Immediately his ears were opened, and the impediment of his tongue was loosed, and he spoke plainly. Then He commanded them that they should tell no one; but the more He commanded them, the more widely they proclaimed it. And they were astonished beyond measure, saying, "He has done all things well. He makes both the deaf to hear and the mute to speak." NKJV

DWJD

- When the Holy Spirit is leading us, He may indicate doing something that may seem strange. Always do what *He* indicates, no matter how strange.
- This may involve doing something as unusual as putting your fingers in someone's ears, spitting, and touching the tongue.
- Always speak to the problem area and command it to be healed. Do it like Jesus did!
- Speak to the deaf and mute spirit, and say something like "Be opened, in the name of Jesus!" You *will* have success, when you obey the Holy Spirit.

Deaf-mute boy healed.

I (John) had the privilege of spending six weeks with Dr. A.L. Gill in Malaysia in 1988. I helped him conduct five healing crusades during this trip. The first major miracle happened in the city of Kuantan, similar to what happened in Mark 7:32-37 above. He and I trained healing teams over a period of three days prior to each crusade. During the final one or two nights, citywide invitations were sent out inviting the public to come and be healed.

One of the healing teams, comprised of two Chinese ladies, was selected to pray for an eight-year-old boy who was a deaf-mute. His mother brought him forward so the ladies could pray for him. The Spirit evidently led them, because they put their fingers into his ears and touched his tongue with their fingers. They commanded the boy's ears to open and his tongue to be loosed. In a matter of minutes he could both hear and speak. His first words mumbled included thanks to "Jesus," in Chinese. His mother was amazed and gave her life to Jesus Christ that night. Ministering healing "two by two" is a biblical principle found in Mark 6.

Mark 6:7-8, 12-13
And He called the twelve to Himself, and began to send them out two by two, and gave them power over unclean spirits. He commanded them to take nothing for the journey except a staff—no bag, no bread, no copper in their money belt. . . . So they went out and preached that people should repent. And they cast out many demons, and anointed with oil many who were sick, and healed them. NKJV

DWJD

- Jesus wants us to minister two by two. It is best to work and minister with someone believing the same as you.
- Where two or more are in agreement, there is more power for ministry. While one is praying, the other is hearing from the Holy Spirit.
- We already have authority over all evil spirits, so use it! We do not go in our own power and authority. We go in the name of Jesus as our authority.
- Travel light. God will supply our every need as we go.
- Notice the order of events: Preach, repent, cast out demons, anoint with oil, and then heal the sick.
- Always carry a vial of anointing oil. It is scriptural, and it gives a point of contact so people can release their faith for healing.

Miracles multiplied.
The trip to Malaysia totally moved me into the absolute realm of the authentic, supernatural healing power of God. There

were only two of us, but a lot happened. It may be hard for readers to grasp the totality of what I am about to relate. I was an eyewitness with twelve rolls of film and one-on-one personal interviews with those healed over a period of six weeks in a phenomenal move of God. Each of the five meetings averaged over four hundred in attendance. I documented over 130 miraculous healings, 190 true conversions to Jesus Christ, and 740 people receiving the baptism of the Holy Spirit. I personally witnessed four totally demon-possessed people set free and returned to their right mind. I documented all of this with photos and a journal as the people testified to being completely healed and set free by the power of Jesus Christ.

Forget the numbers.

Jesus said we would do greater things than He did. We experienced this personally in Malaysia. The two of us, working separately at times, were experiencing simultaneous miracles. Church leadership and trained healing teams would then go into action praying for the sick. By this time, multiple miracles were manifesting all over the auditorium. We were experiencing the "greater works" and did not realize it. I tried to keep track of everything, running from one healing team to another, praying for the sick, and taking pictures. I was overwhelmed with joy and wonderment that this was really happening. I was once again experiencing the authentic manifestation of a God who loves to heal the sick. Suddenly in the middle of the miracles, it came to me. Forget the numbers! Just enjoy doing what Jesus did!

I lost count.

Somewhere during the fifth week I lost count. I tried to reconstruct the numbers later as I reviewed my audiotapes, pictures, and journal. At that point I heard myself say, "Tonight was incredible. We experienced twenty people getting saved, many more got baptized in the Holy Spirit, and a whole bunch of people received all kinds of healing miracles. Praise the Lord!"

Today, I will occasionally revert back to my old ways and try to keep track of who got what. The Holy Spirit will gently remind me it is His business. He says, "John, forget the numbers and just keep doing what Jesus did. I'm keeping track. We'll review everything after the final trumpet has sounded."

The Book of Acts is Not Finished

The following stories are representative of what continues to happen in and around our ministry. We never stop being totally surprised and thrilled when God decides to intervene and heal somebody. We often desire that more pastors and Christian leaders would experience what we do, especially in America. In our exuberance, we sometimes will give an unsolicited testimony to them about an incredible miracle that just happened a few days ago. They look at us with a blank stare, slightly smiling, wanting to believe, but giving the impression that we may have "stretched" the story a bit. They sometimes make us feel slightly guilty for testifying to the great things the Lord is doing. Believers, the book of Acts is not finished! Healing and miracles are more numerous today than they were in the book of Acts! We hope the following stories will build your faith.

Biker gets healed.
Recently, we conducted a workshop on hearing God's voice and healing the sick. A biker attended the workshop and responded to an invitation to receive prayer for healing. He said his body hurt all over from being hit and partially run over by a truck while riding his Harley. He also said he could not breathe properly from crushed ribs and a history of smoking too much. When asked what he wanted God to heal first, he said, "All of it, today!" When we hear a response like that, we immediately begin to pray. John laid hands on his chest and commanded healing to manifest in the name of Jesus Christ. Then John said, "Take a deep breath." He did. To his amazement, he could breathe deeper than ever before and there was no pain in his body. He immediately began to tell everyone about God healing him, and he began witnessing to anyone who would listen. We called the pastor of the church a

month later and asked how the biker was doing. The pastor confirmed that the man was still healed and was continuing to witness to anyone who would listen.

Business executive begins screaming!

One day I (Sonja) was sitting in my office when one of the executives limped through the door. I took one look at him and knew he was in a great deal of pain. He said, "Sonja, I've got spasms in my back, and I'm leaving to go to the doctor." I expressed my concern and asked if he needed someone to drive him to his emergency appointment. He thanked me, but said he was sure he could make it and turned to leave. As he did, he had another spasm, and he began screaming from the unbearable pain.

All of the vice presidents' offices were down one hallway, and we all had ceiling-to-floor glass windows by the doors. As my colleague began screaming, all eyes from the work area outside my office focused on my friend.

That's impressive!

I jumped up and ran around my desk because he looked like he might pass out. As I reached him, I said I did not know what to do except pray. He yelled, "Anything! Anything!" I laid my hands on his back and commanded the muscles to relax and the pain to subside, in Jesus' name. I then said, "You were asking me about speaking in tongues the other day, and I'm going to pray that way also." He again responded, "Anything! Anything!" I interceded for just a few moments in my spiritual language, and then he began to straighten up—the pain was gone! Slowly turning around, his eyes were as big as saucers as he exclaimed, "That's impressive!" I told him I serve an impressive God! As I glanced out of my office, I saw many curious stares and smiles at my brand of "First Aid."

This co-worker and his wife and little daughter began to attend a little community church across town where they lived. The pastor apparently did not preach a clear salvation message, but over the months that followed, I was privileged to confirm this man's salvation as he continued to ask questions. What a joy!

One morning he rushed into my office and asked if I had a minute. Of course I did, and he related how the night before his daughter was running such a high fever that they were bundling her up to rush to the emergency room at the hospital. All of a sudden he remembered how I had prayed for him. (Now remember, he had not received any teaching on divine healing—his only experience was in my office that day). He said he gathered his little one into his arms and told her he thought Jesus wanted to heal her. She had been learning about Jesus in Sunday School and in childlike faith agreed with her daddy. He said he shouted, "Fever, get out of her!" Then he remembered I had said, "In Jesus' name!" so he added that to his heartfelt prayer. His eyes were glistening with tears of joy as he related how the fever broke, she was healed, and things were normal that morning.

True Christianity that expresses the power of God in our everyday lives gets people's attention. It should be the norm to see healings wherever they are needed and done in such a way that people are drawn to salvation and "gifts of healing" in their own lives.

Woman healed of uterine cancer.
One day we had a woman come to us for prayer after the Sunday morning service. She had been diagnosed with uterine cancer and she was going the next day for a pre-operative appointment. She was terrified by the whole ordeal. We prayed a simple prayer and cursed the cancer in Jesus' name and commanded healing to her uterus. She seemed relieved and left in much better spirits.

A couple of months later she rushed up to us with the wonderful news that she had been healed. No sign of cancer and no surgery! We rejoiced with her.

Why is everyone not healed?

As we drove to lunch that Sunday, we were so happy for our friend's good news, but we also discussed once again the mystery of healing. As we shared in chapter 1, we do not have all the answers. We just know that we are to pray and leave the results up to God.

Recently, a dear friend of ours died from cancer. We had contended for healing with her and her husband for over four years. Yet, she went to be with Jesus. The following morning, I was asking the Lord about her death. I recorded the following thoughts in my journal: "Sonja, your and My friend, Nina, fought a good fight, and she has been received into glory where every question has been answered, every doubt cast off. Everything, yes everything, now makes perfect sense to her. For those of you who are still in this dimension, you can only rest in My faithfulness and know that one day it will also make perfect sense to you."

Grace healings and the sovereignty of God.

God remains sovereign. When He decides to miraculously heal someone without any help from any other person, that remains His choice. We call that a "grace healing." Perhaps the person who was sick looked to God, prayed a simple prayer, and "wham" they were healed! We wish God would do that more often. Then this book would not have been necessary. The truth is, the Lord has provided a means by which His body, working with the Holy Spirit, can facilitate healing in those coming to Him in faith. He is not only able to heal us, He is willing. We contend in prayer with the best understanding and leading we have and leave the rest in the hands of a gracious and loving Lord.

When they are not healed.

God in His infinite wisdom has the answer for those who are not healed. This remains a mystery to any honest minister who preaches that Jesus Christ is our Healer. Our experience is that not everyone is healed. Many are, but not all. We must defer to the One who in the very beginning said to the nation of Israel and to us:

Exodus 15:25-26

. . . There the LORD made a decree and a law for them, and there he tested them. He said, "If you listen carefully to the voice of the LORD your God and do what is right in his eyes, if you pay attention to his commands and keep all his decrees, I will not bring on you any of the diseases I brought on the Egyptians, for I am the LORD, who heals you." NIV

When we carefully examine the God of the Old Covenant, there were sometimes conditions surrounding the God who heals. Jesus Christ inaugurates the New Covenant with better promises, one of which is healing. He is the same sovereign God of both covenants. We must rely on His mercy and not on our desire, our effort, or our faith formulas. The Bible says:

Romans 9:14-16

What then shall we say? Is God unjust? Not at all! For he says to Moses, "I will have mercy on whom I have mercy, and I will have compassion on whom I have compassion." It does not, therefore, depend on man's desire or effort, but on God's mercy. NIV

To not include this biblical principle in our discussion regarding divine healing is to ignore the sovereignty of a loving God who ultimately decides who receives healing and who does not. We pray for the sick, not because He guarantees healing; we pray because He has declared that He is willing! The final outcome rests with Him.

151

Blind woman healed.

We were with the Lahu tribal people in northern Thailand and were teaching about the God who heals. After the preaching, an older blind woman was led to the front for prayer. One of our team members was Steven Darrow who owned a large software company in the Northwest. He and his wife, Dorinda, had been through our training, and they were full of faith. Steven and a missionary from Australia began to pray for the woman. In a short while, she began looking around in wonderment as her vision returned. This notable miracle caused quite an uproar in the village. Two days later, a witch doctor showed up at the meeting. He had heard of the astounding things that were happening. (His story is related in chapter 6). The thrilling thing for us about this story was to see a corporate executive healing the sick! We are all called to do what Jesus did.

Lame-from-birth woman walks.

Steven's wife, Dorinda, was quite timid about ministering healing when she first arrived in Thailand. However, the gift of faith came upon her, and she was fearless! A woman was brought for prayer who had been lame from birth. Her legs hung limply, even turned backwards, when she was held upright. Dorinda and another team member, Kathy Knox, practically ran to the woman, took her from those that were holding her up, and began to minister. The gift of faith on Dorinda expressed itself with commands in Jesus' name for healing and strength to manifest in the woman's legs. A creative miracle was needed, and they believed for one!

To the village people's utter amazement, the woman began to receive strength, her legs turned forward, and she began to haltingly take assisted steps. Soon Dorinda was out a few feet in front beckoning the woman to come to her, much as a baby learning to walk. She took her baby steps to Dorinda. It was a tremendous healing for the woman and an unforgettable experience for all of us.

Native Americans learn to heal the sick.

We assisted an internationally known evangelist, Dr. A.L. Gill, in conducting a healing crusade on the Rose Bud Indian Reservation at Mission, South Dakota. We spent several evenings teaching the Christians how to heal the sick. They practiced on each other during the teaching sessions, and those who needed healing were healed. That stirred their faith for others, and they were ready to minister when the first night of the crusade began.

After the preaching, the people came forward for healing and John had all of our two-person healing teams ready. It was exciting to see people who had never before prayed for the sick, until our training, do so with great results.

Rancher's rotator cuff healed.

An older man, a rancher, came for healing. The doctor had diagnosed a torn rotator cuff in his shoulder. He was in so much pain he was not able to do his work. After prayer, he had full motion of his shoulder, and he was extremely happy.

The next evening I (Sonja) was greeting the people as they were arriving. I recognized the rancher, and I asked him how his shoulder was doing. He said he had worked all day and it felt great! I then asked him if he would be willing to tell the people what had happened.

I have never done such a thing.

I saw stark terror in his eyes at the thought of getting up on the stage and using a microphone to testify about his miracle healing. "Oh, no, Ma'am. I have never done such a thing. I just couldn't!" I explained how it would likely help the faith of others and perhaps they, too, would be healed. He was such a humble man and obviously loved the Lord, so I finally persuaded him.

Before the preaching the next evening, we had several people testify to the healing that they had received. When the little old rancher's time came, he said, "I know you folks are like me when you see healing stuff on TV, and you wonder if it's the real thing or not. Well, last night my shoulder was healed—I had a torn rotator cuff. You believe me! I'm telling you I was healed, and I'm not putting you on!" The audience broke into approving applause. They all knew this humble little man who was testifying to God's healing power at the hands of his neighbors who were on the healing teams.

Child healed of bleeding eczema.

We are coaches over home groups for our church, and we occasionally visit the other groups we oversee. We recently learned of a tremendous healing that happened through prayer at one such meeting.

A single mother of three had a beautiful two-year-old that was covered with bleeding, oozing sores due to eczema. She was not responding to any of the medication, and the doctors were confounded. Meanwhile, the condition was worsening. We gently prayed a simple prayer and commanded healing to manifest in the child's body. From that hour healing began, and over the next several days she was completely healed and has had no recurrence. Jesus is our Healer!

Yes, you can heal the sick!

We hope by reading these accounts, your faith will be stirred to heal the sick just like the people we have been telling you about. Likely, you just need a little practice with some people who know how much the Lord wants to use you. Learning how to heal the sick requires a progressive revelation of what Jesus promised to every one of His followers. Those who have submitted themselves to the baptism of the Holy Spirit simply need to begin to release gifts of healing whenever it is appropriate.

It is "gifts," not "gift."

When a believer receives the gift of the Holy Spirit, "gifts" (plural) of healing are immediately available to be released to those who are sick. Other gifts are also available to be given away to those who need them. With a little training, believers can begin to operate in any gifts the Holy Spirit deems necessary for each occasion. When a believer decides to step out in faith and begin praying for the sick, the Holy Spirit is there to help complete the ministry. The Holy Spirit disperses gifts of healing when and where He sovereignly wills. This is promised in 1 Corinthians 12.

1 Corinthians 12:7, 9, 11
Now to each one the manifestation of the Spirit is given for the common good. . . . to another *gifts of healing* by that one Spirit, . . . All these are the work of one and the same Spirit, and he gives them to each one, just as he determines. NIV

DWJD

- When the Holy Spirit indicates He is willing to start healing people, gifts of healing are already being dispersed.
- Note: Healing gifts are not a single great gift for special individuals.
- Gifts of healing are available to whoever wants to believe and steps out in faith and begins to pray for the sick.

There are no "special" ministers with privileged "inside" information—though some well-publicized evangelists would want you to believe to the contrary. The Scriptures are open for any believer to read and believe what is promised. Jesus promises that every Christian can pray for the sick and believe God for healing. As we close this chapter and move on to hearing God's voice, we pray that you will move from doubt and timidity to doing what Jesus said you could do. He promised it. So, He will help you do it.

Let's Practice

- James 1:22 says to *DO* what we have heard (read).
- Consider doing what is recommended in this chapter by referring to the "Let's Practice" in Appendix B, page 324.
- Do the Ministry Skill Assignment entitled, "Learning How to Heal the Sick."

Chapter Four

Ministry Skill Four

HEARING FROM GOD

Jesus Christ says His followers will hear His voice. The Spirit-baptized believer is in direct relationship with the Holy Spirit and is a primary candidate to hear directly from God. In this chapter, we will examine the biblical references and accounts of people hearing and obeying God's voice. We will learn how to hear from God and to do what He says.

Hearing God's voice is a spellbinding experience. He knows how to grab our attention. He surprises us. He speaks in ways so unexpectedly, so spontaneously, that we attribute the voice to Him. Though irrational to modern thinking and extremely difficult to prove, deep down we know we are hearing from the Holy Spirit. When we were born of the Spirit we were given "ears to hear." We can now hear what the Spirit is saying to the church. Christians are continuing to hear from God in a multitude of ways. Whether direct or indirect, God's voice is being heard. He speaks through His Word, through sermons, other Christians, prophecy, books, tracts, tapes, Christian music, and even multimedia. By design, we have dedicated this chapter to hearing from God in a personal way. We will concentrate on personally hearing the voice of the Holy Spirit. Jesus says:

John 10:27
"My sheep hear My voice, and I know them, and they follow Me." NASB

John 18:37
". . .Everyone who is of the truth hears My voice." NASB

John 10:16

"I have other sheep, (*He was speaking about the Gentiles)* which are not of this fold; I must bring them also, and they will hear My voice; and they will become one flock with one shepherd." NASB

God is speaking to us. Hearing His voice is a privilege granted to those who believe. No matter how long it takes, we must discover how to clearly hear God's voice and then obey what He tells us to do.

We must hear His voice and do what He says.

The most important factor in doing what Jesus did is hearing His voice and doing what He says. If ministers are looking for the key to fruitful ministry, this is it. The most effective way to meet the needs of those around us is to have God tell us what the *real* need is and then have Him reveal the solution. That is how Jesus did it. As we stated in the introduction, John 5:19-20 is foundational to this book. We believe the secret to Jesus' perfect ministry of healing and setting people free was because He did everything by revelation.

John 5:19-20

". . . Truly, truly, I say to you, the Son can do nothing of Himself, unless it is *something He sees the Father doing*; for whatever the Father does, these things the Son also does in like manner. For the Father loves the Son, and shows Him all things that He Himself is doing; and the Father will show Him *greater works* than these, so that you will marvel." NASB

God always knows the source of everyone's problems and how they got into the situation. Whether physical, emotional, or spiritual, God knows everything about everyone and holds the solution to each need. When we approach Him with a sincere heart, crying out for an answer, God not only listens, He may reveal the solution.

Psalm 142:5-6

I cry to you, O LORD; I say, "You are my refuge, my portion in the land of the living. Listen to my cry, for I am in desperate need; . . ." NIV

Jeremiah 42:6

"Whether it is pleasant or unpleasant, we will listen to the voice of the LORD our God . . ." NASB

We need to hear from God regardless of what He might say. We will receive His words any way He wants to deliver them. Like young Samuel we say, "Lord, speak, for your servant is listening" (see I Samuel 3:10). For those who have paid the price and have disciplined themselves to hear from God, answers will come. However, for the majority of believers, it is difficult to personally hear God's voice. This chapter is intended to help those desiring to hear directly from God.

John Learns to Hear from God

They seemed a little "spooky."

The first time I (John) heard a Christian say, "God speaks to me," I thought they were nuts. After all, I held a Bachelor of Science degree in Business Administration. If you could prove it scientifically, fine, but do not try to convince me of something I cannot understand. To me, the thought of hearing directly from an unseen God was incomprehensible. I was a brand new believer and wanted everything God had for me. But, all this was new. I was naturally skeptical of those who said they could have a two-way conversation with God. They seemed a little "spooky" to me at the time. I wanted God to speak to me in an authentic encounter—something I knew was real and not some bogus experience.

So I prayed, "God, speak to me like You do to these other Christians. I'm one of Your sheep. I want to hear Your voice. So, speak." There was no answer. No matter how hard I listened, there was silence. After a few months, I presumed these people were God's anointed. They must be super-

159

spiritual to have the privilege of hearing directly from God. I found out later that every Christian could hear from God. We just had to learn how. We needed to incorporate some personal disciplines into our lives that allow us to hear. I was to discover how to hear by obeying Scriptures that would lead me into a deep, personal relationship with Him. Though it would take years to master, I had the rest of my life to work on it. I sought out Christian leaders who had successfully made the journey. Perhaps they could guide me to where I could hear. I will relate the next story from the perspective of how I perceived things as a brand new Christian.

It was a startling experience.
The very first FGBMFI meeting I attended was a luncheon near downtown Seattle. It was a startling experience. They asked for any first-timers to stand and introduce themselves. That was easy. What came next was unexpected. After giving my name and what I did as a businessman, they asked how long had I known the Lord. I said, "About a week." I was surprised as the whole room erupted into applause. I graciously smiled, sat down, and wondered what I had gotten myself into. Then they began to not only sing songs I did not know, but everyone raised their hands and sang with their eyes closed. Then they seemed to murmur and hum some words in unison until the guy right next to me started talking like a chipmunk. With a machine-gun style and shrill voice, he uttered foreign words that made no sense. Everyone kept their hands in the air, listening. Then there was silence. Weird.

Thus saith the Lord.
All of a sudden, on the far side of the room a rather large Jewish man said, "Thus saith the Lord. . . ." The rest of the message spoke directly to my heart. Up to that time I wanted to get out of there. However, I could understand these words and they made me feel good. I wanted to stay and hear more. It was like he really was speaking on behalf of God. I did not understand the protocol for this kind of meeting, but I knew this man had somehow heard from God and was relating what he had heard. Afterwards, I was introduced to this man.

160

His name was Larry Alhadeff. He seemed nice, outgoing, and not weird at all. That is, until he and the other men firmly gave me brotherly "bear hugs." That was hard for me to do. I was taught to stay away from men like this.

I left the luncheon and returned to work in a state of excitement. I did not understand what had happened. All I knew was that Larry heard God's voice and spontaneously related the words to us. Within me I was blessed, even though I was having difficulty interpreting what was happening. I wanted to return to their meetings and find out what else they knew about God and especially how I could hear God's voice. I later found out that I had encountered the spiritual gifts of speaking in tongues and the companion gift of interpretation of tongues as described by Paul in 1 Corinthians 12. This began my journey towards a supernatural God that speaks to His people.

1 Corinthians 12:7-11
But to each one is given the manifestation of the Spirit for the common good. For to one is given . . . various kinds of tongues, and to another the interpretation of tongues. But one and the same Spirit works all these things, distributing to each one individually just as He wills. NASB

The Holy Spirit distributes supernatural gifts each time Christians gather. We should remain open and available to receive or give words that are prompted by the Holy Spirit.

The school of trial and error.
I started to grow in my understanding of the Bible. I would read and meditate in it and then watch, listen, and try to apply it to my life. I would experiment with the things Jesus said we could do. Something wonderful was happening. I was gradually being led into a deeper understanding of how God speaks to His people. First, I watched as others were hearing

from God. Second, I compared what I was witnessing to passages in the Bible. They seemed to be the same. Then I tried to listen to God for myself. As I tried to do what I saw the other men doing, it did not work very well. At first, the words that I thought were from God turned out to be my own thoughts. The majority of the "revelations" ended in disappointment and frustration. I was learning through trial and error.

One of my early Bible teachers said we should journal what we think God may be saying. So, I sat down, prayed, and asked God to fill my mind with His thoughts. By faith, I began to record paragraph after paragraph of what was transpiring in my mind. I thought, "Wow, this is tremendous!" I invited a longtime friend of the FGBMFI, Pastor Harley Goodwin, to my home to examine my work. He reviewed the many pages of hot "revelations." He had baptized me in water the year before, so I respected his spiritual input.

It is about half God and half you.
After reading my stuff, he smiled and said, "Brother John, some of this sounds good. But, it's about half God and half you. If I were you, I'd throw it all in the trash. That means your soul nature is competing with your spirit. If you don't know what the Bible says, you record what you think it says and what you want to hear. The result is a mixture of what *you* want God to say with parts of what His Word already says. This is dangerous. Instead, allow His Word to renew your mind to what He's already established as truth and obey what the Word already says." I threw all of it away and started reading the Bible in earnest.

I slowly began to differentiate between religious zeal and operating with the gentle coaxing of the Holy Spirit. I was learning valuable lessons by stumbling through the process. Delivering what we think are inspired words from the Lord in the presence of discerning and mature leaders is a safe way to learn. Allowing mature believers to critique your words is a sound way to learn what is and is not from the Lord. The same Holy Spirit is upon everyone. By allowing the Lord to give a positive witness to the majority of those present, agreement is reached, confirming the authenticity of the content. This may have to be done over and over again. Time is needed to truly hear from God. We need others to confirm the words we are hearing from God. It is critical to have mature Christians around us that will correct, critique, and guide us in the process. This also affords us the opportunity to judge ourselves: Am I teachable and submitted to authority?

How Do You Prophesy?

During the early years of attending all kinds of FGBMFI meetings, I noticed that quite a few men would spontaneously deliver inspired words from God to those gathered. Sometimes these words would be for the whole group, other times for individuals. I asked the president of the chapter how I could learn how to do this. His response was puzzling at first. He said, "Brother, you can't give it out unless you have it in you." I asked what he meant by that. He wisely said, "You cannot speak on behalf of the Lord until He has something to draw from. You must spend a lot of time renewing your mind in the Word of God." I said, "I want to do this." He said, "The best way to deliver an encouraging word is to know the Bible backwards and forwards. That comes with years of meditating and memorizing the Word of God." That sounded like a lot of hard work. That is what the pastor told me. There must be an easier way. The Scriptures say meditation is the key.

Psalm 119:15-16
I will meditate on Your precepts and regard Your ways. I shall delight in Your statutes; *I shall not forget Your word.* NASB

163

Meditation and memorization of the Word of God are sure ways to build a reservoir from which the Holy Spirit can draw. The Lord uses His Word implanted in our hearts to bring forth phrases that resonate God's plan for our lives.

Dick Mills.

A prophet came to town from California. His name was Dick Mills. He was an frequent speaker at major FGBMFI meetings. I watched him minister. I had never seen a prophet before. To me he was amazing. He would stare at various individuals, point to them and say, "What is your name? The Lord has a word for you." He would then repeat their name and spontaneously quote a series of Scriptures from both the Old and New Testaments. Another person would follow him around writing these Scriptures on a notepad and pass them to the person. We would look these up later and marvel at the confirming nature of the words to our personal lives.

Walking Bible.

Dick knew the Word of God so well that he was literally a walking Bible. He had committed hundreds and hundreds of Scriptures to memory and would rely on the Holy Spirit to recall them as he fixed his gaze on certain individuals. He knew the importance of fixing his gaze on people before delivering what God had given him to speak. We will revisit this hidden ministry truth later. We see the scriptural precedence in Acts 3.

Acts 3:4-6

But Peter, along with John, *fixed his gaze on him and said*, "Look at us!" And he began to give them his attention, expecting to receive something from them. But Peter said, "I do not possess silver and gold, but what I do have I give to you: In the name of Jesus Christ the Nazarene—walk!" NASB

Concentrating on a person's need may open the way to hear from God. It takes practice to do this. The Lord desires to meet our needs, and He may use mature believers to confirm His intentions.

Young man, stand up.

Dick looked my way, pointed to me and said, "Young man, stand up, give me your hand. The Lord has a word for you." I stood up, told him I was John, and took his hand. He said, "John, the word of the Lord to you is:"

Joshua 1:9

"Have I not commanded you? Be strong and courageous! Do not tremble or be dismayed, for the LORD your God is with you wherever you go." NASB

Genesis 28:15

"Behold, I am with you and will keep you wherever you go, and will bring you back to this land; for I will not leave you until I have done what I have promised you." NASB

Exodus 4:12

"Now then go, and I, even I, will be with your mouth, and teach you what you are to say." NASB

DWJD

This is a safe approach in giving guidance to people's lives. Jesus will use people like this to confirm what the Lord may be speaking to our hearts. Scripture is the best starting place to receive guidance for our lives.

He finished with a short exhortation about how God was going to use me in a future ministry. I wrote these in my first Bible and recopied them over and over through the years.

A confirming word.

Within six months, another prophet came through town. His name was Dick Joyce and he had a similar ministry. Like Mills, he pointed at me and asked me to stand. Then he spontaneously gave me a set of Scriptures that exhorted me in much the same way as Dick Mills had previously. He said, "I see a man called to serve the Lord. The word to you is this:

Isaiah 42:18-19

Hear, you deaf! And look, you blind, that you may see. Who is blind but My servant, or so deaf as My messenger whom I send? Who is so blind as he that is at peace with Me, or so blind as the servant of the LORD? NASB

Philippians 3:13

Brethren, I do not regard myself as having laid hold of it yet; but one thing I do: forgetting what lies behind and reaching forward to what lies ahead. NASB

Ezekiel 12:25, 28

"For I the LORD will speak, and whatever word I speak will be performed. It will no longer be delayed, for in your days, O rebellious house, I will speak the word and perform it," declares the Lord God. "Therefore say to them, 'Thus says the Lord God, "None of My words will be delayed any longer. Whatever word I speak will be performed,"'" declares the Lord God. NASB

Luke 21:15

"I will give you utterance and wisdom which none of your opponents will be able to resist or refute." NASB

Colossians 4:3

. . . God will open up to us a door for the word, so that we may speak forth the mystery of Christ, for which I have also been imprisoned: . . . NASB

One way the Lord confirms His intentions for us is by delivering the same or supporting Scriptures through two or more mature Christians who are unknown to each other. The Lord does this to assure us that He is personally speaking to us.

At the time, I did not understand the significance of these two prophetic encounters. God's plan for my life was just beginning to unfold.

Be Full of the Word

By this time I knew these two men were hearing from God. There was too much compelling evidence. The presence of the Holy Spirit accompanied their activities. There seemed to be an unusual atmosphere of faith and sense of expectation as these men delivered what God gave them. Then it dawned on me. These men were full of the Word of God. They had spent years memorizing thousands of Scriptures. No wonder they were anointed. God's Word had renewed their mind. It was like they really were speaking on behalf of God because they thought like God's Word. This revelation hit me like a flash. This may be my answer. I wondered what would happen if I would memorize Scripture. It certainly could not hurt. I did not know the Bible all that well anyway.

Combining business with pleasure.

I was an account representative for a large business envelope manufacturing company in Portland, Oregon. My sales territory included all the counties from north Seattle to the Canadian border. I had attended many business seminars to sharpen my sales and marketing skills. A principle that was recalled to me was how to acquire a new personal sales skill. The presenter said if you would practice it for twenty-one days it would become a part of your daily life, thus improving your presentation. I decided to apply the same principle to memorizing Scripture. I selected my favorite Scriptures from both the Old and New Testaments. I then spoke each Scripture seven times into a tape recorder. I would do this until I filled a ninety-minute tape. Then I would start a new tape. I was treasuring the Word of God in my heart.

Psalm 119:10-11

. . . Do not let me wander from Your commandments. Your word I have treasured in my heart, . . . NASB

The Word of God is permeated with the presence of the Holy Spirit. It will never pass away. It is eternal. It is alive. When we memorize His Word, we are replacing human understanding with eternal truth that will change our thinking to the way God thinks.

I listened to myself.

During my drive time to and from work and between appointments, I would listen to nothing but Scripture. By the end of twenty-one days, I was amazed at how easy it was to speak the complete series of Scriptures out loud as I was hearing it. After only hearing the first few words, I could perfectly finish speaking the Scripture. What was remarkable to me was after only six months, I had memorized 130 key passages from the Bible. I must have been led by the Holy Spirit to do this. The passages I chose to memorize were eternal promises pertaining to salvation, eternal life, the power of the Holy Spirit, healing, deliverance, and what Jesus said we could do. I still can recall most of them today, word for word.

Then something wonderful began to happen. What I had prayed for came to pass. As people would ask for prayer or be concerned about their situation, I would suddenly know a promise from Scripture that would meet their need. The Holy Spirit would often recall a set of Scriptures that would be the answer to people's problems. It happened so naturally I felt confident that the Lord was speaking through me. He was using the deposit of His Word in my spirit to bless others. It was extremely gratifying. The Lord was using me in a way I never thought possible. Finally, I was hearing God's voice in a safe and reliable way. It was like I was being used as an echo of the written Word of God when and where it was needed.

I Heard the Voice of the Holy Spirit

I will never forget the first time I delivered an "inspired" word from the Holy Spirit at a public gathering. It happened in a FGBMFI luncheon at the Galilean Restaurant in north Seattle. During worship, one of the leaders gave a public message in tongues. The master of ceremonies told us to wait until there was an appropriate interpretation of the message. We needed to be in order and understand what the Lord might be saying. We waited and waited. In the meantime, I was enjoying the Lord's presence on the other side of the room. It seemed the Lord was causing an explosion of words and accompanying pictures to manifest in my mind. It was great. I was having my very own Holy Ghost party.

1 Corinthians 14:27
If anyone speaks in a tongue, let there be two or at the most three, each in turn, and let one interpret. NKJV

It is best to allow the Holy Spirit to use more than one person when the gifts of tongues and interpretation are manifesting together in a public gathering.

"What do I do?"
The man standing next to me received a word of knowledge that I had the interpretation to the message in tongues. He firmly nudged me with his elbow saying, "Brother, you have the interpretation. Give it!" I opened my eyes and said, "What do I do?" He said, "Just speak what you are hearing and seeing in the Spirit." The party was over. With hesitant words I related to the group what I had just seen and heard. It must

have been inspired because there erupted spontaneous applause to the Lord of lords. For the first time in a public setting, I had heard the voice of the Lord and was privileged to deliver what He wanted said. The Holy Spirit had created an atmosphere that brought edification to those gathered.

1 Corinthians 14:26

How is it then, brethren? Whenever you come together, each of you has a psalm, has a teaching, has a tongue, has a revelation, has an interpretation. Let all things be done for edification. NKJV

God, the Holy Spirit, is present when believers gather. Everyone should come expectant and ready to contribute something from the Lord that will edify and build up those who are gathered.

Gaining sensitivity to the Holy Spirit.

The more I memorized the Word, the more God would use me to give an encouraging word to others. As the months and years rolled on, I noticed an ever-increasing sensitivity to the ministry of the Holy Spirit. This happened as I prayed with certain individuals. It was as if I knew things about their life and how best to pray for their situation. It was sparked into action when I either looked directly at them or laid my hand on their shoulder. It took a long time of trial and error to master cooperating with the Holy Spirit in this way, but I kept doing it. Sometimes I heard correctly, sometimes not. When I hesitated and failed to obey the subtle leading, I would immediately know I was grieving the Holy Spirit. He gently lets us know when we hesitate and begin doubting His leading. If we continue doubting too long, the anointing ebbs away and we are left feeling miserable.

The safe approach.

I have learned how to apologize when I miss what God wants to do. Christians are quick to forgive you when you are trying to obey God's voice. I recommend the "safe approach" to anyone who is not sure they are hearing correctly. It will go something like this: "Sir, I may be wrong. But, I would like to tell you what I 'think' I am hearing from the Lord. Is that O.K.?" When we approach ministry like that, people will most always respond with, "Go ahead." After delivering the word I ask, "Did that make any sense to you? Did the word fit your situation?" I allow them to respond honestly. I am ready to ask forgiveness if I missed God. We have discovered that 95 percent of the time it is God leading us. We are apologizing less and less as we learn to do it right.

The occasions of disobedience were also becoming less. I was gaining confidence to minister as I thought I was being led. Eventually, I decided to go ahead and assume I was being led by God's voice. Whether it was a weak leading from the inner voice or the firm, commanding voice of the Holy Spirit, I made a declaration to go ahead and act on what I thought was manifesting in my mind. At the same time, I always remained open for critique from those to whom I ministered. I wanted to obey Paul's admonition in Ephesians 6.

Ephesians 6:18
. . . pray at all times in the Spirit, . . . NASB

Jesus said believers would speak in tongues. Paul says that when we speak in tongues we are actually praying in the Spirit. Praying in tongues allows the Holy Spirit to activate our mind to hear a response from God.

Praying in tongues.
Ephesians 6:18 is a primary avenue to hear from God. It is not an option. Praying in tongues is a must and should be pursued aggressively. The more we pray in the Spirit, the more we will hear from God. When coupled with memorization of Scripture, praying in tongues keeps the channel open to hear God's voice on a daily basis. This is part of

abiding in Christ. To abide means to get so close to the Lord that we will pray unselfishly.

John 15:7

"If you abide in Me, and My words abide in you, ask whatever you wish, and it will be done for you." NASB

DWJD

Jesus desires for us to pray using His words as we ask for things. Praying in the Spirit allows us to pray with His words that are abiding in our spirit nature. When we do this, we are praying His words and asking according to His will. In this way, He will do whatever we ask.

Pray at all Times in the Spirit

I learned a vital truth from a number of leaders in the Charismatic movement during the 1970s and 1980s. They all agreed on one thing. I can still hear their teaching: "The way we hear from the Holy Spirit is to pray at all times in the Spirit. If you are not praying in tongues at every opportunity, then you are really missing God's best." They would challenge us to pray in tongues for as long as possible. I remember what happened whenever I exceeded about a half-hour praying this way. Something happened within me. It was as if I became supercharged deep within me. I experienced a feeling of spiritual euphoria. It was as if I was connected with the Holy Spirit in a way otherwise not possible.

1 Corinthians 14:2, 4

The one who speaks in a tongue does not speak to men but to God; for no one understands, but in his spirit he speaks mysteries. . . . He who speaks in a tongue edifies himself, . . . NKJV

Paul strongly encourages believers to pray in tongues at every opportunity. The more we do this, the more the mysteries of God begin to flow from our spirit nature, thus edifying and recharging us for ministry.

Stop and listen.

Believers who are willing to pay the price of spending quality time praying in tongues will inherit a little known promise found in 1 Corinthians 14. Whenever I pray for extended times in the Spirit and then stop abruptly and listen, I can hear words of praise and adoration to the Lord in my mind. Intelligible words emit from the Spirit of my mind that concur with what I have just been praying in tongues. I assume this is most often the interpretation of the mysterious words I have been praying.

1 Corinthians 14:13-14

Therefore let one who speaks in a tongue pray that he may interpret. For if I pray in a tongue, my spirit prays, but my mind is unfruitful. NASB

DWJD

- Paul reveals a profound truth about praying in tongues. He says that anyone speaking in tongues should pray that he may interpret what he is saying.
- Praying in tongues is a supernatural transaction generated from our spirit nature, not our mind.
- Paul encourages us to allow the Holy Spirit to interpret what we have been praying so our mind can understand what was said.
- Whenever we are alone we should practice this way of praying.

Personal worship.

The context of 1 Corinthians 14 is almost exclusively related to the public gathering of the church body. But how does one learn how to express these gifts when they arrive at church? May we suggest practicing at home? If we cannot learn how to edify ourselves, how can we ever learn how to edify the church? Let us attempt to apply the principles of speaking in tongues and interpretation of tongues in the safety of our own home, alone.

An exciting way to pray.
The preceding Scripture says we can expect to receive the interpretation of what we have been praying in unknown languages. It says, ". . . pray that he may interpret." I discovered this while alone with God, praying for prolonged times in the Spirit. I would pray, "Lord, what am I saying?" Words would manifest in my mind. So, I would speak these back to the Lord. The words were most often praise, exaltation, and magnification of the Lord. They seemed to be words that needed to be said to the Lord. This became a regular exercise that strengthened my faith and belief that I was on track. I eventually concluded that I was hearing what the Holy Spirit was saying. He then encouraged me to express these words to the Father. It was as if the Holy Spirit was giving me the kind of words that would bless and magnify the Father more than what I could come up with.

Caution.
I also found that when I continued to exercise faith and speak words that were manifesting in my mind, occasionally the message would pertain to things the Lord wanted me to do. The communication was personalized and intended for me to apply to my situation. There is a danger in accepting words that come this way as being from God. In our zeal to hear from God we must always test the words we are hearing, especially if they apply to us personally. I learned quickly to write down what I thought the Holy Spirit was saying. As I wrote I would always pray, "Lord, if this is from You, please confirm it any way You want." I would never act on the message until I received multiple confirmations. A good indication we are hearing from the Holy Spirit is when we hear the same message or see the same images

in our thoughts and dreams over and over again. This is especially true when we pray for extended times in tongues.

When confirmation comes.

As soon as God confirmed what He had said, I learned to immediately act on what He wanted me to do. With few exceptions, the leading turned out to be from the Lord. When He multiplies His confirmations, you can be more assured it is from Him.

Psalm 119:105-106

Your word is a lamp to my feet and a light to my path. I have sworn and I will *confirm* it, . . . NASB

1 Peter 5:10

After you have suffered for a little while, the God of all grace, who called you to His eternal glory in Christ, will Himself perfect, *confirm*, strengthen and establish you. NASB

DWJD

When it is Jesus wanting you to do something, the Holy Spirit will cause multiple confirmations to manifest, giving us the assurance that it is from Him. Most confirmations will be a spontaneous surprise. This is a major clue the confirmation is from the Lord.

How This Works Out in Our Daily Lives

Hearing God's voice can be a great advantage to staying on course in our daily lives. It would be wonderful if we could hear His voice hour-by-hour like Jesus did. That is just not how it works for most Christians. Even the most spiritual, most mature, and most holy pastors we know do not hear from God like Jesus did. We do not, but we want to. All of us should be working toward this goal. If every Christian leader were totally honest, we would have to admit we are a long way from hearing the Father's voice like Jesus did. Knowing it is possible is the driving force that keeps us seeking an even closer, more personal relationship with the Heavenly Father. The following are some real-life examples of how we have heard from God and attempted to obey.

We must be deliberate.
Learning to hear God's voice requires deliberate action on our part. I (Sonja) am a Word person, and by being in the Word daily for almost forty years, the Holy Spirit as Teacher has taught me many wonderful spiritual principles. I have learned from the Word what pleases God and how I can show Him I love Him. Learning to hear God's voice through His Word is not only exciting, it can shape the very direction our lives will take. The following Scriptures have guided me through the years.

Hebrews 4:12
For the word of God is living and active. Sharper than any double-edged sword, it penetrates even to dividing soul and spirit, joints and marrow; it judges the thoughts and attitudes of the heart. NIV

1 Samuel 15:22
"To obey is better than sacrifice, . . ." NIV

John 14:15
"If you love me, you will obey what I command." NIV

The Word of God is living and active and supernatural. God makes it clear in His Word that we show Him we love Him by our obedience. Therefore, we must know His Word so we can live a pleasing life before Him. It also allows Him to speak boldly to us through His Word.

Renewing the mind.

Over the years He has dealt with my (Sonja's) sinful, carnal behaviors through His Word. It is as if a spiritual spotlight shines on certain passages and causes them to illuminate and give me personal insight, conviction and understanding. This is the supernatural nature of the Bible as revealed by the Holy Spirit.

On many occasions it has been a fierce struggle between my soul nature (mind, emotions and will) and my spirit. One of the greatest areas of spiritual warfare is self-justification. What stinking thinking that is! I always wanted to be right, always wanting my point of view to prevail. The following incident reveals how I have struggled in this area.

Corporate executive needs to hear from God.

I was employed as a corporate officer of an electronics corporation, and I enjoyed my job very much. As the company grew, the Board of Directors agreed with the top executives that it was time to hire a new Chief Executive Officer to take the company to the next level. In this reorganization, four new executives were hired. In my position I had to interface with each of these people on a daily basis.

Since I had always had excellent working relationships with their predecessors, I naively assumed it would be business as usual. What a rude awakening I experienced! From day one, the new "inner circle" began to shut me out. Since I was dependent upon them for timely information to do my job, I was in a most untenable situation. As the weeks progressed, the situation went from bad to worse. Nothing I did or said seemed to change things. It was obvious: they not only did not like me, they wanted me out of there.

I was fervently praying about the deteriorating circumstances in which I found myself, and I had no answers, no reasons why. I had watched the job I loved deteriorate into one that was miserable, to the point that I was dreading going to work. It all came to a head one Friday afternoon when the data I needed for a Board of Directors' meeting was not forthcoming, consequently making my report late. The rude way I was told that the information would not be available until the following Monday was "the last straw."

Fire was shooting out of my eyes!

I became so angry I think fire was shooting out of my eyes! Shaking with violent anger, I somehow managed to mumble something like, "I cannot believe you can be so unprofessional!" I then went into my office and slammed the door with all my might. Every wall in the executive suite shook at the force of my fury. I grabbed my briefcase and purse, threw the door open, marched out, and slammed the door again. By then, I had everyone's attention. Thank God, no one said a word as I stomped out to my car and left for the weekend.

Very few times in my life have I been so completely out of control. It was sickening. We had planned a weekend trip to a quaint Bavarian town in eastern Washington. I vented my anger and frustration, my self-justification, my uncontrolled soul nature to poor John. It became clear I had three choices:

1. I could resign and leave the company I had helped build along with the lucrative stock options, bonus programs, etc.
2. I could stay and fight them on their own terms. After all, I reported directly to the Chairman and personally knew all of the directors of the board. I could cause my "enemies" considerable grief and feed the demon of self-justification.
3. I could stay, and through God's grace, be myself—not responding in like manner.

After I was finally able to calm myself to where I could listen, I went to the Bible and was led to:

1 Corinthians 13:4-7

Love is patient, love is kind. It does not envy, it does not boast, it is not proud. It is not rude, it is not self-seeking, it is not easily angered, it keeps no record of wrongs. Love does not delight in evil but rejoices with the truth. It always protects, always trusts, always hopes, always perseveres. NIV

This paragraph is one of the most powerful passages in the entire Bible. Jesus, as my perfect example, exhibited this type of love. How we need Him and His love!

He spoke through His Word once again.

I had been rude, self-seeking, easily angered and was keeping a record of every little offense! I was extremely sensitive to how I was being treated. That kind of love the Apostle Paul wrote about can only come from God. I asked Him for it, and He immediately softened my heart. He spoke through His Word once again. I felt led to purchase a small, but meaningful gift for the woman who had treated me so rudely on Friday.

I was myself as I walked into the office on Monday morning and put the beautifully wrapped gift on the woman's desk as I said a cheery "Good morning!" Honestly, her mouth dropped open as I walked into my office. She obviously was ready for a knock-down-drag-out encounter, and my actions totally disarmed her.

I quit the ugly self-justification.

Things began to change that very day. I quit the ugly self-justification and determined that if the Lord allowed me to continue to be treated badly, then He must need to work some things into or out of my character, and I would declare, "Your grace is sufficient."

Two months later, one of the executives stuck his head in my office and asked if he could meet with me in a few minutes. As I said, "Of course," I honestly thought to myself, "What now?" This particular man had been especially abrasive in our communications.

He thought I was a phony.
I went to his office, sat down on the other side of his desk, and braced myself. He began by thanking me for coming, and said he needed to tell me something before he went into the matter he wanted to discuss. I nodded my head, and he proceeded to tell me that he had not liked me from the moment he laid eyes on me. He thought I was a phony—no one could be that cheerful and considerate day in and day out. However, he had come to the conclusion that I was who I appeared to be and that he had been mistaken. He then leaned forward, smiled, and said the most unbelievable thing: "Actually, Sonja, I really like you!"

I was dumbfounded, speechless, and sat there in utter amazement as he moved on to the matter he wanted to discuss. It involved a very serious situation with one of his employees, and he wanted my advice on how to handle it. Together we were able to come up with an excellent solution that was a win-win for the employee and the company.

My remaining time at that company was enjoyable. We all ended up being friends and supportive co-workers. Yes, we can hear the voice of the Lord through His Word and His Holy Spirit for our everyday life experiences! The following story relates a more dramatic way the Lord can speak.

"John, I Call You to Preach the Gospel!"

Isaiah 6:8
Then I heard the voice of the Lord saying, "Whom shall I send? And who will go for us?" And I said, "Here am I. Send me!" NIV

One of the highest callings that any man or woman can have is being called to preach the Gospel. When we hear God's voice, personally calling us to proclaim the Full Gospel, we should have only one response: "Yes Lord! Here am I, send me!"

Jack-in-the-Box.

It was noon on November 3, 1975. I (John) had just been handed my lunch at the drive-up window of a Jack-in-the-Box drive-in near downtown Seattle, Washington. I decided to save time by eating lunch in my car because I had a busy day of making sales calls. Parking close to the ordering window, I unwrapped the biggest, juiciest hamburger on the menu. As I put it up to my mouth, God's voice suddenly filled the car. He said, "John Decker, I call you to preach the Gospel!" Shocked, I lost my grip on the burger. The tomatoes, lettuce, and onions fell to the napkin on my lap. Then He said it again: "John Decker, I call you to preach the Gospel!" Stunned, eyes wide, and holding my breath, I stared at the big plastic Jack-in-the-Box statue with the two-way speaker on his chest. The voice was not coming from the speaker. The speaker was the King of kings and the Lord of lords! I slowly placed what remained of the burger back into its box.

Ask for confirmation.

A pastor once told me to always ask for multiple confirmations if you think the Lord is speaking to you about a major life change. This one qualified. I said, "Lord, if that's You speaking, this is very serious. I want You to confirm what I think You said, three times!" I thought if I made it hard for God I could really know for sure if it was Him. I barely finished my question when I heard, "Drive up to the park on the top of the hill and I will confirm it!" The voice was so clear, so forceful, and so spontaneous that I started the car and drove to the park. Turning off the engine, I said, "O.K., what now?" Again, as before, His words loudly exploded inside my head. He said, "Turn to Hebrews chapter 3." I fumbled around the boxes of envelope samples in the back seat and finally found my Bible. Turning to chapter 3, my eyes immediately fell on:

Hebrews 3:7-8
. . . the Holy Spirit says, "Today, if you hear His voice, do not harden your hearts as when they provoked Me, as in the day of trial in the wilderness." NASB

DWJD

A jolt went through my inner man with the words, "John, I am speaking!" This is one of the ways you know God is speaking to you.

I knew the Holy Spirit was personalizing this passage to me. I said, "O.K., that's one confirmation." Then He said, "Turn the page!" I turned the page. There it was again, not only once but two more times!

Hebrews 3:15
". . . Today if you hear His voice, do not harden your hearts, as when they provoked Me." NASB

Hebrews 4:7
". . . Today if you hear His voice, do not harden your hearts." NASB

DWJD

When the Holy Spirit speaks, He may repeat the same message over and over until we accept it as from God.

I said, "O.K., that's twice." Then I was startled when I heard a loud knocking on the passenger side window. I jerked to the right and saw the face of my prayer partner smiling at me. He motioned for me to unlock the door. I could not believe what was happening. Sitting down he said, "God told me to drive up here, find you, and tell you that He is calling you to do something very important."

I said, "O.K. God, that's three."

When I told him what was happening and that he was the third confirmation God had orchestrated to get me to believe it was Him, we began to pray and cry together. With hands raised, sitting in the front seat of my car we began praising God and rejoicing that the Lord had boldly called me to preach the Gospel in such a convincing way that I knew it was Him. This bold encounter with God was just the beginning of a series of events that put me into the equipping ministry. The following Scriptures showed me that Peter had a bold encounter with the Lord where he was told something three times.

Acts 10:13-20

And *a voice* came to him, "Rise, Peter; kill and eat." But Peter said, "Not so, Lord! For I have never eaten anything common or unclean." And a *voice* spoke to him again the second time, "What God has cleansed you must not call common." *This was done three times.* And the object was taken up into heaven again. Now while Peter wondered within himself what this vision, which he had seen, meant, behold, the men who had been sent from Cornelius had made inquiry for Simon's house, and stood before the gate. And they called and asked whether Simon, whose surname was Peter, was lodging there. While Peter thought about the vision, *the Spirit said to him,* "Behold, three men are seeking you. Arise therefore, go down and go with them, doubting nothing; for I have sent them." NKJV

DWJD

- This is one of the best Scriptures in the New Testament regarding how the Holy Spirit can speak to the believer today.
- We can also expect the Holy Spirit to arrange circumstances that will coincide with His commands like He did in this passage. He does this to create a momentum that will convince us that it is the Lord speaking.
- Then we simply obey what we heard. Take time to meditate on the details in Acts chapter 10.

More confirmations.

It was but a few months later, after I spoke at the Tacoma Chapter of the FGBMFI, where a man I had never seen before appeared in front of me. He took my hand, and looking deep into my eyes he said, "The Lord says to you to be bold as never before. You shall not delay any longer. You shall preach the Gospel in the mighty power of the Holy Spirit. The power of Almighty God shall be in you and in your words!" I closed my eyes for a moment and began thanking the Lord. When I opened my eyes, I could not see the man. I quickly went looking for him but to no avail. The other men did not know who he was or where he came from. This began a series of similar confirmations over the next two years that firmly convinced me to surrender my life to preach the Gospel. I finally did it in the spring of 1977. I began to understand the mysterious way the Holy Spirit works. I saw in Acts 13 where the Holy Spirit spoke concerning Barnabas and Saul.

Acts 13:1-3

Now in the church that was at Antioch there were certain prophets and teachers: Barnabas, Simeon who was called Niger, Lucius of Cyrene, Manaen who had been brought up with Herod the tetrarch, and Saul. As they ministered to the Lord and fasted, *the Holy Spirit said*, "Now separate to Me Barnabas and Saul for the work to which I have called them." Then, having fasted and prayed, and laid hands on them, they sent them away. NKJV

When we get serious about hearing from God, He will reward those who diligently seek Him. Fasting, praying, and ministering to the Lord are scriptural ways to create an atmosphere where we can hear the Holy Spirit. In this case, the Holy Spirit boldly confirmed Barnabas and Saul's call to become apostles to the Gentiles. The same can and should be happening to us.

How I Learned to Hear God's Voice Through Journaling.

I (Sonja) often ask pastors and leaders at our workshops if they are regularly hearing the voice of the Lord. Almost without exception, all hands are affirmatively raised. I then asked them if they remember from one day to the next what He has told them. That gets some inquisitive looks. Next, I ask them if they would agree that, yes, the Lord is speaking to us, but because we are not disciplining ourselves to record what He is saying, we cannot remember what He told us yesterday. His thoughts become intermingled with our own, and there is no clear message.

Besides reading the Word, the most significant way I have learned to hear and know His voice is through recording what I hear Him saying to me. I have been journaling for almost forty years. Every morning I read my Bible and then I write down my worship (simply exclaiming God's worthiness), my thoughts, and often my prayers. Next, I discipline myself to listen for His voice, and I diligently record what I am hearing and the impressions I am receiving.

Lord, is this really You?

I remember early on when He told me something that was going to happen. I could hardly believe it. In fact, I put a big asterisk in the margin with a note that said, "Lord, is this really You? It seems so preposterous!" Now imagine my amazement when that very thing came to pass a short time later! I remember thinking, "It was You! It was You, Lord! Even though I doubted at the time, it was Your voice!"

Over the years, this has happened time and time again. This is my vital, one-on-one connection time with the magnificent, triune, Godhead—Heavenly Father, Lord Jesus Christ and the precious Holy Spirit.

His voice can be heard around the world.
On one of our mission trips to the refugee camps in Northern Thailand, John was wearing a money belt that contained all of our cash for the team's expenses. On our trip back to the no-star hotel this particular afternoon, it was extremely hot, and John removed the money belt. He put it over the back of the seat directly in front of him. When we returned to the hotel and I stretched out on the bed, His voice immediately called my attention to John's missing money belt! John had left it in the van. He raced down to the van, and by God's grace, it was where he had left it.

He was addicted to pornography.
One Sunday morning we arrived early at a church in California where we were to speak. The pastors introduced us to the worship team, and we discussed how we wanted to close the service. One young man on the team was like a son to the pastors, and John and I both immediately liked him. He was cute, personable, and very talented.

There was a tremendous response to our altar call—people accepted Jesus as their Savior, many were healed, and another group was baptized in the Holy Spirit. In the midst of all that wonderful ministry, my eyes fell on this young man I described earlier. On a human level, we both had instantly liked him, so I was shocked when I discerned that he was addicted to pornography and living a life of deception. I mulled this over for a few minutes and then I went to John and shared what I had heard. He had not picked up on that, so I thought I was not hearing correctly.

A few more minutes passed, and I knew I had to say something. He walked over to the woman pastor who was standing next to me and was talking much like a son with his mother. I took a deep breath, breathed a prayer, and then asked him if I could ask him a question. "Sure," he said, never imagining what I was about to expose. "Are you hooked on pornography?" I asked. He looked like someone had just hit him with a two-by-four. The color drained from his face, and he burst into tears. "Yes! It's true, I'm just sick about it."

He was sleeping with two young women!
I immediately went and got John, told him what I had heard was true, and asked him to come minister to the young man. John got the associate pastor to assist him and for accountability after we left. It was an ugly story. He had played around with porn, got addicted, and was currently sleeping with two young women in the congregation! It was unbelievable! What a web of deception he had allowed Satan to weave. John dealt with the unclean and lying spirits and set accountability in place. We then shared with the senior pastors who were also blindsided and brokenhearted by this revelation.

Sad to say when we checked back on the situation, we learned that the young man had left the church. Apparently, he was still struggling and he was not able to resist the temptations. We know that men often need a strong program and/or support group to break this kind of bondage. We are finding this deplorable conduct in more and more churches. How we need the revelation gifts of discerning of spirits and words of knowledge and wisdom so we can unmask the enemy and get people the help they need. Oh, that a holy reverence for God's house would fall upon us!

Supernatural strategies.
Recently, the Lord challenged both of us to enter a fresh and very serious phase of spiritual warfare and intercession. He indicated that if we would dedicate a significant amount of time each day praying in and with the Holy Spirit, He would

reveal glimpses of future events. Not that we would become prophets, but that we could direct our energies to stay as close to God's will as possible. The Lord also indicated that if we paid the price to stay in close, intimate relationship with Him that He would reveal the strategies of the enemy before they happen. We would be able to sidestep potential tragedy and stay on track with God. He said we would need to join the ranks of the truly committed intercessors for this to become a reality.

Paying the price.

True intercessors pay an enormous price to stay in touch with the Lord. It is neither cheap nor intermittent. It is a serious undertaking, often for life. It is a thankless business to spend hours of quality time crying out before God on behalf of others, some who are enemies of the cross. The alternative is not attractive. We would be on a course of a comfortable life of status quo, business as usual, and an occasional blessing because of the grace of God. We are reminded of the Scriptures that say obedience is better than sacrifice. So we have chosen intercession as the best course of action. We are spending more and more time entreating the Lord, exercising our spiritual languages, and listening for His response. The rewards are worth the price.

We have only just begun.

We are beginning to hear incredible things that will affect our future and the future of those affiliated with our ministry. Our journals are filling and our spirits are rejoicing for what the Lord continues to reveal. We are both approaching our mid-sixties as of the writing of this book. We become more energized as each year passes. We have learned one truth that keeps us going: hearing God's voice is the key to productive ministry. He knows the end from the beginning. He knows where each of us will be five or ten years from now. If we will surrender everything we are and ever will be into His hands, it is easy for Him to catapult us into exactly what He wants us to do. It is easy for Him to place us precisely where

He wants when we constantly remind Him that is only where we want to be.

Let's Practice

- James 1:22 says to *DO* what we have heard (read).
- Consider doing what is recommended in this chapter by referring to the "Let's Practice" in Appendix B, page 325-326.
- Do the Ministry Skill Assignment entitled, "Hearing from God."

Chapter Five

Ministry Skill Five

HEALING THE SICK BY REVELATION

Jesus healed the sick by doing what He saw the Father revealing through the Holy Spirit. We will learn how to do the same in this chapter. When we follow the Holy Spirit's leading and obey what He is revealing in regard to praying for the sick, healing will manifest and miracles will result.

Jesus only did what He saw the Father doing. It is reasonable for us to believe that Jesus operated perfectly by revelation knowledge emanating from the Father. It would then stand to reason that even though He was moved by compassion, the only people He healed were those the Father selected. Sometimes it was the whole crowd. Other times "many" were healed. Sometimes only one received healing. From this, we can begin to understand the reason everyone He prayed for was healed. It was because in the Father's infinite wisdom and foreknowledge He will have mercy and compassion on whomever and whenever He chooses. The only ones Jesus prayed for were those revealed by the Father through the Holy Spirit.

John 5:19-20
Then Jesus answered and said to them, "Most assuredly, I say to you, the Son can do nothing of Himself, but what He sees the Father do; for whatever He does, the Son also does in like manner. For the Father loves the Son, and shows Him all things that He Himself does; and He will show Him greater works than these, that you may marvel." NKJV

> ## DWJD
>
> Learning how to heal the sick by relying on the leading of the Holy Spirit is a difficult skill to master. Yet, it is the way Jesus conducted His healing ministry. He wants us to learn how to do it like He did. It is available to every Spirit-filled believer around the world. More and more believers are discovering the Holy Spirit's willingness to guide them to those who will be healed.

Whenever God starts revealing, He starts healing.

We have coined the above phrase to explain a more sure way to minister healing to others. Whenever we receive a word or picture from God regarding the situation about those around us, God is initiating ministry. If we act on these impressions, the people most often receive the things God is revealing. This is especially true regarding healing. We firmly believe this is the key to supernatural ministry. We should always pray for those requesting healing. However, without a leading from the Holy Spirit, we are not surprised when our prayers yield no visible result. We should always remain expectant because of God's willingness to heal. But, when we are operating with an authentic word or revelation from the Holy Spirit, the healing most always manifests.

Stop and listen.

Healing of chronic disease, serious pain, or life-threatening ailments needs to be carefully confirmed by a thorough medical examination. We want our testimony to be based on fact, not emotion. Whenever and however God wants to heal us is just fine. But, every minister should learn this truth: Whenever God starts revealing things about people around us, stop and listen. Then act on what is being revealed and minister accordingly. Everyone gets blessed and God gets all the glory.

Matthew 10:19-20

". . . do not worry about what to say or how to say it. At that time you will be given what to say, for it will not be you speaking, but *the Spirit of your Father speaking through you.*" NIV

DWJD

Jesus reveals how to conduct ministry. He says we should be so connected with the Holy Spirit that He will give us what to speak. We are to rely on the Spirit of the Father speaking through us to those in need. This is the way Jesus wants us to respond when we find ourselves in front of people asking God to heal them. Only do what you hear from the Father.

Obey the Word and the Spirit.

The Word of God authorizes us to heal the sick. The Holy Spirit tells us when and to whom healing will manifest. The Word tells us we can, the Holy Spirit tells us when.

God initiates the ministry.

When God starts revealing specific words, thoughts, pictures, or symbolic images that are relevant to the people to whom we are ministering, we should carefully observe what is being revealed. It only takes seconds to stop, watch, and listen. When we proceed with the revelation and act on what we are discerning, the healing is only seconds away. The only thing God requires is strict obedience to what is being revealed. When we obey and act on what we are being shown, the healing most often manifests. This is because we are not initiating the ministry, God is. Both the person and the minister know it was all God. Everyone is quick to give God all the praise for initiating and completing the healing. We see below in 1 Corinthians 12 that it is the Holy Spirit who manifests these supernatural gifts through God's people for the common good.

1 Corinthians 12:7-10

"But to each one is given the manifestation of the Spirit for the common good. For to one is given *the word of wisdom* through the Spirit, and to another *the word of knowledge* according to the same Spirit; to another faith by the same Spirit, and to another gifts of healing by the one Spirit, and to another the effecting of miracles, and to another prophecy, and to another *the distinguishing of spirits*, to another various kinds of tongues . . ." NASB

- Jesus wants His ministers to operate by revelation, just like He did.
- When the Holy Spirit comes upon believers, He imparts various gifts. Three of these gifts allow us to minister to others by "seeing or hearing" what needs to be done from God's perspective.
- These are called revelation gifts because the Holy Spirit is revealing hidden wisdom, knowledge, and spiritual activity to us.
- When we minister to others, acting on these revelations, we are ministering according to God's perfect will. We will examine the distinguishing of spirits in the next chapter.

The lady wearing the blue blouse.

Recently, while teaching a Ministry Training Centers (MTC) pastors' workshop in Abidjan, Ivory Coast, Africa, I (John) received a word of knowledge. The Holy Spirit wanted to accentuate what I was teaching about ministering by revelation by giving a real-life example to all of the pastors and leaders. The Holy Spirit gently interrupted my teaching by saying, "John, I want to heal someone." I stopped what I was doing, closed my eyes, and waited for further words from the Lord. I told my interpreter to tell the pastors, "The Lord wants to heal someone. Let's wait on Him." With my eyes still closed, in my mind I began to see a woman wearing a blue blouse. I had to assume she was in the gathering of pastors. Then I saw the woman rubbing her back as if in pain. That was it. No more words or pictures. I have learned that when this happens I do not try to analyze the word of knowledge. In faith, I quickly act on what I am receiving. I said, "There is a lady here with severe back pain and God wants to heal you. You are wearing a blue blouse. When you come forward, God will instantly heal you!"

She came up smiling.

I have also learned to be very bold when a revelation is manifesting because the Lord is initiating the miracle, not me. The wait between when you call out what you think the Lord is saying and when the people finally respond seems like an eternity. In this case, she only took thirty seconds to get up and come forward. Greatly relieved and once again full of faith, I laid one hand on her shoulder and said, "I command the back pain to go! In the name of Jesus Christ, amen!" Then I told the interpreter, "Tell her to bend all the way over, the pain is gone!" Not knowing French, I encouraged her by smiling and quickly bending over myself a few times to give her the idea. She bent over and came up smiling. She said the pain was all gone. She demonstrated it by swaying back and forth and up and down. She came to us during the break and thanked us over and over again. She had been in unbearable pain for a long time. We took a picture of her for our newsletter and promised her a copy.

Defining the Word of Wisdom

The word of wisdom is a divine revelation from God revealing to man His plan and best course of action for a given situation. This wisdom is communicated spontaneously from God to man, through the Spirit, revealing how to proceed in His will. It provides wholeness, restoration, peace and/or strength to overcome in times of perplexity, trial, persecution or danger.

It will reveal the future.

The word of wisdom and the word of knowledge are very similar. The word of wisdom will reveal what God's will is concerning what should or will happen. It will reveal what the future should be, either in a few minutes, days, or months. We are to simply obey what we are either seeing or hearing from the Holy Spirit. God's infinite wisdom is revealed in the form of what He desires to be accomplished. When we hear or see correctly about what is yet to come, we simply act out what we are hearing or seeing. That is what Jesus did. We are working with the Spirit of truth (Holy Spirit) who will tell us what is yet to come.

John 16:13-14

"But when he, the Spirit of truth, comes, he will guide you into all truth. He will not speak on his own; he will speak only what he hears, and *he will tell you what is yet to come.* He will bring glory to me by taking from what is mine and making it known to you." NIV

DWJD

- Just prior to or during prayer for others, the Holy Spirit will begin to reveal what you should do or say in the form of pictures or words in your mind.
- He is revealing what is "yet to come." When we obey and proceed according to what is being "made known to us" through the Holy Spirit, we will experience a miracle.
- It takes a lot of trial and error and hours of practice to master cooperating with the Holy Spirit in this way.

What is heard or seen.

We will see pictures in our mind of what should happen. We will hear instructions of what to do about the people standing in front of us. We are given God's will in advance. We are being given what God desires to happen. We may not understand it at the moment. Our mission is to obey in faith and fully trust that God knows what He's doing. The word of wisdom very often will manifest with the word of knowledge. The two go together. God will reveal the root problem and then give us the solution, all in one word. This is exciting when it happens. The minister seems to be suspended for a moment in total dependence on God's will as it is being revealed. God is calling all the signals. We simply act out His signals and bring His will into fulfillment in the natural realm.

The lady with the white headband.

While teaching an MTC teacher intensive in Malawi, Central Africa, I (John) received a word of wisdom. During the Sunday pre-service prayer, the Holy Spirit began to reveal that I was to preach on healing. I had prepared a good sermon, but the Lord had a better one in store. While praying, in my mind I saw a lady with her hair piled on top of her head and held together with a white headband. I kept seeing her over and over. I said, "Lord, what am I seeing?" All I heard was, "I'm going to heal her." The Lord seldom gives me any more details than I need to know. I went into the service looking all over for the lady with the white headband. She was not there. I began preaching on divine healing and was about half way through when I began to think, "Well, Lord, I guess I missed You on this one." Then the door opened and another group of people came in. There she was! I preached ten more minutes and then I heard, "John, call her forward."

Through the interpreter I said, "There is a lady here with a white headband, and God wants to heal you." People began looking all around for the lady. I saw her and another woman begin to argue with one another. The lady with the white headband kept shaking her head no. I thought, "Oh no, Lord, is she really the one?" Then the Holy Spirit gave me the rest of the word of wisdom. I have learned to proceed with what is given to me even though it may only be a part of the unfolding picture. He said, "Yes, that's the one. She has pain in her ovaries and is afraid. I will heal her."

New ovaries.

Wow! Now I knew what to do. With boldness I looked at her, pointed to her and repeated what I had just heard from the Lord. She looked amazed, hesitated for a moment, then got up and came forward. I had Sonja lay hands on her lower abdomen as I prayed. Because the Lord always heals what He reveals, I boldly prayed, "In the name of Jesus Christ, I command brand new ovaries in this woman. Satan, you cannot have her. I command you to loose her, now! Pain leave, now! In the name of Jesus Christ, amen!" I told the interpreter to tell her she was healed and to go get a doctor's report to confirm it. She said the pain was no longer there and she would go get the doctor's diagnosis. She returned at the end of the week and announced to everyone that the doctor said she no longer had the ovary problem and she was given a clean bill of health.

Jesus is our perfect example.

Jesus perfectly operated in words of wisdom as an example for us. He did these things as a man, filled with the mighty power of the Holy Spirit. He was demonstrating how to operate in the supernatural by relying totally on the Holy Spirit. He said we would do the same things He did. In all four Gospels there are beautiful examples of Jesus operating by revelation from the Father. Below are two examples of "seeing" into the future by words of wisdom.

John 11:1-4

Now a man named Lazarus was sick. He was from Bethany, the village of Mary and her sister Martha. This Mary, whose brother Lazarus now lay sick, was the same one who poured perfume on the Lord and wiped his feet with her hair. So the sisters sent word to Jesus, "Lord, the one you love is sick." When he heard this, *Jesus said, "This sickness will not end in death. No, it is for God's glory so that God's Son may be glorified through it."* NIV

197

Matthew 26:33-34
Peter replied, "Even if all fall away on account of you, I never will." "I tell you the truth," Jesus answered, *"this very night, before the rooster crows, you will disown me three times."* NIV

- In both of these examples Jesus is showing us how to cooperate with what the Father is revealing through the Holy Spirit.
- He repeated what He was hearing and seeing from the Father.
- We should do the same when the Holy Spirit begins revealing words of wisdom and knowledge.
- We repeat or act out what we are hearing and seeing the Father do through the Holy Spirit.

The lady from South Whidbey Island.
When I (John) first began operating by revelation it was a scary experience. Stepping out and doing something like this takes a lot of courage. I remember a particular dinner meeting where I was the speaker for the FGBMFI in 1977. The Holy Spirit urged me to call out a woman for healing while I was speaking. This was new to me. I thought I heard the Holy Spirit say, "She needs healing. Speak to her." I kept on telling my story, not wanting to make a fool of myself. But, every time I looked her way the same inner urging would prompt me to speak to her. I had seen this done by mature speakers and evangelists at these kinds of meetings and on television. Now it seemed God was testing me to see if I would obey.

I may be wrong, but . . .
In faith, I stepped way out of my comfort zone and said to her, "I may be wrong, but sister I believe you need to be healed. Right?" To me, the next five seconds of silence seemed like an eternity as everyone awaited her response. With a surprised look, she said, "Yes, I do." With incredible

relief, my faith re-engaged. I stepped off the platform, laid hands on her, and said, "Be healed in the name of Jesus Christ!" Whatever was wrong, it only took a moment of stretching and bending for her to exclaim, "It's gone! The pain's all gone!"

God knows everything about everybody.

God changed the course of that meeting. People spontaneously came forward to be prayed for. Other healings must have taken place. I do not remember. But, I will never forget the lady from South Whidbey Island. The event showed me something new. The Holy Spirit always knows everything about everybody. He chose this meeting to activate a word of wisdom and knowledge through a vessel that was almost too scared to do anything about it. I learned a big lesson. Whenever He starts revealing who needs healing they get healed! When we relinquish our agenda for His and obey His voice, miracles begin to happen.

Philip received a word of wisdom.

The Holy Spirit spoke directly to Philip and told him God's plan in advance. He was to take a hike on the road to Gaza. When he got to a certain point, the Holy Spirit delivered a second word of wisdom to go to the eunuch's chariot. His obedience was rewarded supernaturally.

Acts 8:26-29

Now an angel of the Lord said to Philip, *"Go south to the road—the desert road—that goes down from Jerusalem to Gaza."* So he started out, and on his way he met an Ethiopian eunuch, an important official in charge of all the treasury of Candace, queen of the Ethiopians. This man had gone to Jerusalem to worship, and on his way home was sitting in his chariot reading the book of Isaiah the prophet. *The Spirit told Philip, "Go to that chariot and stay near it."* NIV

DWJD

- We can expect the Holy Spirit to speak to us exactly like He did to Philip.
- The voice of the Holy Spirit will be strong and directive when you are ministering to others. The key is to *expect* Him to speak.
- We do this by constantly asking for direction and revelation by praying in tongues and asking for direction before and during ministry to others.
- Pray, "Lord, what do You want to do next? Lord, what do You have for this person? Lord, how do I pray for this person?"
- Just do what Jesus did.

Paul received a word of wisdom.

In times of intense ministry or even in distress, the word of wisdom is a welcomed revelation from the Spirit of God. Paul received advance information that no one was going to die because of the storm raging against the ship he was on.

Acts 27:21-25

After the men had gone a long time without food, Paul stood up before them and said: "Men, you should have taken my advice not to sail from Crete; then you would have spared yourselves this damage and loss. But now I urge you to keep up your courage, because not one of you will be lost; only the ship will be destroyed. Last night *an angel* of the God whose I am and whom I serve stood beside me and said, *'Do not be afraid, Paul. You must stand trial before Caesar; and God has graciously given you the lives of all who sail with you.'* So keep up your courage, men, for I have faith in God that it will happen just as he told me." NIV

DWJD

- We may not get a visit from an angel, but the Holy Spirit is always with us to give insight and information concerning the outcome of our current situation.
- He knows the end from the beginning and will reveal what we need to know to minister healing and comfort to those God places before us.

The revelations do not have to be dramatic.

Our receiving a word of wisdom may not be as dramatic as with Jesus, Philip, or Paul. But, we can receive foreknowledge that will show us the way into God's perfect will. We simply expect the manifestation to come in the timing and at the discretion of the Holy Spirit. This gift is very helpful when we are ministering to people and we do not have a clue as to what to do. By keeping our mind focused on what heaven wants, there will be times when heaven will respond.

Best Girlfriend Receives Best Gift!

My (Sonja) best girlfriend is Janie Gibson. She has been my best girlfriend since junior high school in 1952. (That is fifty years!) Although we have not lived in the same town since college days, we have remained the dearest of friends. Can you imagine exchanging fifty birthday and Christmas gifts! I have lovely things all over our home that daily remind me of her. We recently agreed we would only give "consumables" (stationery, etc.) from now on.

It was like I knew it was the right time.

Back in 1970, Janie and her husband were visiting in our hometown, and I was concerned that they did not yet personally know the Lord. They both had attended church while growing up but never understood the need for a personal Savior. I sensed they were open as I shared about the wonderful experience I recently had with the Holy Spirit baptism. It was like I knew it was the right time.

Then came the Holy Spirit baptism.
I invited them to our home Bible study. Janie wanted to come, but Glynn was hesitant. After a little gentle persuasion, he finally agreed to accompany Janie. I cannot remember exactly what we talked about or studied, but at the close of the meeting, we asked them if they would like to invite Jesus into their hearts and receive Him as their personal Savior. They wholeheartedly responded, and it was a joyous time for all of us. I later had the privilege of leading them and another couple into the Holy Spirit baptism. It was wonderful to share this additional, common ground in our friendship.

We have since walked through some extremely difficult life experiences together. One involved their infant grandson, Brittain, who developed Kawasaki disease and was in critical condition at Children's Hospital in Seattle for four months. I remember going into his room with his parents, Brian and Kim Gibson, and speaking healing over his swollen, lifeless little body. I kept declaring, "Brittain, one day I will watch you play basketball."

A spirit of death.
In the middle of the night, I received a call from Brittain's daddy, Brian, my godson. The doctors had said Brittain would not live through the night and Brian was literally sensing the spirit of death in the room. Frantically, he said, "Sonja, what do I do? I'm not willing to let him go!" I silently prayed and then instructed him to put everyone out of the room except Janie, his grandmother. I then explained his spiritual authority as head of his household and instructed him to exercise that authority by submitting himself to God in prayer. He was then to boldly address the spirit of death in the name of Jesus Christ and command it to depart. He hung up the telephone and did exactly what I had told him. Even though Brian had limited understanding about this level of spiritual warfare, he acted in total and bold faith, and the spirit of death departed! Little Brittain had a worldwide prayer covering that resulted in his total recovery. As of this writing he is seven years old, and he plays basketball!

Defining the Word of Knowledge

The word of knowledge is a divine revelation originating with God about situations either past or present of which God makes us aware. This knowledge is communicated spontaneously from God to man, through the Holy Spirit, to bring clarification, wholeness, and restoration to the lives of those present.

Words come spontaneously.

The word of knowledge comes in the form of words directly from God and is given to us by the Holy Spirit. These words spontaneously manifest in the spirit of our mind. Sometimes the words are weak. Other times the words are strong, depending on the urgency and nature of the situation. The word of knowledge is communicated directly from the Holy Spirit. Because it is spontaneous and will relate to a current situation of ministry, we can assume it is from God. We act on what the words reveal.

God reveals the past and the present.

God sees all and knows all. A word of knowledge reveals the missing facts that are needed to complete the information so we can conclude a situation of ministry. We can use an analogy by picturing a very large symphony. God is the conductor. We are the gifted players with our many instruments. Each of us has a part to play, but we await His cues and timing to release our gifts and talents. When the time is right, He gives us a sign in the form of words that fits perfectly into the melody of ministry. The following Scripture illustrates how Peter operated by words of knowledge given by the Holy Spirit.

Acts 8:18-24

Now when Simon saw that the Spirit was bestowed through the laying on of the apostles' hands, he offered them money, saying, "Give this authority to me as well, so that everyone on whom I lay my hands may receive the Holy Spirit." But Peter said to him, "May your silver perish with you, because you thought you could obtain the gift of God with money! You have no part or portion in this matter, for your heart is not right before God. Therefore repent of this wickedness of yours, and pray the Lord that, if possible, the intention of your heart may be forgiven you. *For I see that you are in the gall of bitterness and in the bondage of iniquity.*" But Simon answered and said, "Pray to the Lord for me yourselves, so that nothing of what you have said may come upon me." NASB

DWJD

- Like Peter, there will be times when we will "see" images or hear the Holy Spirit say, "That person is in the gall of bitterness and in the bondage of iniquity. Have them repent of their wickedness."
- We immediately respond to the revelation by telling them what the Lord just revealed and have them do what the Lord said to do.

Apply it to the situation.
The information pertains to certain facts that must be known so we can clearly understand what needs to be done. For instance, we may be praying for someone to be healed and nothing seems to be happening. Suddenly we hear the words, "He has not forgiven his brother." We immediately and boldly apply this information. We do it with wisdom and sensitivity. We could say, "I am sensing that you have not forgiven your brother. Am I correct?" Their response will confirm whether we heard correctly or not. Our prayer ministry will take a definite turn for the better from that point forward.

The Yelm experience.
My (John) most phenomenal meeting for operating by revelation was in Yelm, Washington in the mid-1980s at a dinner meeting of the FGBMFI. While eating fried chicken, the Lord's voice strongly manifested in my mind. He said, "Go outside, behind the building. I want to tell you what will

happen tonight." The chicken was good, but hearing from God was much better. I got up from dinner and went outside. It was pitch black, even more so behind the building. I felt my way around back and stood staring at some distant lights. I prayed in tongues for awhile and then said, "What did You want to tell me, Lord?" As I stared into the night, I heard the Lord say, "I want to do many things tonight. If you will obey Me without hesitation, I will cause My glory to be revealed. You must rely totally on Me and obey My voice in everything that happens." I said, "Yes, I will!"

God's agenda can be specific.
I went back in and sat down. As I began to eat a little more chicken, I looked around the room at each person. When I fixed my gaze on certain ones, the voice of the Lord would manifest words in my mind for that person. Things like, "That one needs Me. She will give her life to Me tonight. I'm going to heal that man's back when you lay hands on him. That couple is having serious marriage problems. They will be set free through a prophetic word I will give that man over there. That lady has an eating disorder and will be set free through prophetic prayer. That couple over there does not know Me. You will call them out, and I will save them."

God does it all.
It was as if I had earphones on and was hearing the Lord speaking loud and clear. I had said "yes" to the Lord, but this was more than I expected. The gift of faith dropped on me just as the president of the chapter introduced Sonja and me. I walked to the podium. I started giving my testimony. Right in the middle of speaking, the Lord interrupted me and said, "Start calling out those I designated. Now!" With total confidence I began, one-by-one to point to those He previously had indicated. I announced to them what the Lord had earlier said about them. Without exception, everyone received what the Holy Spirit said they would. Couples received salvation, many people were healed, the lady was completely set free of the eating disorder, and many people

were baptized in the Holy Spirit. God initiated everything and used me in the process.

Notice the fruit of the word.

We can always assess if our prayer ministry is productive by the fruit that results. We are surprised how many times it was the Holy Spirit delivering a word of knowledge. Our humanness will resist proceeding with information that seems to come out of nowhere. As we become more experienced, we can look back and see that God was leading us more than we thought. Sometimes we may have to wait weeks or months for reports to filter back to us on the times we acted on an unsure word of knowledge. This is more reason for us to simply obey what we think we are hearing and believe God to come to our rescue. It is better for us to step out and believe God for the impossible than to play it safe so we can avoid being embarrassed.

Jesus saw their faith.

The following account of healing shows how Jesus "saw" men's faith by revelation and then healed the man. Jesus also "perceived in His spirit" what the scribes were thinking.

Mark 2:2-12

Immediately many gathered together, so that there was no longer room to receive them, not even near the door. And He preached the word to them. Then they came to Him, bringing a paralytic who was carried by four men. And when they could not come near Him because of the crowd, they uncovered the roof where He was. So when they had broken through, they let down the bed on which the paralytic was lying. *When Jesus saw their faith*, He said to the paralytic, "Son, your sins are forgiven you." But some of the scribes were sitting there and reasoning in their hearts, "Why does this Man speak blasphemies like this? Who can forgive sins but God alone?" But immediately, when *Jesus perceived in His spirit that they reasoned thus within themselves, He said to them, "Why do you reason about these things in your hearts?* Which is easier, to say to the paralytic, 'Your sins are forgiven you,' or to say, 'Arise, take up your bed and walk'?

But that you may know that the Son of Man has power on earth to forgive sins"—He said to the paralytic, "I say to you, arise, take up your bed, and go your way to your house." Immediately he arose, took up the bed, and went out in the presence of them all, so that all were amazed and glorified God, saying, "We never saw anything like this!" NKJV

DWJD

- Jesus gives us an example of how to rely on the Holy Spirit. Jesus responded to the revelation of faith in the paralytic and his friends. We can only "see" faith in someone through the gift of the word of knowledge.
- The Holy Spirit must tell us when a person is ready to be healed. Jesus "saw" their faith and proceeded to heal the paralytic by speaking words of authority, "Rise, take up your bed, and go home!" The healing was instant. We should do the same.
- The Holy Spirit also revealed the negative perceptions in the hearts of the religious leaders. Jesus showed us how to rely on the Holy Spirit to reveal what was going on and how to deal with it.
- Forgiveness and healing were considered impossible to the listening Pharisees.
- The Pharisees' mindset was that *BOTH* were impossible. The Holy Spirit led Jesus to perform *BOTH* to make His point: God can both forgive sin and heal the sick. We should allow Him to do the same through us.

Do it like Jesus did.

When you preach and teach like Jesus did in the above passage, the power of God will manifest. When it does, power is available for healing and deliverance. Even when the faithless, critical people are there, the power of God is present to effect miracles. Jesus ignored them. So should we. Act within the anointing, and flow with what the Holy Spirit is indicating. When you see their faith, act within what they are expecting. Jesus came into agreement with what the men were expecting to happen—healing! So, minister to those demonstrating faith. Bypass those who are not operating in faith. God desires to accomplish His works through us to cause astonishment and awe in people to open their eyes to receive Christ as Lord and Healer. The Holy Spirit points directly to Jesus Christ. We must be careful to glorify God at the signs and wonders He causes to happen.

Doing the Supernatural Stuff

The late John Wimber coined the phrase, "Doing the Stuff," in 1985 in his book, *Power Evangelism.* As a new Christian he asked a pastor after a service, "When do you do the stuff?" He was referring to healing and miracles that he had just found in the Bible. He never got a satisfactory answer.

Sonja and I recently taught a one-day seminar on "Doing the Supernatural Stuff" at a Foursquare Western District Pastors' Conference in central California. One of the pastors wanted to attend but could not, so he invited us to Carson City, Nevada to re-teach the same seminar at his home church. The seminar was composed of four areas that seem to be overlooked in many churches: 1) How to lead other believers into the Holy Spirit baptism; 2) How to heal the sick; 3) How to minister by revelation knowledge; and 4) How to set people free from demon bondage. The morning sessions resulted in fifteen leaders receiving the Holy Spirit baptism and many people being healed of all kinds of problems. The afternoon session became even more exciting as the Holy Spirit began to cause words of knowledge and wisdom to flow freely among the people.

We are not special.

During the teaching on how to release revelation gifts, the Lord began giving both Sonja and me words of knowledge and wisdom regarding specific healings the Lord wanted to do. Each time it would happen, Sonja and I would say, "Hey, we are not special. All of you leaders can do this. It just takes a lot of nerve to be willing to be wrong a few times as you learn how to move with the Holy Spirit." We would then put them into groups of ten leaders so they could practice releasing words of knowledge and wisdom for each other.

During the main afternoon session, God began to do some awesome things. John announced that there was a lady needing a healing on her lower shin. The Holy Spirit was specific as to which leg and where the sore was located. A lady close to the front boldly stood up and said, "That's me! I've had a terrible staff infection on this shin." She then pointed to her right shin and began to pull up her pant leg. She said, "Oh, my Lord, it's gone! The black sore is all gone!" The big black-looking sore had been there for a long time, but God had just taken it away. This was a notable miracle for all to see. We took a picture of her for our newsletter, showing us where the skin was now normal and scar free.

We try to get the audience involved whenever the Holy Spirit starts revealing things. One way we do this is to call out what the Holy Spirit is indicating He wants done. If it is some kind of healing, we have the people with that particular problem come forward and stand up front. Then we ask for those who have never prayed for the sick to come and face the ones needing healing. Because the Lord always heals what He reveals, it always amazes both the ones praying and the ones receiving when God heals everyone. This is one of the best ways to demonstrate that God is in charge and not the one ministering.

In pain for thirty years.

One such case involved an older gentleman dressed in western clothes. The Lord revealed that there were people with pain, starting in their backs and going down their legs. About five people, including the older gentleman, responded. I (John) then called forward five believers who had never experienced divine healing through their hands. Sonja matched them up, leading them in the prayer of faith, and we watched as God healed them. The pain left instantly in all but the gentleman in western attire. Having everyone else sit down, I asked how long the pain had been in his back and legs. He said, "Thirty years!" I asked how many times had he been prayed for. He said, "I've lost count. Probably a hundred times." His way of responding indicated he did not have much faith.

Suddenly the Holy Spirit said to me, "Infirmity, it is a spirit of infirmity." Without hesitation I said, "The Lord has just revealed that we are dealing with a spirit of infirmity. I am going to loose you and you will be healed." We laid hands on his back, and I commanded the spirit of infirmity to leave in Jesus' name. I said, "Tell me when all the pain is gone." He said, "It's going!" I said, "Amen. And it will continue until it's all gone." Over the next half-hour he kept testing his back and legs and announcing the percentage of pain that was leaving. He finally said, "It's 99 percent gone. I think what's left is just stiffness from never being able to bend over." With that, we all gave the Lord a long and loud praise of thanksgiving for what He accomplished in Carson City.

What is revealed is healed.

Christians in the West like to focus on all the sick and hurting people that never seem to receive their healing. The revelation gifts, especially the word of knowledge, change all this. When the revelation gifts are in operation, the healing statistics go from 50/50 to 100 percent. Whenever a true word of knowledge is involved in ministry to the sick, the person always receives their healing. It happens immediately or within a few hours or days. It can be said that whenever God begins to reveal, He heals. We can trust the Holy Spirit to do what He says. When He comes upon us and reveals a word of knowledge concerning a person's bodily condition, healing is imminent. God is directly involved. We simply obey and get out of the way. Healing will manifest.

Jesus operated perfectly.

Jesus is the author and finisher of our faith. He authored the word of knowledge and showed us the perfect way to operate in it. Jesus said we could do what He did. How do we do it? We do only what we see the Father doing. This will come in the form of words or images in the word of wisdom and knowledge just like Jesus received them.

John 5:19-20

Jesus gave them this answer: "I tell you the truth, the Son can do nothing by himself; *he can do only what he sees his Father doing*, because whatever the Father does the Son also does. For the Father loves the Son and shows him all he does. Yes, to your amazement he will show him even greater things than these." NIV

DWJD

We should come to the place where we pray, "Lord, I want to do only what I see the Father doing by the Holy Spirit. Help me to do that." Then we can pray, "Lord, show me even greater things than these. I want to do what Jesus did!"

The Lord knows the source of the sickness.

When we are praying for the sick we often are not sure what is causing the sickness or pain. Sometimes the person does not know either. It could be a virus, a chemical imbalance, heredity, or even a spirit. The Lord always knows. So, we should wait to hear from Him. When we do, the healing will always manifest. Below is the same story from the combined

211

perspective of both Matthew and Mark. Notice that Jesus ignored the people's request to have Him lay His hands on the deaf-mute. Instead, He followed the instructions from the Father and put His fingers in his ears, spat, and touched the person's tongue.

Mark 7:31-37 Matthew 15:29-31

Mark 7:31-37: Again, departing from the region of Tyre and Sidon, He came through the midst of the region of Decapolis to the Sea of Galilee. (Matthew 15:29-30: . . . and went up on the mountain and sat down there. Then great multitudes came to Him, having with them the lame, blind, mute, maimed, and many others; and they laid them down at Jesus' feet, and He healed them.) Then they brought to Him one who was deaf and had an impediment in his speech, and they begged Him to put His hand on him.

And He took him aside from the multitude, and put His fingers in his ears, and He spat and touched his tongue. Then, looking up to heaven, He sighed, and said to him, "Ephphatha," that is, "Be opened." Immediately his ears were opened, and the impediment of his tongue was loosed, and he spoke plainly. (Matthew 15:31: So the multitude marveled when they saw the mute speaking, the maimed made whole, the lame walking, and the blind seeing; and they glorified the God of Israel.)

Then He commanded them that they should tell no one; but the more He commanded them, the more widely they proclaimed it. And they were astonished beyond measure, saying, "He has done all things well. He makes both the deaf to hear and the mute to speak." NKJV

- We need to proceed as the Holy Spirit is leading us. When the Holy Spirit is leading us, we only do what He indicates.

- This may mean we proceed in an unusual way. Here, Jesus followed what the Father was indicating by putting His fingers in the person's ears, spitting and touching his tongue. At the same time, He said to him, "BE OPENED!" We should do the same, when and *if* the Holy Spirit is truly leading us.

- Note: Jesus returned to Decapolis, a region where previously people did not want Him. Now, the people were no longer afraid—they wanted His ministry of healing. This was because the demoniac had been delivered of spirits and had spread the Gospel that Jesus was the Christ (see Mark 5:18-20).

Ministry Examples

The Chiang Mai healing crusade.

I (John) was the main speaker at a two-night healing crusade in Chiang Mai, Thailand in early 2002. Our associate ministers Greg and Karen Fry also shared and ministered at this crusade. The first evening, God healed between twenty-five and thirty people of pain, asthma, infections, eyesight, and high fevers. There were so many miracles happening that we quickly prayed for everyone who came forward. There were three separate instances where the Holy Spirit spoke to me that spirits were causing people to experience severe headaches or chronic pain in their bodies. As soon as I would look these people in the eyes, the Holy Spirit would firmly say, "Spirit of infirmity is causing it." When I commanded the spirits to leave, the people would be instantly healed of their sickness.

Deaf men instantly healed.

The second evening, I waited on the Holy Spirit to identify and initiate what kind of healing was to be done. Twenty-five people were healed in about an hour as the Holy Spirit called out various pains and illnesses. Again, spirits caused some of the people's problems. The Holy Spirit graciously healed these people after the spirit was identified and commanded to loose them. The highlight of the evening was two men who were 85 to 90 percent deaf in both ears. They responded to the Holy Spirit's invitation to come and be healed of deafness. The first man came up, took out his hearing aids, and said he was ready to be healed. Greg and I began to pray for him with no success. We stopped and wondered what we needed to do. The Holy Spirit quietly said to me, "It's a spirit of deafness." I smiled at the man, and looking intently into his eyes, I said, "You foul spirit of deafness, be gone!" Total hearing was instantly restored to the man.

Spit on your fingers.
The other deaf man was closely watching the first deaf man receive his hearing. As soon as he saw the miracle, he quickly maneuvered his way to be next in line. His faith was high and he was ready. I had the interpreter yell into his ear, "How long have you been deaf?" He said, "Twenty years." I looked at Greg and Karen, and we agreed that this was easy for God.

The Holy Spirit then firmly spoke to me and said, "Spit on your fingers, put them into the man's ears and say, 'Be opened!'" Without hesitation I obeyed. I spit on both of my index fingers, put my fingers in the man's ears, and loudly said, "Be opened, in the name of Jesus!" It took the man about a minute to realize he was hearing perfectly without his hearing aids. He, too, was instantly healed by the power of God. I realized this is what Jesus did in Matthew 15:29-31 and Mark 7:31-37. Greg, Karen, and I went back to our hotel praising God for the incredible move of the Holy Spirit those two nights. We later discovered that many of those people who were healed now belong to the Foursquare Church and have made Jesus Christ their Savior. We had learned how to hear from the Father and obey what He wanted us to do so He could bless many of His people.

The Holy Spirit speaks the words He hears.
The word of knowledge is the Father speaking to us through the Holy Spirit. We are hearing the words the Holy Spirit is hearing from the Father. We are hearing words and seeing things that the Father wants us to hear and see.

> **John 16:13-14**
> "But when he, the Spirit of truth, comes, he will guide you into all truth. He will not speak on his own; *he will speak only what he hears*, and he will tell you what is yet to come. He will bring glory to me by taking from what is mine and *making it known to you*." NIV

DWJD

- Jesus is telling us how He interacted with the Father through the Holy Spirit. He is revealing to us how to do what He did.
- He waited to hear words from the Father that were relayed to Him by the Holy Spirit.
- He was hearing words that revealed what was yet to transpire.
- He was hearing the Father's perfect will in advance!
- We can expect the same when we pay the price to serve God with all of our heart, mind, and soul. We can do what Jesus did!

Miracles in south Seattle.
A few years ago, Sonja and I were invited to teach on how to heal the sick at a large Foursquare church south of Seattle, Washington. We always pray, study, and seek the Lord before attempting to teach on the miraculous. We placed our agenda before the Lord and reminded Him and ourselves that He can do anything He wants in every meeting. We felt confident and ready as we drove up, parked, and proceeded to the pre-service prayer gathering with the leaders in charge. During the prayer time I noticed the chairperson of the event was really sick. She almost did not come because

of unusual pain in her body and a severe headache. The others turned to her and said, "Let's pray over her now so she can enjoy the meeting." We all agreed and began to pray. As I approached her, the Holy Spirit said, "Not now, John. I will heal her later." Wondering what He meant, I backed off and prayed in the Spirit. No one seemed to notice that I was the only one not laying my hands on her.

The Holy Spirit took charge.

The meeting started with great worship. I noticed there was standing room only with a lot of the youth sitting on the floor of the platform near where we were teaching. As usual, Sonja and I continued to sing and pray in tongues up until time to teach. There was a strong anointing as we taught. Then the Holy Spirit began to take charge. I heard Him say, "Call the chairperson to the stage." I obeyed. Then He said, "Ask who would like to be used in healing and invite the first one to raise their hand to come and pray for her." I obeyed. A young lady down front and to the right quickly raised her hand. Others followed but were too late. I said, "You were the first. Come up here." She came up and I had her lay her hands on the chairperson and repeat a prayer after me. She did exactly what I told her, word for word. Then I said to the lady who prayed, "Ask her what is happening."

The new recruit said, "What's happening?" The chairperson said, "Oh my! Oh my! It's gone! The pain's gone and my headache is gone, too. I'm healed! God just healed me!" The crowd broke into spontaneous praise and applause. Faith rocketed throughout the auditorium. I asked the recruit, "Who did that?" Over the microphone she quickly said, "Jesus!" We found out later she had been a Mormon who had just got saved the Sunday before. Many of the church folks knew that and were praising God and rejoicing for using a new Christian like her to heal the sick. It gave great hope to everyone that God is not a respecter of persons when it comes to praying and believing for miracles.

Forbid the pain to remain.

I heard the Holy Spirit say, "Have them pray for each other and I will heal them." We had planned to individually pray for those needing healing, but the Holy Spirit changed the agenda. I instructed anyone who had noticeable pain in his or her body to stand. About seventy-five people stood. I said, "Those around them stand and lay hands on those with pain and say this after me: 'In the name of Jesus, pain I command you to leave this body. I forbid this pain to remain. I call it done. In the name of Jesus Christ, amen!'" I then asked for everyone to check their body and to sit down if the pain was gone. Over three-quarters of them sat down. The crowd again erupted in applause. I asked the people still standing to allow those around them to again pray like before. We did this two more times. After this, three remained standing. I instructed those three to allow the others to minister to them until they were healed. They, too, went home feeling better than when they came.

Examples of Words of Knowledge

Everybody gets to participate.

These kinds of meetings are faith builders to many Christians who never get a chance to practice what the teachers are teaching. The Holy Spirit has led Sonja and me to get as many in the audience as possible to personally experience the healing power of God. By encouraging them to minister and pray for those needing healing in an atmosphere where the Holy Spirit is directing the meeting, multiple miracles are sure to manifest. Instead of the evangelist being the focus of power, the people look more to Jesus Christ as the source of power and miracles. When Sonja and I step aside and allow the Holy Spirit to freely work through us, it is obvious to everyone that Jesus wants to use anybody and everybody to get the job done. This way everyone gets blessed and God gets all the glory. That is the way it should be.

Peter relayed a word of knowledge.

Peter received a word of knowledge from the Holy Spirit and he spoke to Ananias and Sapphira. It was confirmed immediately as coming from God when both died in front of him.

Acts 5:1-4

Now a man named Ananias, together with his wife Sapphira, also sold a piece of property. With his wife's full knowledge he kept back part of the money for himself, but brought the rest and put it at the apostles' feet. Then Peter said, "Ananias, how is it that Satan has so filled your heart that you have lied to the Holy Spirit and have kept for yourself some of the money you received for the land? Didn't it belong to you before it was sold? And after it was sold, wasn't the money at your disposal? What made you think of doing such a thing? You have not lied to men but to God." NIV

Matthew 12:32

"Whoever speaks a word against the Son of Man, it shall be forgiven him; but whoever speaks against the Holy Spirit, it shall not be forgiven him, either in this age or in the age to come." NASB

DWJD

- Jesus mentored Peter. Peter heard Jesus say whoever speaks against the Holy Spirit will not be forgiven.
- Peter also had learned from Jesus to act on whatever the Holy Spirit revealed.
- In this case, the judgment of God was pronounced against a man and his wife who lied about giving everything to the work of the Lord when they in fact held back money for themselves.
- The presence of the Holy Spirit was so strong that death came to both of them.
- We must be careful at all times so we do not lie to the Holy Spirit.

Ananias relayed a word of knowledge.
Paul was rescued from blindness by a Damascus disciple named Ananias. The Holy Spirit told Ananias facts he did not know about Paul. Then the Spirit told him what to do with the word of knowledge—to speak the word to Paul.

Acts 9:10-12

In Damascus there was a disciple named Ananias. The Lord called to him in a vision, "Ananias!" "Yes, Lord," he answered. The Lord told him, *"Go to the house of Judas on Straight Street and ask for a man from Tarsus named Saul, for he is praying. In a vision he has seen a man named Ananias come and place his hands on him to restore his sight."* NIV

DWJD

Whenever we hear the Holy Spirit call us by name and give strong instructions for us to do something, we must obey.

Paul healed the sick by a word of knowledge.
Paul received a revelation about a crippled man having enough faith to stand up and be healed. Paul obeyed what he was hearing from the Holy Spirit, and a miracle healing manifested.

Acts 14:8-10

In Lystra there sat a man crippled in his feet, who was lame from birth and had never walked. He listened to Paul as he was speaking. Paul looked directly at him, *saw that he had faith to be healed* and called out, "Stand up on your feet!" At that, the man jumped up and began to walk. NIV

DWJD

- Here is an excellent example of a word of knowledge manifesting to Paul that resulted in a man lame from birth being totally healed.

- The only way we can "see" a person having the faith to be healed is through the Holy Spirit's gift of a word of knowledge.

Miracles in Korea.

Recently, Sonja and I were invited to conduct an MTC Teacher Intensive near Seoul, Korea. Sixty pastors and leaders attended the weeklong training. During one of the healing workshops, a woman in leadership came forward complaining of chronic sickness and depression that had plagued her for years. The moment she looked at me (John) a word of knowledge manifested in my mind. I heard the Holy Spirit say, "She has a spirit of infirmity. Command it to go and she will be healed." I obeyed. I spoke to the spirit and said, "Spirit of infirmity, you are bound. I command you to loose this woman in the name of Jesus Christ!"

Before I could say anything else she fell to the floor, writhing and rolling from side to side as she coughed repeatedly. I left her there and went on praying for others who had lined up for prayer. Eventually, I returned to where the woman was now lying still, seemingly free of whatever had her bound. The next day, she returned with a big grin on her face announcing that she was totally healed of her sickness and was totally free of the depression. She had slept the whole night through for the first time in years without using the usual drugs.

She called her sick sister.

The woman leader was so elated for what Jesus had done that she called her Buddhist sister who was going in for back surgery the next day. Her sister had been in excruciating pain for months and was desperate for relief. At the first break in the meeting, the woman leader led us over to where her sister was lying on a pew, unable to sit up without terrible pain. As I set my gaze on her, the Holy Spirit said, "Tell her I love her so much that I will heal her back. All she needs to do is acknowledge that the Lord Jesus Christ is her

Healer." This was relayed to her through our interpreter. She nodded her head "yes."

At that moment I commanded her back to be healed in Jesus' name. I then said, "You may stand up now. The pain will be gone." She had a bewildered look on her face as she slowly sat up, then stood up, slowly twisting back and forth expecting pain. She then looked at us with a smile and boldly exclaimed, "There is no more pain. I've been healed by God!" A woman pastor promptly led the sister into a prayer, asking Jesus to become her Lord and Savior. I had obeyed a word of wisdom and knowledge that led to this woman being healed and saved by the grace and power of God.

Contend for the best.
As ministers, we must pursue God until we are operating competently in words of wisdom and knowledge. These gifts are available to any serious believer. They can be the difference between victory and defeat. We should contend in prayer, meditation in the Word, and even fasting until we begin to hear from God. Consecration brings revelation. When we get serious about being able to minister by the leading of the Spirit of God, powerful ministry begins. Operating in words of knowledge and wisdom will produce the kind of results Jesus experienced.

Remember, Jesus and His Word have already declared that we can heal the sick. We only have to wait for the Holy Spirit to indicate to whom and when. Learning to work in harmony with the Holy Spirit and His gifts to heal hurting people is the most rewarding service to our fellow man we can ever experience. There is none better. It places us in the passenger seat as the Holy Spirit drives the car. We are along for an exciting ride that will take us on a journey of matchless ministry.

The next chapter is the final step in learning how to cooperate with the Holy Spirit in setting people free of demon bondages. Jesus did not prioritize physical healing over spiritual healing. He treated both with equal compassion and concern. We shall learn to do the same as He did.

Let's Practice
- James 1:22 says to *DO* what we have heard (read).
- Consider doing what is recommended in this chapter by referring to the "Let's Practice" in Appendix B, page 327-328.
- Do the Ministry Skill Assignment entitled, "Healing the Sick by Revelation."

Chapter Six

Ministry Skill Six

DEALING WITH DEMONS

The subject of demons is often complex and misunderstood. Jesus intended for His followers to learn how to deal with demons and set people free of the bondages demons cause. This chapter is divided into two parts: Demons in Foreign Lands and Setting the Captives Free in America.

Demons in Foreign Lands

As I (John) entered the door of the meeting place, two ushers were carrying a demon-possessed woman to the back of the auditorium. They were holding the young woman tightly by both arms as she was screaming, spitting, and twisting her body uncontrollably. The worship service had started, and apparently the demons did not like people worshiping the Lord Jesus Christ.

It happened in Africa.
We were in Abidjan, Ivory Coast, West Africa, where Sonja and I were assigned different churches in which to preach. We had just finished five days of teaching over one hundred French-speaking pastors on effective discipleship principles from our *Ambassador Series*. As I entered my assigned meeting place, I saw the ushers dealing with a demonized lady. I then remarked, "Well Lord, this ought to be interesting." The Lord had already told me to preach on healing. I wondered what else He had in mind.

I presented the Gospel to this newly planted church of over one hundred people, emphasizing that Jesus wanted to heal people of all sorts of diseases and pain. Working through an interpreter, the Holy Spirit began revealing words and pictures to me of what He wanted to do. I would repeat what the Lord revealed and began calling people to the front for prayer. First to come was a woman with severe pain in her right elbow. As I obeyed, prayed, and commanded the pain and stiffness to leave, it did. The Holy Spirit singled out eight people with chronic lower back pain. Again, all were healed within minutes. As three more women were being healed of foot pain, the demonized woman in the back of the church began screaming at the top of her lungs. I was really distracted by all the screaming, but the congregation seemed unconcerned. I tried to remain cool and give the impression that I had everything under control. As I glanced back there, I suddenly felt compassion for the woman.

The blood of Jesus is the key.
I put the healing service on hold and began a short teaching on how God loves demonized people so much that He sent His Son to set them free. I also preached that all believers have been authorized and empowered to cast out demons. The message seemed appropriate. I taught that the blood of Jesus was the source of the power that sets people free of spiritual bondages. The moment I mentioned the blood of Jesus, the demonized lady went absolutely crazy. It took three people to restrain her.

I asked the pastor if it would be all right if they brought her to the front. He signaled the ushers and they brought her forward and tried to set her in a chair. She stiffened out like a board and refused to sit normally. She would not look at me, twisting her head from side to side, continuing to scream, spit, and hiss at everyone. In English, I said, "Look at me." When she did, I saw the demon's cold stare glaring at me through hollow eyes. I said, "Be quiet and come out of her!" Immediately, she stopped screaming and became as docile and manageable as any normal person. I did not receive any further instructions from the Holy Spirit so I had the ushers take her back to her seat. I have learned to stop when the

Holy Spirit is silent. No more screaming. No more distractions came from the woman.

She left.

The service concluded with more worship. I then began to pray for a long line of those who were in pain or were sick. God began healing people like He normally does. The demonized woman apparently left quietly as I was praying for the sick. I learned later from an elder that the woman was a member of the church. She suddenly started having these strange outbursts in church about a month prior and was becoming progressively more out of control. He was not sure how this single woman became this way, but suspected she got involved in some kind of ritualistic sexual activity.

I left with a different attitude about demonized people. It was as if I was allowed to experience what Jesus did so many times as illustrated in the Gospels. To Him, the demon-possessed were viewed in the same category as the broken-hearted, sick or those in pain. They all needed to be free and well. In Luke 4, Jesus Christ's mission is stated clearly. He wants His followers to continue the same mission.

Luke 4:18-19

"The Spirit of the Lord is upon Me, because He has anointed Me to preach the gospel to the poor; He has sent Me to heal the brokenhearted, to proclaim liberty to the captives and recovery of sight to the blind, to set at liberty those who are oppressed; to proclaim the acceptable year of the Lord." NKJV

DWJD

- Our mission is fulfilling the Great Commission by doing the same things Jesus did. We are to preach, heal, set the oppressed free, and give Jesus Christ all the credit.
- We are to set at liberty those who are oppressed of the devil by removing the demons that are oppressing them.

Let's examine the same narratives from the Gospels.
Jesus' methods of setting people free of spiritual bondages are clearly observed in the Gospels. In this chapter, we have compiled the same Gospel stories into a single composite rendition of the event. Where Matthew, Mark, and Luke tell the same story, we will show it as a single Scripture with inserts of chapter and verse where the other Gospel writers might differ slightly or expand the story. Then we will follow up with "DWJD" application points with suggestions for how we might do the same as Jesus did.

Jesus sets the pattern.
The following Scriptures depict an early event in the ministry of Jesus Christ. It reveals the beginning of a series of prayer and ministry patterns of how Jesus set free those in spiritual bondage. We will closely observe how Jesus set people free and then offer suggestions of how we might employ the same patterns in ministering to people today.

> **Matthew 8:16-17** Mark 1:32-34 Luke 4:40-41
> Matthew 8:16-17: When evening had come, they brought to Him many who were demon-possessed. And He cast out the spirits with a word, (Luke 4:40: . . . He laid His hands on every one of them) and healed all who were sick, that it might be fulfilled which was spoken by Isaiah the prophet, saying: "He Himself took our infirmities and bore our sicknesses." (Luke 4:41: And demons also came out of many, crying out and saying, "You are the Christ, the Son of God!" And He, rebuking them, did not allow them to speak, for they knew that He was the Christ.) NKJV

DWJD

By studying these Scriptures, we can begin to observe the more obvious approaches and methods Jesus used in dealing with the demonized. When we study how He did it, we can learn a great deal on how we can set people free the same way.

Here are some observations for us to consider:

- Those who were sick or demonized were brought to Jesus. Jesus did not have to go looking for this kind of ministry. People knew they could count on getting healed or delivered because of His reputation. Today, people are looking for anyone who knows how to set people free who are in similar situations. As the church, we need to rise up and do what Jesus did by setting these people free.

- People will bring the sick and demonized to whoever is operating in the authority given by Jesus Christ.

- When faith is present, we are to minister in the authority granted to us in the name of Jesus Christ.

- Demons will often acknowledge the presence of the Holy Spirit upon us *before* others recognize that the power of God is present. Spirits may respond by "crying out" and challenging anyone who is operating in spiritual authority.

- Speaking words of authority to the spirits that inhabit men and women will set them free. The words that Jesus firmly spoke were simple and to the point. In later verses He will say words like "Come out of him" or "Be gone."

- Jesus did not permit demons to speak. Likewise, we should rebuke the spirits and command them not to speak.

- Luke indicates that laying on of hands may be employed while healing the sick or setting people free from spiritual bondages.

- These Scriptures plainly demonstrate that Jesus is the fulfillment of Isaiah's prophecy when He set people free and healed those who came to Him.

Witch doctor set free.

In chapter 3 we gave an account of an older, blind woman in the Lahu tribe of northern Thailand being healed. News of this notable miracle traveled quickly through the jungle. Two days later there was quite a stir in the village when a witch doctor came looking for us. The tribal people were amazed when they learned that he wanted help from the God who had healed the blind woman.

Our team members, Steve Darrow from the USA and an Australian missionary, began to interview the man through interpreters. His arm was paralyzed and contorted, and his heart was racing with uncontrollable palpitations. He told them he had heard of the Christian God when he was a youth, but he had forsook following Him and sought the power of witchcraft instead. However, he now knew the demons had turned on him and were going to kill him. How marvelous is our God to have us in Thailand at that very time so this man might hear of God's miracle-working power. Our Father's mercy, grace, and compassion are limitless!

Steve and the missionary first took authority over the demons and commanded them to leave the man, which they did. It was amazing to see his arm unfold as the paralysis left his body. Then, instinctively, he raised both arms above his head in surrender and praise to God.

The villagers were utterly amazed.
Next, they both led him into repenting of his sin and renouncing the witchcraft he had practiced for so many years. He then asked the Lord Jesus Christ to come into his life and become his Savior and Lord. Next, he received the Holy Spirit baptism and began to speak in unknown languages. The villagers were utterly amazed as they watched all of this transpire.

In those tribal societies, supernatural activity is a part of their daily lives prior to converting to Christianity. However, it is totally fear- and power-based. They are always trying to appease the evil spirits so they will not harm them, their loved ones, or the other villagers. The witch doctors exercise demonic control over these people and keep them in abject fear. Needless to say, when they see the one and only true Creator, the Christian God, taking authority over the witch doctor and evil spirits, they rejoice. Our God not only sets them free, He gives them love, joy, and peace. No wonder Jesus called His message the Good News!

Faith, Authority, and Discerning of Spirits

The Holy Spirit graciously imparts the ability to discern spiritual activity that may be manifesting near us. This ability comes in the form of one of the supernatural gifts of the Holy Spirit called the discerning of spirits described in 1 Corinthians 12:10.

1 Corinthians 12:7-11
But the manifestation of the Spirit is given to each one for the profit of all: for to one is given the word of wisdom through the Spirit, to another the word of knowledge through the same Spirit, to another *faith* by the same Spirit, to another gifts of healings by the same Spirit, to another the working of miracles, to another prophecy, to another *discerning of spirits*, to another different kinds of tongues, to another the interpretation of tongues. But one and the same Spirit works all these things, distributing to each one individually as He wills. NKJV

- The gifts of discerning of spirits, supernatural faith, and the words of knowledge and wisdom are the tools needed to deal with demons. Without them our ministry will be greatly hampered.
- To activate these gifts, we simply ask the Holy Spirit to cause them to manifest whenever we confront suspicious spiritual activity.

Shooting in the dark.

We need the gift of discerning of spirits and/or the gifts of the word of wisdom and knowledge to deal with demons. We define the gift of discerning of spirits as the supernatural perception to distinguish the source of spiritual activity. This gift clearly reveals whether the activity is divine, human, or demonic in origin. The supernatural gifts of the word of knowledge and wisdom will also reveal the same information. Trying to identify and cast out demons without these gifts is like conducting target practice in total darkness. You know the target is out there somewhere, so you keep firing and hoping that you will hit something. These gifts are the spotlight that shows you how to hit the bull's-eye.

Supernatural faith comes with the revelation.

The supernatural gift of faith also comes into play when we encounter demons. Upon discerning the presence of an unclean spirit, God imparts supernatural faith that causes us to become fearless in the face of any kind of demonic activity. This kind of faith is imparted to us so we can firmly take charge of the situation and aggressively command the spirits to depart. If we try to proceed in our own faith and understanding, fear may be present. Demons know when we are fearful. They will take advantage of any fear or timidity we express. To be successful, we need to operate by instructions from the Holy Spirit and in the supernatural faith God gives us.

Jesus gave every follower authority to cast out demons.

Let us begin our path of becoming equipped to deal with demons. First, we will examine Jesus' teaching regarding the authority He gave every believer to cast out demons. We will also examine why this authority was given in the first place. No one can read the New Testament without seeing where Jesus gave His disciples the clear and indisputable authority to heal the sick and cast out demons.

Upon our first observation of the Scriptures printed below, we immediately assume it is just for the twelve disciples following Him at the time. Our early instruction probably reinforced this assumption. We thought, "He couldn't mean me. Besides, demons are a thing of the past. This surely doesn't apply to us today. Jesus must be describing a spiritual problem unique to simple-minded people of those times."

Not so. When we connect John 14:11-14 with the Scriptures below, we are faced with the biblical fact that all believers in Christ have been given the power and authority to not only heal the sick but to command spirits to depart.

Matthew 10:1 Mark 3:13-15   Luke 9:1-2
Matthew 10:1: And when He had called His twelve disciples to Him, He gave them power over unclean spirits, to cast them out, (Luke 9:1: . . . gave them power and authority over all demons, . . .) and to heal all kinds of sickness and all kinds of disease. (Mark 3:14-15: . . . and that He might send them out to preach, and to have power to heal sicknesses and to cast out demons.) NKJV

Matthew 28:18-20
And Jesus came and spoke to them, saying, "All authority has been given to Me in heaven and on earth. Go therefore and make disciples of all the nations . . . teaching them to observe *all things* that I have commanded you; . . ." NKJV

DWJD

- Jesus gave all of His followers power and authority over demonic spirits, to cast them out, and to heal all kinds of sickness and disease. This was taught to the first generation of disciples.

- He then commands Christian leaders to teach each successive generation of disciples to observe all things that Jesus told them to do (including casting out demons).
- By Jesus giving all believers the power and authority to overcome "all" demons, there are no categories of demonic spirits that are excluded.
- Upon believing this truth and accepting the challenge to go, we become the "sent ones."
- Jesus has already commissioned His followers to go into the entire world. As we go, we are to make disciples, teach, baptize, heal the sick, and cast out demons.
- There is only one conclusion. We are to obey and go do these things.

What if you do not know how?

That is why we wrote this book. There seems to be a universal lack of knowledge and understanding regarding how to deal with demons. This is especially true in the thinking of the Christians in the West. Since the turn of the twenty-first century there has been a plethora of endorsements pertaining to seeking a "higher spiritual awareness."

Hundreds of books, movies, and television shows unashamedly promote the existence of extraterrestrials, horrific manifestations of apparitions rising from the dead, and spirit guides coming to lead us into a higher consciousness, connecting us to the realm of the netherworld. They all lead to the same place: the outstretched arms of the one whose only goal is to kill, steal, and destroy lives. The empowered Christian is the only hope for a world totally and completely mesmerized with the "good life" of doing whatever feels good and not being accountable to anyone, especially the Lord Jesus Christ. The Bible warns us about this kind of disobedience. This kind of lifestyle eventually leads to a trap door of spiritual bondage as described in the following Scripture:

Galatians 5:19-21

Now the works of the flesh are evident, which are: adultery, fornication, uncleanness, lewdness, idolatry, sorcery, hatred, contentions, jealousies, outbursts of wrath, selfish ambitions, dissensions, heresies, envy, murders, drunkenness, revelries, and the like; of which I tell you beforehand, just as I also told you in time past, that those who practice such things will not inherit the kingdom of God. NKJV

- Any of the above actions of the sinful nature, if practiced long enough, may attract demonic spirits. When we accept Christ and truly repent of any and all of these things we are set free and will inherit the kingdom of God.
- If we ever return and practice any of these things, after accepting Christ, we could eventually attract a demonic spirit and fall into spiritual bondage.
- Whenever a person comes to know the Lord personally, then *afterwards* decides to betray Him, or decides to blatantly defy Him by engaging in open disobedience, the enemy has the right to enter them.
- Judas is a good example. As long as Judas was following Jesus and doing what was expected of him, he was protected from the evil one. The moment he openly betrayed Jesus, Satan "entered" him (Luke 22:3) and eventually caused him to commit suicide.

Some People Need to be Loosed!

Whenever a demonic spirit is given an opening to establish a stronghold in a person's life, the entrance is achieved through deception. It can happen through open disobedience to God's commands and/or choosing to live a life mentioned above in Galatians chapter 5. When this happens, the person is susceptible to demonization. If not addressed, the spirit can eventually cause peculiar physical problems. One such problem is identified in the Bible as a "spirit of infirmity." The person may need to be loosed from the spirit that is causing the physical abnormality. Neither the best medication nor professional counseling offered by the medical community will heal the person if the condition is sourced in a spirit. Only aggressive prayer in the name of Jesus Christ will heal them. Jesus addresses this particular spirit in John 5:5 and in the Scripture below.

Luke 13:11-17
And behold, there was a woman who had a spirit of infirmity eighteen years, and was bent over and could in no way raise herself up. But when Jesus saw her, He called her to Him and said to her, *"Woman, you are loosed from your infirmity."* And He laid His hands on her, and immediately she was made straight, and glorified God. But the ruler of the synagogue answered with indignation, because Jesus had healed on the Sabbath; and he said to the crowd, "There are six days on which men ought to work; therefore come and be healed on them, and not on the Sabbath day."

The Lord then answered him and said, "Hypocrite! Does not each one of you on the Sabbath loose his ox or donkey from the stall, and lead it away to water it? So ought not this woman, being a daughter of Abraham, whom Satan has bound—think of it—for eighteen years, be loosed from this bond on the Sabbath?" And when He said these things, all His adversaries were put to shame; and all the multitude rejoiced for all the glorious things that were done by Him. NKJV

DWJD

- Special note: Spirits can cause various kinds of sickness, disease, pain, or debilitating kinds of deformities. In this case it was Satan who had her bound, manifesting in a severe curvature of the spine. The Bible identifies these spirits as having the ability to "bind" people in their physical body.

- However, not all sickness and disease are caused by spirits. This is why we must rely on the Holy Spirit's revelation gifts to discern between a true medical problem and one that is caused by a spirit.
- Jesus saw her in the crowd and selected her over everyone else who might have been sick. (Remember, Jesus only did what was revealed by the Father).
- Jesus called her to Him, wanting close contact so He could lay hands upon her.
- Jesus *spoke* words of faith and deliverance directly to the woman, saying, *"Woman you are (loosed) freed from your sickness."*
- She was *made erect* immediately and began *glorifying* God.
- The Christian has been given the authority to "loose" people from the spirits that are causing physical deformities.
- When we encounter someone who has a similar physical problem, we should pray in the Spirit and remain very sensitive for specific direction from the Holy Spirit.
- When you have a *sure word* of direction from the Holy Spirit, then act immediately. We *always* have the authority to do it. But, the *power* is released when we obey the Holy Spirit's instructions.
- Just like Jesus, we must learn to operate in the Father's timing, direction, and His will before we proceed. We will always operate in total victory when we immediately respond to what the Holy Spirit wants us to do.
- When the Holy Spirit says, "Release the person from the bondage. It is caused by a spirit of infirmity," then *DO IT*, just like Jesus did.
- *Lay your hands upon them* just like Jesus did.
- *Speak* words of deliverance over them just like Jesus did. You can say the same words Jesus used, *"Be loosed from your sickness."*
- If you were acting on instructions from the Holy Spirit, you will witness a miracle.

Plundering the strong man's house.

The Bible refers to the "strong man" as a reference to a demonic spirit. They only appear to be strong if we are ignorant of the authority and power given by Jesus Christ. Jesus has made His followers far superior and much stronger than any demonic spirit. The religious leaders in Jesus' time were totally ignorant of the authority and power He had over demons. They were oblivious to the fact that He was delegating the same authority and power to all of His disciples. This is still true today. Some religious leaders are unknowingly attributing the episodes of the Holy Spirit's successful deliverances to a modern-day version of Beelzebub, which is still the prince of demons (see the following Scriptures). We must be very careful to give all the credit to God for loosing people from demon bondage.

Luke 11:14-23 Matthew 12:24-30 Mark 3:22-30
Luke 11:14-23: And He was casting out a demon, and it was mute. So it was, when the demon had gone out, that *the mute spoke*; and the multitudes marveled. But some of them said, "He casts out demons by *Beelzebub*, the ruler of the demons." Others, testing Him, sought from Him a sign from heaven. But He, *knowing their thoughts*, said to them: "Every kingdom divided against itself is brought to desolation, and a house divided against a house falls. If Satan also is divided against himself, how will his kingdom stand? Because you say I cast out demons by Beelzebub. And if I cast out demons by Beelzebub, by whom do your sons cast them out? Therefore they will be your judges."

"But if I cast out demons with the finger of God, (Matthew 12:28: . . . by the Spirit of God, . . .) surely the kingdom of God has come upon you. When a strong man, fully armed, guards his own palace, his goods are in peace. (Mark 3:27: and Matthew 12:29: No one can enter a strong man's house and plunder his goods, unless he first binds the strong man. And then he will plunder his house.) But when a stronger than he comes upon him and overcomes him, he takes from him all his armor in which he trusted, and divides his spoils. He who is not with Me is against Me, and he who does not gather with Me scatters . . . . NKJV

DWJD

- Jesus was always firm and consistent when He identified demonic activity in people. We should do the same. Persistence in allowing the Holy Spirit to reveal what kind of spirit is manifesting will always result in victory.
- Spirits that cause a person to be mute should be addressed as a "mute spirit." We command the mute spirit to come out and the tongue to be loosed in the name of Jesus Christ. It is the power of the Holy Spirit coming upon the person that sets them free.
- Be prepared to have "religious" leaders accuse you of being "of the devil" when you get involved in deliverance. When they attribute the work of the Holy Spirit to the devil, they are extremely close to blaspheming the Holy Spirit and will have to give an account for it. Refuse to argue with them, but do pray for them. Ignore their ignorance and continue setting people free.
- The "strong man" Jesus refers to is the principal demon that controls a person's behavior. When you have on the full armor of God and the name of Jesus on your lips, the demon cannot overcome you.
- Be sure to confirm the person's salvation and lead them into the Holy Spirit baptism.
- This is critical so their spiritual "house" will be full of God. If not, the house will be "swept and clean" with no armor and without the Holy Spirit guarding the house. The person is left vulnerable for the demon to come back and overcome them.
- If you do not fill the house and get rid of the first bondage in their life, more demons will eventually take up residence in their mind and they will be worse off than before (see Matthew 12:43-45).

- Note: Being "bound" works two ways. The principal demon (strong man) cannot plunder our house (mind and body) unless he first binds us with various bondages: rebellion, addictions, disobedience against God, etc. Conversely, we cannot plunder the strong man's house unless we first bind him in the name of Jesus. We then release the person from whatever is binding them by having them surrender to and obey God. This includes submitting to salvation, water baptism, baptism in the Holy Spirit, and doing God's will.

The Reality of Spirits

Spirits can cause people to be mute.

Over the years we have observed many cases where spirits are the source of a person's inability to speak. The person may want to speak, but the spirit has bound them so they believe they cannot. Many came to Jesus with this problem as outlined below.

Matthew 9:32-33

As they went out, behold, they brought to Him a man, mute and demon-possessed. And when the demon was cast out, the mute spoke. And the multitudes marveled, saying, "It was never seen like this in Israel!" NKJV

Matthew 12:22-23

Then one was brought to Him who was demon-possessed, blind and mute; and He healed him, so that the blind and mute man both spoke and saw. And all the multitudes were amazed . . . . NKJV

- The people came knowing that Jesus could set them free. The mute must come in faith, desiring to be set free.

- A spirit can cause muteness. Again, this requires the gift of discerning of spirits to be absolutely sure.
- Jesus teaches us to "cast out" the demon of muteness by firmly speaking to it.
- Bystanders will marvel and be amazed when the person begins to speak. We must be quick to initiate thanksgiving to God for setting the person free.
- Ignore any "religious leaders" that speak negatively about you and your deliverance team. Always respond in love. We can diffuse the situation by asking the person who was truly delivered to share what happened with the religious leaders.

The little girl named "No Speak."

One of the many mission teams we took to the hill tribes in northern Thailand consisted of two evangelists, a lady pastor, a CEO of a high-tech company and his daughter, and Sonja and myself. Our mission was to teach one week in a Lahu tribal village and one week in a Karen tribal village. Our goal was to equip the Christians to fully understand and operate in the authority given by Jesus Christ. We did it like Jesus did. We taught the Word, preached the Gospel, and healed the sick. During one of the afternoon sessions, Dawn, the daughter of the CEO, felt strongly that a little mute girl she had befriended would be healed if we would pray for her.

The little six-year-old had been given the name "No Speak" by the Lahu tribe because she had been mute since she was an infant. Her parents gave us permission to pray for her. The Lord led us to have Steve Darrow, the CEO, and the Lahu pastor pray for her. Steve and the pastor laid hands on her and Steve commanded the spirit that had the little girl bound to be gone. Steve prayed, "You mute spirit, I command you to loose this girl in the name of Jesus Christ. I loose her from the curse put on her by this tribe. Be gone, in Jesus' name!" We released her to go play with the other children, but told them to come and tell us when they heard her say anything. Later the same day, the children all came running back yelling, "She's speaking, she's speaking!" That evening the children helped her sing the praise songs for the first time in her little life. Dawn renamed her "Joy" instead of "No Speak." We serve an awesome God!

Malaria healed.

While we were ministering to the Lahu tribe, a woman from Burma came into the village wanting to be healed of malaria. She had walked for many miles over the mountains for she had heard there were miracles happening in the Lahu village that week. She looked terrible: gaunt, yellowish skin, and so weak she could not stand. The minute she sat down the Holy Spirit said to me (John), "It's a spirit. An unclean spirit is the source of the symptoms. Cast it out!" Using two interpreters, I immediately commanded the unclean spirit to come out of her. In a matter of minutes her skin became normal, she began to smile, and strength returned to her body. She thanked us and briskly walked away. One of the interpreters was a Thai Foursquare pastor. He was overwhelmed, weeping with joy and amazement. He said, "We hear all these stories from other Christians about Jesus healing people. This time I have seen the glory of God for myself. I have witnessed a miracle with my own eyes. That woman had malaria. I saw Jesus heal her! Praise God!" The following passages describe how Jesus set a boy free from a mute spirit that was causing symptoms similar to epilepsy.

> **Mark 9:14-29** Matthew 17:14-21 Luke 9:37-42
> Mark 9:14-29: And when He came to the disciples, He saw a great multitude around them, and scribes disputing with them. Immediately, when they saw Him, all the people were greatly amazed, and running to Him, greeted Him. And He asked the scribes, "What are you discussing with them?" Then one of the crowd answered and said, "Teacher, I brought You my son, who has *a mute spirit.* (Matthew 17:15: ". . . for he is an epileptic and suffers severely; for he often falls into the fire and often into the water.")

(Luke 9:39: ". . . a spirit seizes him, and he suddenly cries out; it convulses him so that he foams at the mouth, and it departs from him with great difficulty, bruising him.") And wherever he seizes him, he throws him down; he foams at the mouth, gnashes his teeth, and becomes rigid. So I spoke to your disciples, that they should cast him out, but they could not." He answered him and said, "O faithless generation, how long shall I be with you? How long shall I bear with you? Bring him to Me."

Then they brought him to Him. And when he saw Him, immediately the spirit convulsed him, and he fell on the ground and wallowed, foaming at the mouth. So He asked his father, "How long has this been happening to him?" And he said, "From childhood. And often he has thrown him both into the fire and into the water to destroy him. But if You can do anything, have compassion on us and help us." Jesus said to him, "If you can believe, all things are possible to him who believes." Immediately the father of the child cried out and said with tears, "Lord, I believe; help my unbelief!"

When Jesus saw that the people came running together, He rebuked the unclean spirit, (Matthew 17:18: . . . the demon, . . .) saying to it, "Deaf and dumb spirit, I command you, come out of him and enter him no more!" Then the spirit cried out, convulsed him greatly, (Luke 9:42: . . . threw him down . . .) and came out of him. And he became as one dead, so that many said, "He is dead." But Jesus took him by the hand and lifted him up, and he arose. (Matthew 17:18: . . . and the child was cured from that very hour.)

And when He had come into the house, His disciples asked Him privately, "Why could we not cast him out?" So He said to them, (Matthew 17:20: . . . "Because of your unbelief; for assuredly, I say to you, if you have faith as a mustard seed, you will say to this mountain, 'Move from here to there,' and it will move; and nothing will be impossible for you.") "This kind can come out by nothing but prayer and fasting." NKJV

DWJD

- Jesus teaches us many things about setting people free in this detailed account from the perspectives of Matthew, Mark, and Luke.
- *Physical symptoms*: These are the same symptoms as epilepsy. We must ask the Holy Spirit to give us the discerning of spirits to know for sure if it is truly a spirit or simply epilepsy at work in their brain. In this case, the spirit seized the boy and caused him to scream. They may shriek, yell, and get very loud. They may convulse violently as if they are being mauled and thrown to the ground. They may foam at the mouth, spitting saliva. They may grind their teeth and become rigid. Finally, they may become so still they may seem to be in a coma.
- Remember, you can only cast out demons when demons are the source of the problem.
- *Unbelief*: Jesus says to both the parent and His disciples that unwavering faith is all that is needed to cast out demons.
- He said, "Everything is possible for him who believes!" We should pray and expect the "gift of faith" to come upon us when we engage in deliverance.
- *Fasting and praying* will often be necessary for us to successfully operate by revelation and by the gift of faith. This should be done just prior to entering into a deliverance session. Some spirits do not come out easily. Prayer with fasting is necessary to weaken, identify, and cast out certain kinds of spirits.

- *Avoid arguments* with religious leaders. New believers tend to get into arguments with religious leaders. This is fruitless. Do not do it.
- *Interview parents.* Determine if medication solves the symptoms. Demons do not respond to medication. Determine exactly what the parents are believing God to do. Never go beyond what they authorize. Everyone must be in agreement.
- *Listen for faith.* In this case the man said, "But if You can do anything!" Listen for faith to manifest in the family involved. Do not proceed until they expect the deliverance to be successful. "Lord, I believe; help my unbelief!"
- *Engage in the deliverance.* Begin by speaking to the spirit behind the physical impairment. If deaf, speak to the *"deaf spirit."* If mute, speak to the *"mute spirit."* Command the spirit to *come out.* Command the spirit *never to return or enter* the person again.
- *Naming a spirit.* We seldom ask spirits for their names. They always lie. We ask the Spirit of truth, the Holy Spirit, for the principal spirit that has the person bound. If revealed, then we address the spirit by name.
- Continued *physical manifestations* during the deliverance are only an indication that spirits are responding to the authority of Jesus Christ. Do *not* focus on the outward manifestations. Listen to the Holy Spirit's instructions!
- When the Holy Spirit says we are done, we are done. We are done not because there are no more outward manifestations. We are done when every member of the team hears the Holy Spirit say, "You are through."
- Have the person promise to stay in close accountability with a mature prayer partner. Have them promise to never return to the same behavior, the same people, or situation that caused the problem in the first place.
- *Debrief.* Use the event as a point of teaching for the team on how to better conduct this kind of session next time.

The demon-possessed boy.

While conducting a weeklong healing crusade in Panang, Malaysia, I (John) encountered many people who were either demonized or demon-possessed. The difference is the degree by which the demons have control of the person. A demonized person can function normally in their daily activities. However, in one or more areas of their life they are unable to control their behavior. Their mental perceptions are very skewed. Demon-possessed people have little or no control of their behavior.

One such case was a mother who brought her demon-possessed boy to the crusade. The boy was out of control. He was about seven years old. His mother held him tight in a bear hug in the back of the auditorium until we called for the sick. Once the altar call was given, she brought him kicking and screaming to the front row. The boy would yell and spit like a wildcat as his mother sat in a chair holding him tightly. We had trained thirty healing teams of two people each to minister healing and deliverance. They were full of faith and ready for anything.

A healing team of two ladies stepped up to the boy, bent over, looked him straight in the eyes and said, "You are bound, in the name of Jesus Christ! Come out of him, now!" The boy stiffened out, screamed at the top of his voice, and slumped over exhausted. Minutes later the deliverance was complete. The boy stood on his feet, leaned into his mother, and looked around in wonderment. It was as if he was seeing the room and everything going on for the very first time. He was completely set free and behaving normally. The mother was so thankful that she gladly prayed with the ladies and invited Jesus into her life. I took pictures of the incident to remind me of the wonderful power God has given believers to set people like this free.

The power of the name of Jesus.

The next night the place was filled with over six hundred people. I was in the back of the auditorium documenting and overseeing the healing teams ministering to the sick and diseased. Miracles were happening every few minutes. When someone got out of a wheelchair they would have him or her walk up on stage and testify to their healing. When twisted or deformed arms, legs, or backs would straighten out they would be ushered up on stage to testify. Faith and excitement were running high in everyone.

I noticed a young man with a puzzled look approaching me. He spoke English so I asked him, "What do you want God to do for you?" Speaking hesitantly, he said, "I haven't been able to sleep. Could you pray for me?" I said, "Do you know Jesus?" The second I said "Jesus," something hit him hard in the chest. I never touched him, but it caused him to stumble backwards and land on the floor. He was laid out for forty minutes. Finally he got up, confessed he had been worshiping the "Goddess of the Sea" and did not know what was happening to him. I quickly shared that Jesus was his only hope. He gladly prayed and asked Jesus to become his Lord. This event demonstrated just how powerful the name of Jesus is toward the demonic strongholds in people's lives.

The Gadarene demoniacs.

Like we have said before, the difference between being de-monized and being totally demon-possessed is the degree by which the demons have control of the person. When a person is demon-possessed, the person has very little if any control of their behavior. They would be classified in the West as being mentally insane and most likely locked up in a mental institution. Those who are demonized can function normally in society but may have great difficulty in a specific role or function in their personal life. That area of their life, if probed or irritated, will cause the person to manifest in strange or aberrant behavior. The following is a case of total demon-possession.

Mark 5:1-20   Matthew 8:28-34   Luke 8:26-39

Mark 5:1-20: Then they came to the other side of the sea, to the country of the Gadarenes. And when He had come out of the boat, immediately there met Him out of the tombs a man with an unclean spirit, (Matthew 8:28: . . . two demon-possessed men, . . .) who had his dwelling among the tombs; and no one could bind him, not even with chains, because he had often been bound with shackles and chains. And the chains had been pulled apart by him, and the shackles broken in pieces; neither could anyone tame him. And always, night and day, he was in the mountains and in the tombs, crying out and cutting himself with stones.

When he saw Jesus from afar, he ran and worshiped Him. And he cried out with a loud voice and said, "What have I to do with You, Jesus, Son of the Most High God? I implore You by God that You do not torment me." For He said to him, "Come out of the man, unclean spirit!" Then He asked him, "What is your name?" And he answered, saying, "My name is Legion; for we are many. (Luke 8:30: . . . because many demons had entered him.) Also he begged Him earnestly that He would not send them out of the country. (Luke 8:31: . . . out into the abyss.) Now a large herd of swine was feeding there near the mountains. So all the demons begged Him, saying, "Send us to the swine, that we may enter them."

And at once Jesus gave them permission. Then the unclean spirits went out and entered the swine (there were about two thousand); and the herd ran violently down the steep place into the sea, and drowned in the sea. So those who fed the swine fled, and they told it in the city and in the country. And they went out to see what it was that had happened. Then they came to Jesus, and saw the one who had been demon-possessed and had the legion, sitting and clothed and in his right mind. And they were afraid. And those who saw it told them how it happened to him who had been demon-possessed, (Luke 8:36: . . . was healed.) and about the swine. Then they began to plead with Him to depart from their region. (Luke 8:37: . . . for they were seized with great fear . . . .)

And when He got into the boat, he who had been demon-possessed begged Him that he might be with Him. However, Jesus did not permit him, but said to him, "Go home to your friends, and tell them what great things the Lord has done for you, and how He has had compassion on you." And he departed and began to proclaim in Decapolis all that Jesus had done for him; and all marveled. NKJV

DWJD

- Jesus teaches us how to approach a demon-possessed person in love and compassion. We then proceed to set them free.
- Spirits know we have authority and power to torment them, and they know certain Christians are a threat to their domain. They will most often challenge us to see if we know our authority. They will speak through the person and may demonstrate their superhuman strength to test the Christian. Even though human effort may not subdue them, the name of Jesus will bind them and keep them from doing us physical harm.
- People engaged in Far Eastern sects and martial arts such as Kung Fu, Tai Kwan Do, etc., are taught how to draw strength from a "master" by focusing on century-old chants that attract demons to help them fight, over-power, and ultimately kill their opponent.
- Demon-possessed people are *loud, obnoxious,* and cannot function normally in society. They go naked, cut themselves, and are forced to live alone.
- Demons do not want to leave the person they inhabit.

- When demons try to negotiate with us, it usually means they know we have power over them. So, be tough just like Jesus, and cast them out. To be "tormented" means to be cast out.
- Neighbors acquainted with the demon-possessed will not understand the significance of a person being delivered from demons. They will be afraid of what is happening. They will ask that we go away, especially if the presence of God threatens their way of life and financial livelihood.
- Luke 8:29: *For He had commanded the unclean spirit to come out of the man.* This infers that the demons did not come out immediately. The demons did not come out until they went into the pigs (see Luke 8:33).
- There will be times when we encounter someone with multiple demons. Listen for specific instructions from the Holy Spirit as to the primary spirit that should be addressed. Otherwise, it may take quite awhile to cast out all the spirits.
- Once the person is set free, strongly encourage them to go to their own neighborhood and give testimony of what God has done and preach the Gospel.

The disciples did what Jesus did.
Let us examine how the early disciples continued doing what Jesus had taught them. They were eyewitnesses of Jesus casting out demons. They, like we, are to accomplish ministry the way Jesus instructed them. They were simply Holy Spirit empowered disciples just like we are. Let us see what kind of results they had in attempting to cast out demons just like Jesus had shown them.

Philip casts out unclean spirits.
When persecution broke out in Jerusalem, the disciples were dispersed to neighboring towns and countries. They had been taught how to do what Jesus did and were now preaching the Gospel in the power and anointing of the Holy Spirit. Philip discovered the authority and power given to him by Jesus Christ.

Acts 8:4-8

Therefore those who were scattered went everywhere preaching the word. Then Philip went down to the city of Samaria and preached Christ to them. And the multitudes with one accord heeded the things spoken by Philip, hearing and seeing the miracles, which he did. For unclean spirits, crying with a loud voice came out of many who were possessed; and many who were paralyzed and lame were healed. And there was great joy in that city. NKJV

DWJD

- *Preaching* the Word stirs up unclean spirits. Philip was preaching what Jesus said to preach in Mark 16:15-20. These signs shall follow them that believe: Healing, casting out of demons, etc.
- *Preaching* caused people to give attention to what Philip was saying. This was the first time they heard that Jesus could set you free from bondages, from being paralyzed, and being lame. There was great rejoicing in that city—not resistance nor argument about doctrine. No. They had joy because their friends and family members were being healed through the name of Jesus!
- The Samaritans saw signs of what Philip was doing.
- When spirits come out, they make a commotion, shouting with a loud voice. We can expect this to happen, but do not allow them to offset the preaching of the Gospel. We are to command them to, "Be quiet!"
- Demons can cause paralysis. When they are cast out, the paralysis is gone.
- Great miracles and signs took place by Philip's preaching, mainly because there was no opposition from religious leaders. The leaders were not there because they did not want to associate with pre-Christian (unclean) people.
- When we get away from the doubt and unbelief of many in the West, healing and miracles are more likely to manifest.

Paul casts out demons.

Paul had been baptized in the Holy Spirit and operated in the authority and power given to him by Jesus Christ. He exercised this power in the next passage to cast out a demon inhabiting a slave girl.

Acts 16:16-19

Now it happened, as we went to prayer, that a certain slave girl possessed with a spirit of divination met us, who brought her masters much profit by fortune-telling. This girl followed Paul and us, and cried out, saying, "These men are the servants of the Most High God, who proclaim to us the way of salvation." And this she did for many days. But Paul, greatly annoyed, turned and said to the spirit, *"I command you in the name of Jesus Christ to come out of her."* And he came out that very hour. But when her masters saw that their hope of profit was gone, they seized Paul and Silas and dragged them into the marketplace to the authorities. NKJV

- Paul gives us a wonderful example of how to cast out demons. This is one of the best Scriptures in the book of Acts on how to do it.
- First, Paul waited long enough to be sure he was dealing with a demon. The Holy Spirit evidently confirmed that they were dealing with a "spirit of divination." This often manifests as a form of religious spirit that always misleads and lies.
- Second, the demon knows who we are and will announce it to whoever will listen. This demon also carried a familiar spirit with it that could tell things about Paul and others that only they knew. We have to be very careful because some of these people will occasionally attend our churches. They are loud, arrogant, and will stop a move of God.

- Third, wait for God's timing to cast it out. Always wait for the Holy Spirit to tell us to "go ahead." Paul waited "many days." Finally, she was disrupting their meetings, so he dealt with it.
- Fourth, this passage is the clearest "how to" in the area of deliverance. We cannot improve on it. "I command you, in the name of Jesus Christ, to come out of her!" It came out "that very hour." Do it just like Paul did it, and we will be doing it just like Jesus did it.
- Finally, get the permission of those with authority over the person. Otherwise, they may cause trouble for you.

Do Not Make it Difficult

There is a tendency for novice Christians to get loud and emotional when they first get involved in deliverance ministry. If we use the above situation where Paul dealt with the demon in the slave girl, we have a wonderful example of how it should be done.

We should not try to improve on it or make it more difficult. Just do what Paul did. Be patient and wait for the Holy Spirit's timing. When the Holy Spirit reveals the activities of the demonic spirit and says to cast it out, then command it to come out in the name of Jesus Christ. Be very firm and stay with it until the Holy Spirit says you are done. We do not have to shout and become physical with the person. That demonstrates to the demon that you are resorting to human or fleshly tactics. Rely on the leading of the Holy Spirit and you will set the person free within a short period of time.

Spirit houses.
Many people have asked us why there seems to be more demonic activity in Third World or developing countries. It is because they are generally more superstitious. Their religions are sourced in the supernatural of the enemy. For instance, in Thailand, a very significant part of their Buddhist religion is the "spirit house" phenomenon. You will see these in most

Thai and some Chinese restaurants in America. Most homes and businesses in Thailand have these beautifully decorated structures for honoring and appeasing spirits. The more successful you are, the larger the spirit house. We will occasionally witness uninformed Christians admiring a spirit house, not realizing its function is to appease demonic spirits.

You can feel the negative energy.
If Christians are sensitive to the spiritual realm, they can actually feel the negative energy coming off the spirit houses. On numerous occasions we have felt the evil presence before we even saw the spirit house. We would sense the negative energy, look around, and sure enough, there it would be.

The idea behind the spirit houses is that the person puts offerings of flowers, food, even Coca-Cola to appease the spirits so they will not harm them. By deliberately inviting the spirits, (whom they think may be relatives or friends who have died), they are in deception and giving demonic spirits the right to inhabit the premises. Paul admonishes Christians to not "be participants with demons."

> **1 Corinthians 10:19-21**
> Do I mean then that a sacrifice offered to an idol is anything, or that an idol is anything? No, but the sacrifices of pagans are offered to demons, not to God, and I do not want you to be participants with demons. You cannot drink the cup of the Lord and the cup of demons too; you cannot have a part in both the Lord's table and the table of demons. NIV

DWJD

- Idols or spirit houses attract demon spirits. People, sometimes unknowingly, are sacrificing to demonic spirits.
- Christians must be diligent to not open themselves up to spirits by visiting temples or admiring spirit houses or any type of idol, large or small.
- This same negative energy can be discerned in occult or New Age gatherings and in and around their bookstores.

Thai Christians have to contend with pre-Christian relatives who bring their idols and witchcraft paraphernalia with them when they come for a visit from another city. There is a reality to this supernatural dimension, and the Christians have to pray and take authority over the spirits that have come with the relatives into their homes. Otherwise, all sorts of occurrences begin to manifest, and the peace of God that normally permeates their homes is disrupted.

There is concentrated demonic activity in the temples.

This may sound far-fetched to some of you reading this, but if you would talk with missionaries and Christians living in these countries, you could easily verify this reality. Another area of concentrated demonic activity is in their watts, or temples. Again, you can feel the negative energy emanating from these places of worship. The worshipers feel the energy, fear it, and are compelled to try to appease the spirits so they will not be harmed. Christians should not visit these demon-infested sites.

It felt like a wet spider web.

On my (John) first trip to Panang, Malaysia, I traveled with Dr. A.L. Gill who was especially sensitive to spiritual activity in and around heathen temples. As we drove from the airport to our hotel, I was sitting in the backseat marveling at all the new sights of this "city of a thousand temples." Sitting in the front seat, Dr. Gill was watching my reactions in the rearview mirror as we drove close to a very elaborate Hindu temple. Without warning, a horrible feeling came over me as I observed the thousands of demonic gargoyles protruding from its steep roof. I felt something like a cold, damp spider web fall upon me. My reaction caused my friend to smile, laugh, and say, "Looks like your spiritual antenna is doing just fine. Keep it fine-tuned and you'll keep out of trouble." He was referring to the gift of discerning of spirits. I became very thankful as the Holy Spirit continually activated this gift the entire six weeks I spent in Malaysia.

We must allow God to demonstrate His power.

Because people in these countries live in the supernatural realm and are enslaved by fear of the demonic spirits, one of the most effective ways to minister to them is in the demonstration of the love and power of God. If we are holding evangelistic meetings for the tribal people in northern Thailand and someone goes into a demonic manifestation, falls on the dirt, and begins slithering like a snake, we better know our authority in Christ. All the eloquent preaching and teaching we learned in seminary will not prevail over this kind of situation. We need to step into the authority given to us by Jesus Christ and allow the Holy Spirit to demonstrate His power through us. Paul knew how to handle situations like this:

1 Corinthians 2:4-5

And my speech and my preaching were not with persuasive words of human wisdom, but in demonstration of the Spirit and of power, that your faith should not be in the wisdom of men but in the power of God. NKJV

DWJD

- Do what Paul did. We exercise our authority by simply commanding them to stop and be quiet in the name of Jesus Christ.
- When the person immediately stops and lies still, that gets the pre-Christians' attention!
- We then preach the Full Gospel message: Jesus Christ, the Son of God as Savior, Healer, Baptizer in the Holy Spirit, and soon coming King.
- After the preaching of the Word, God is always faithful to heal the sick and set people free from the demonic.

When the tribal people *see* and *experience* the power of God and discover it is greater than any demonic spirit, they accept Jesus Christ as the One and only true God, the Creator! Hallelujah!

Pray over hotel rooms.
During my mother's final illness, I (Sonja) did not go with John on one of the mission trips to Thailand. I was staying at a hotel in Vancouver, Washington near where my mother was convalescing. As a matter of rule, we always pray over our hotel rooms and "sanctify" them through the name and blood of the Lord Jesus Christ.

This particular night I was tired, and I forgot to pray. In the middle of the night I awoke with a demonic spirit trying to smother me. I was terrified and could barely get the words out, "In the name of Jesus Christ, I command you to leave!" I repeated this multiple times, but it would not lift off of me. Finally, I said, "I am covered with the blood of Jesus, and you must depart!" And it did. The bizarre thing about this incident is that I rolled over and went back to sleep! Only the peace of God could explain that.

I (John) thought I was going to die.
While staying in a hotel in Mae Sai, Thailand, next to the Myanmar border, I neglected to take authority over any spiritual "residue" that usually lingers in the rooms. About 3:00 a.m., I awoke with a sudden and very acute pain in my abdomen. I stumbled to the bathroom in an effort to rid myself of the pain. Nothing seemed to help. Collapsing back in bed I began to feel extremely weak and began to shiver uncontrollably. Fear hit me. I thought, "This is serious. There's no hospital here. I could die of this."

Then the Holy Spirit interrupted me with, "Take authority over the spirit!" Immediately I said loudly, "You foul demon. I command you to loose me and get out of here! I take authority over you and forbid you to stay upon me. In the authority of the blood of Jesus Christ, be gone! All spirits in this room are bound. You cannot stay. I command all of you out of here in the name of Jesus Christ!" I did not care if the people in the next room could hear me. This thing was trying to kill me! Within minutes the pain left and the shivering stopped. I rolled over and slept like a baby the rest of the night.

Are there demons in America?

We have been exploring demonic bondages in the Third World countries. Now we turn to America. There has been an increase in demonic activity in the USA. As Christians, we must face the reality of spiritual entities and the power they hold over certain people. Beginning in the 1960s, we have watched the moral fiber of our nation disintegrate before our very eyes. Entrance points for hoards of demons have come through:

- Embracing eastern religious systems
- Exploring the occult, witchcraft, and New Age philosophies
- Increasing violence and sex depicted on TV and in movies
- Internet pornography and illicit sexual perversions
- Drug and alcohol abuse

If we are to truly do what Jesus did, we cannot ignore the subject of demonic activity upon humans. To the contrary, we need to examine closely what role we need to play to be able to set free those who are being held captive by Satan. Demons are at work worldwide. Jesus commissioned Christians to cast out demons wherever we find them holding people in bondage. The remainder of this chapter brings the issue closer to home, right here in America.

Setting the Captives Free in America

Demonology 101.

The following story was my (John) introduction to the world of spirits. It began in Everett, Washington during the mid-1970s. My good friend Ken Miracle introduced me to a man in his seventies who had a reputation for healing the sick, prophesying, and operating in the revelation gifts of the Holy Spirit. His name was Reverend Jesse Raymond. He was a frequent speaker in full gospel churches, healing conferences, and the Full Gospel Business Men's Fellowship International (FGBMFI). We met at a luncheon meeting of the FGBMFI in Everett, Washington. He conducted Christian counseling in an office in the back of his Lighthouse Christian Bookstore in the north part of town. He invited me to visit his store on my next sales trip to that area.

I dropped in one Friday afternoon and was spellbound by all of his stories about miracles that he had experienced while preaching the Gospel. I will never forget what happened next.

Come out!

His afternoon counseling appointment entered the store. Jesse asked me to stay and watch the store as he counseled the man. I was happy to help. The man carried a well-worn Bible, said he was a Spirit-filled believer, and that he came to receive help with some "personal concerns." Jesse's office was in the back of the store. It had a large glass window between the office and the book displays. I could see everything that was happening, but could barely hear what was being said. That is, until I heard Jesse say, "You will have to come out of him, now!"

I quickly looked into Jesse's office. Jesse seemed relaxed as he leaned back in his big office chair. On the other side of his desk was the man sitting, leaning forward with his elbows on his knees, eyes red, scowling at Jesse, growling, gagging, and coughing. The hair went up on the back of my neck. I did not understand what I was seeing. Fear hit me. I wanted to get out of there, fast!

Then the phone rang. I ran to answer it. They needed to speak to Jesse. It was urgent. I motioned through the glass that it was really important. Jesse got up, opened the door, came to the phone and said, "John, go in there and take over for me. I'll only be a minute." I must have looked like a four-year-old seeing the real Frankenstein for the first time.

Jesse just smiled and said, "Don't worry. Just speak to the spirit in the name of Jesus! I'll be right back." He pushed me into his office and I fearfully sat down in Jesse's chair.

He just stared at me.
Having only the desk between Satan and me was not very comforting. The red-eyed man just stared at me, breathing heavily. I could not say anything. I froze. Finally, I managed a weak, "In Jesus' name, you stay where you are. I command you to sit there!" He just stared at me. I was really getting nervous. I quietly prayed, "Please, Lord, get Jesse back in here. Hurry, Lord!" Then the guy gave out a very loud groan and a half growl that petrified me. Finally, Jesse walked in with a small wastebasket, gave it to the man, and said, "Come out you foul, perverse spirit, all the way out. Now! In the name of Jesus Christ!"

I motioned Jesse to please take his seat as I backed up to the far wall. I watched closely as the man gagged, convulsed, and coughed into the wastebasket. This happened three or four times. Then he collapsed back into his chair, sighed deeply, wiping his chin, and finally said, "It's gone! It's gone! It's all gone!" Jesse said, "Yes, it's gone." He looked at Jesse, and asked, "How did you know what it was?" Jesse said, "The Lord told me when you first walked in here today. He said that you've been deeply into pornography for years and you opened the door to a lying and perverse spirit."

I was stunned. He was a charismatic Christian, spoke in tongues, and attended church. I thought Christians could not have demons. That is what I believed. I was terribly confused. After the man left, Jesse recommended some books on the subject and invited me back to discuss my findings. I left in amazement. I did not have a clue what to think. Boy, did I have a lot to learn about the spirit world. One thing was for sure. Christian or not, I had witnessed firsthand the visible grip of spiritual bondage that an entity had on the man. I also witnessed the awesome power of the name of Jesus setting the man free from the clutch of a powerful demonic spirit.

Can a Christian Have a Demon?

When the subject of demons comes up, it seems Christians ask the same question: "Can a Christian have a demon?" After more than thirty years of studying this issue, our answer is this: A Christian is given the freedom of choice. If they choose to associate with people that participate in evil deeds or choose to disobey God and continue to live a destructive lifestyle of sin and wanton pleasure, they open themselves up to demonic entities. It may take a long time, but eventually they can become demonized. The bottom line is that Christians cannot have it both ways. Either we live for God or live for ourselves. The choice is ours.

This is shocking!

To many, it may come as a shock to discover that Christians can have demons. There are those who argue that Christians cannot have the Holy Spirit and demons at the same time. What they fail to teach is that demons reside in the soul nature (mind, will and emotions) and in the body, not in the human spirit. When we receive Christ, our spirit nature is made new and becomes alive with the Holy Spirit. However, our mind is not made new. It needs to be "renewed" day-by-day. People who say they believe in God but have no knowledge of biblical truth are susceptible to the lies of Satan. If we do not know what the Bible says, we remain vulnerable to a "different spirit." Paul warns Christians to be very careful not to be corrupted by a different spirit.

2 Corinthians 11:3-4

But I fear, lest somehow, as the serpent deceived Eve by his craftiness, so your minds may be corrupted from the simplicity that is in Christ. For if he who comes preaches another Jesus whom we have not preached, or if you receive a *different spirit*, which you

259

have not received, or a different gospel, which you have not accepted, you may well put up with it. NKJV

DWJD

- Those seeking spiritual insight in the wrong place open their minds to spiritual corruption.
- Cults are successful in recruiting unsuspecting people by preaching "another Jesus" and a different gospel. Jehovah's Witnesses and Mormonism are two from a long list of cults that emanate a "different spirit."
- We are safe when we strive for mainstream Christian orthodoxy that is based on centuries of carefully researched theology accepted by a large majority of respected scholars.
- A "different spirit" is instruction that sounds good or feels good to the soul, but is cloaked with deception and eventual bondage to an ideology that leads away from the Gospel of grace into spiritual oppression.

---

1 Timothy 4:1-3

Now the Spirit expressly says that in latter times some will depart from the faith, giving heed to *deceiving spirits* and *doctrines of demons*, speaking lies in hypocrisy, having their own conscience seared with a hot iron, forbidding to marry, and commanding to abstain from foods which God created to be received with thanksgiving by those who believe and know the truth. NKJV

DWJD

- Believers who know the truth of God's Word will not be led astray by spiritual legalism, deception, or doctrines of demons.
- Those who do not know what the Bible says are susceptible to persuasive con artists that masquerade as preachers, interested only in their own moneymaking agenda.

- Cults may start with good intentions, but if their leaders are not grounded in Christian orthodoxy, deceiving spirits and doctrines of demons will soon be their teachers.
- The gifts of discerning of spirits, words of wisdom and knowledge, and a broad understanding of the Bible are the best defense a Christian has to avoid being deceived by cults.

Mental abuse.

We learned in Psychology 101 that the human mind, given the right set of negative circumstances, could be influenced to a point of becoming mentally unstable. We believe that abrupt trauma from severe physical or mental abuse can create mindsets of deception. Events such as witnessing a murder or victimization such as being beaten as a child, forced sexual acts, rape, or homosexual attack can impair, injure, or even twist a person's mind to accept a warped belief system or lies that skew their thinking. If left to fester, these mindsets will remain with a person all their life. Accepting Christ and becoming born again will erase most of these unhealthy lies from the mind. However, in the case of severe mental abuse during childhood or adolescence, there can remain a "hook" in the deep recesses of the mind. If not dealt with through a concerted effort of aggressive renewal of the mind, the deep-seated lie or fear will be a magnet for a demonic spirit.

Christians who understand how the enemy works in these areas of mental abuse and deep wounds in our soul nature, should be willing to reach out in love to those who are bound or in opposition to sound theology. We endeavor to do this according the following Scripture:

2 Timothy 2:24-26

And a servant of the Lord must not quarrel but be gentle to all, able to teach, patient, in humility correcting those who are in opposition, if God perhaps will grant them repentance, so that they may know the truth, and that they may come to their senses and escape the snare of the devil, having been taken captive by him to do his will. NKJV

DWJD

- Carnal Christians who continue to oppose sound teaching from the Word of God and disobey God could eventually fall into the snare of the devil and be taken captive by him to do his will.
- Genuine repentance is required to reinstate a person who is backslidden and bound by the snare of Satan.

Forgiveness and repentance expose the enemy.
When a person embraces a lie of the enemy by holding unforgiveness, it attracts a lying entity. When they forgive those who caused the problem, there is an immediate emotional release and spiritual freedom that floods their soul. Similarly, when a person truly repents of any part they played in a major sinful act that took place either before or after coming to Christ, an emotional deliverance takes place. In both of these situations, a release from spiritual bondage takes place, and the person is loosed from any influence of a demonic spirit. If they refuse to repent, the devil will keep them in his snare. This will often result in a gradual slide towards demonization.

John's new quest.
Along with learning how to heal the sick, I was now determined to learn all I could about the unseen realm of spirits. As described in chapter 3, learning how to heal the sick was a long process. Learning about spirits became a parallel learning process. The more I learned about healing, the more the subject of spirits became evident. Divine healing operates in and through the Holy Spirit. Discerning and casting out demons also operates in and through the Holy Spirit. Both are a measurable result of the divine working of a loving God who wants His people to be free. He wants all of us (spirit, soul, and body) to be free to worship Him unencumbered.

If we pursue a healing ministry, we will eventually face demonic spirits. It just happens. Our purpose here is to crush the fear of the subject of deliverance and to equip believers to effectively deal with demonic spirits when they surface.

Ignoring demons is dangerous.

The most effective weapon our enemy uses is deception. If Satan can convince Christians to avoid the issue by ignoring what Scripture tells us about the existence of harmful spirits, then Satan wins. We have all heard comments from various Christian leaders who attempt to discredit those engaged in deliverance ministry. Likewise, we can all testify of the zealous few engaged in the fanatical excesses that give deliverance ministries a bad reputation. Pastors and leaders need to wisely inform their congregations of the existence of demons and their potential influence on Christians. Ignoring the subject allows demonic spirits to set traps for the uninformed and cause havoc within the church.

Churches are often the place troubled people look for help. We receive calls from desperate people who cannot find a Bible-based deliverance ministry in their city. It saddens us that we cannot recommend a single ministry in their area. This should not be so! This is why we are committed to establishing Ministry Training Centers (MTC) in local churches where teams of qualified people can be equipped to do this type of ministry. Skilled lay ministers can be used to relieve the already overworked salaried pastoral staff. Many churches use our MTC graduates as their prayer ministry teams and for hospital visitations. Pastors know they can trust those in their church who have been given biblical training and hands-on experience through the MTC training.

We don't know how!

We believe the hearts of Christian leaders are saying, "We don't know how! Show us an authentic approach that is biblically based, and we may consider getting involved." The

Bible is full of references where Jesus gave His followers the power and authority to loose demonic strongholds in people's lives. The promises have not passed away. We strongly advocate that Christian leaders should honestly research the subject enough to teach a balanced message regarding the existence of spirits and the influence they may have on Christians. To not teach this in the course of normal Christian discipleship will, by default, keep congregations from learning the truth about spirits. The result will most often lead to uninformed fears of the whole subject and perpetuate the myths of why we should avoid dealing with demons.

As we enter the spiritual complexities of the twenty-first century, we must equip the saints with knowledge and understanding regarding the wretched strategies of an enemy who is capturing unsuspecting Christians with lies, lust, and lascivious living.

Demonic Oppression

We cannot count how many Christians, Spirit-filled Christians, who have come to us with demonic oppression. Many times we are able to trace the source to a childhood incident of abuse or victimization by a family member or friend.

Spiritual transference.
In sexual abuse, there generally is a spiritual transference from the abuser who usually has a perverse/unclean spirit. Even though the child or young person is the innocent victim, the transference takes place. In those cases when the precious victim comes to Christ and receives salvation, they surely are forgiven of all of their confessed sins. However, until the perverse/unclean spirit has been directly addressed and commanded to leave by the power and authority of Jesus Christ, it continues to have influence in the person's life. In the case of a woman, it can be subtle; e.g., dressing slightly suggestively. Men are excessively drawn to them, and they do not know why.

264

If it is a man who has been victimized, he may turn to homo-sexuality or be enslaved to progressive levels of pornography. By that, we mean the insatiable appetite of the unclean spirit drives him from one level of perversion to another until he may be actually involved in child pornography—one of the most vile and perverted forms of sin. We have made an ob-servation that when a man and woman who have had the above-described experiences come in contact with each other, there is an unnatural magnetic drawing to one another. They cannot explain it, because it is on a spiritual level—the two demonic spirits are being drawn to each other.

Why me?

If the woman has become a Christian, but has not experi-enced deliverance from this kind of spiritual activity, she will often make comments such as:

- "I get so sick of guys staring at me and coming on to me—even supposedly happily married Christian men."
- "Why me? Why don't the guys at the office go after the younger, prettier girl I work with?"

Likewise, the man who has become a Christian but has not been set free of a skewed perspective of his sexuality will have a warped view of women and sex in general. If not dealt with, they can be prone to engage in unnatural sexual activity leading to bisexual or homosexual acts. Achieving a healthy marriage with a satisfying sexual expression becomes a dis-tant dream.

These precious souls need to be set free by the power of the blood of Jesus Christ and the authority He has given us over such evil, tormenting demonic spirits.

Wrong theology keeps some people bound.
There are many wonderful Christians who believe that demonic spirits cannot torment born-again believers. But the Word and our ministry experience prove this is a very dangerous position. If you believe that, and find yourself tormented by a spirit and no matter how much you try to stop a compelling, sinful, destructive behavior, you simply cannot, what do you do? We think that may have been what happened to a very prominent American evangelist and a very well known pastor of an evangelical megachurch in the Seattle area. If our theology disallows Christians from being delivered from demonic spirits, then those who are enslaved are without hope. We do not believe that those Christians we have described are "possessed." However, they certainly are "oppressed" of the devil and need to be set free.

Catholic priest set free.
One time we were doing a seminar on the Holy Spirit for a charismatic Catholic group. Every Friday night an older priest would stand in the back of the room and listen. We assumed he was simply monitoring our teaching. One evening, he came to the front of the room after the service and approached me (Sonja). We had been teaching about demonization, and he began a conversation about the subject. He related a recurring experience he was having at night when he went to bed. Shortly after turning the lights out, a dark and foreboding presence would come upon him, almost crushing his chest. He asked me what I thought the source could be. I immediately responded that it sounded demonic to me and asked if he would like prayer. This humble man said "yes," and John and I discreetly went with him to another room, identified the spirit, prayed a prayer of deliverance, and he was set free. The next week he returned to the meeting with a beautiful smile and a good report. The spirit had not manifested since we prayed! How gracious is our God!

Internet pornography.
With the advent of Internet pornography, many men, even Christian men (pastors, priests and leaders) have become addicted in the privacy of their offices. The progression often

goes like this: Out of curiosity, he taps onto a website, and a flood of filth pours out before him. The Holy Spirit immediately convicts him, and he may log off, but the sensual images continue to replay in his mind. Before long, he is back on line being seduced deeper and deeper into the cesspool. All the while, the Holy Spirit is talking with him, warning him, grieving over his behavior. It is likely that all the man would have to do to be set free at this time would be to cry out to God. He would need to truly repent (turn from it), tell his wife and another man for accountability, and immediately install a foolproof filter on his computer. We see in 1 John that we must confess our sins to experience forgiveness and to be purified from this kind of unrighteous behavior.

1 John 1:8-10

If we claim to be without sin, we deceive ourselves and the truth is not in us. If we confess our sins, he is faithful and just and will forgive us our sins and purify us from all unrighteousness. If we claim we have not sinned, we make him out to be a liar and his word has no place in our lives. NIV

Repentance is required to be converted to Christ. Repentance is also necessary to stay free. Failure to continue repenting from sin gives demons permission to invade our mind.

What happens when a man ignores the Holy Spirit?

If the man ignores the conviction of the Holy Spirit and he continues in his sinful behavior, at a certain juncture a perverse/unclean spirit *has a right* to attach itself to the man in that area of his life. Now the behavior has become compulsive, and the man cannot stop! He is now under the influence of that evil spirit and more often than not, the perverse spirit's companion, the lying spirit, also invades his personality. He is now enslaved in sin and must have the power of those spirits broken over his life. Otherwise, it will be a downward spiral ending in destruction.

What is the mission of the Christian?

Christians need to be educated about spirits and how they work. Jesus expected His followers to accept the challenge He set before them. The first thing all Christians must learn is the mission that Jesus set before us. When we understand where and what we are commissioned to do, we can begin to learn how to fulfill the requirements necessary to become a well-balanced and effective minister. We explored the obvious commands of Jesus Christ in chapter 1. In Acts, the first chapter, Jesus commands His followers not to go preach or go into the entire world until they have been baptized in the Holy Spirit. In chapter 3, we concluded that the follower of Christ who is baptized in the Holy Spirit is in a preferred position to operate in the supernatural of God. If we are to heal the sick and cast out demons, then we must be full of the Holy Spirit.

Boot Camp Discipleship

During the early disciples' three-year boot camp of learning these things, they went out simply trusting in Jesus' commands and authorization. It worked for them, even though the day of Pentecost was many months away. The Holy Spirit had not yet fully come upon them. How much more can you and I, baptized in the Holy Spirit, work miracles in Jesus' name today? This is illustrated in the next passage by Jesus sending His new recruits to the marketplace and commanding them to do things they had never done before.

Matthew 10:5-8 Mark 6:7-13

Matthew 10:5-8: These twelve *Jesus* sent out (Mark 6:7: . . . two-by-two, *and gave them power* over unclean spirits.) and *commanded* them, saying: "Do not go into the way of the Gentiles, and do not enter a city of the Samaritans. But go rather to the lost sheep of the house of Israel. And as you go, preach, saying, 'The kingdom of heaven is at hand.' Heal the sick, cleanse the lepers, raise the dead, *cast out demons*. Freely you have received, freely give." (Mark

6:12-13: So they went out and preached that people should repent. And *they cast out many demons*, and anointed with oil many who were sick, and healed them.) NKJV

DWJD

- When the Holy Spirit sends us out, we can trust His leading and His power to accomplish what He wants, whether it be healing or casting out demons.
- When we preach the Full Gospel, it will produce opportunities to heal the sick and cast out demons.
- When we preach that people should repent of sin, it may cause a "clash of kingdoms" between light and darkness.
- Those held in Satan's bondages might need demons cast out of them. We should be prepared to do this and set them free.
- We should have a bottle of anointing oil with us while ministering. It is a scriptural symbol of the presence of the Holy Spirit. Demons may openly resist the use of oil on a person. Use oil when the Holy Spirit says to.

John enters boot camp.

During the early years of attending banquets of the FGBMFI, there were plenty of opportunities to pray for all kinds of sicknesses and disease. Sometimes there were more people wanting prayer than businessmen available to pray. We had to spread out and work alone. I did not know the wisdom of Jesus' strategy of ministering with a partner, "two-by-two." A little Native American mother pulled her six-foot-three-inch, 295-pound son to where I was praying. He had the long, dark braids and was dressed in tribal-style clothing. She appeared very intent on getting her boy some serious prayer. She said, "My boy needs help. He is acting very strange. He thinks he sees things trying to get him." I laid my hands on him and began praying in tongues. With my eyes still closed, in my mind I saw a large lobster-type claw gripping his entire midsection. I opened my eyes and could not see anything, but with my eyes closed I could still see it. Then I heard the Holy Spirit say, "He is bound by a spirit."

He growled and bent over.

Up until this time, I had never tried to cast out a spirit. But, I was already into the situation and felt the Holy Spirit was helping me. So, with all the authority I could muster, I said loudly, "In the name of Jesus, I bind you, you foul spirit!" This big Indian boy let out a bloodcurdling growl and bent down, almost touching his knees. Immediately, I knew I was in over my head. I quickly looked around for help. I needed a partner, someone who knew what to do next. The big Indian remained bent over, half-groaning and half-growling.

Then I spotted Phil, got his attention, and waved him over to where I was ministering. Phil Israelson had been on a couple of airlifts to Central America, and I remembered him telling of his experiences with demonic spirits. I knew he would know what to do. I was operating in the power and authority, but did not have the experience to complete the ministry.

He got up smiling.

Phil came over and said, "What's the problem?" I said, "He's got a demon and needs your help." Phil smiled at me, turned to the young man, laid hands on his back and firmly took authority over the situation. He prayed, "In the name of Jesus Christ, I command you lying spirit to come out of him!" He did this three times. Suddenly this big guy let out a long growl, finishing with a long sigh, and fell backwards hitting the floor with a healthy thud. He laid there for about five minutes and then got up smiling. He and his mother thanked Phil and discussed what the young man needed to do to remain free. Phil led him in a prayer confirming his salvation and then led him into the Holy Spirit baptism.

After they left I thanked Phil for helping me. I was full of questions, and he gave me some very valuable tips should I find myself facing demonic activity again. It was not but a couple of months later when I again was confronted with a demonized person. This time I knew what to do. The person was set free. It worked just like Phil had taught me. Thank God for ministers who will mentor us in doing things right.

Joy comes when we experience success.

There is great satisfaction when you are part of the process of setting people free from spiritual bondages, especially Christians. We just shake our heads with compassion when we see uninformed or immature believers caught in destructive lifestyles. We see the great turmoil, oppression, and agony they are facing. They are unable to shake themselves loose from what is binding them. They are desperate. They have tried everything, and nothing seems to work. They pray and pray without relief. Though people under the influence of demonic spirits can function well at work and even at home, the bondage disallows them to function in a specific area of their personal life. It is a great privilege to know and understand that, in Christ, the demons are subject to us and they must obey our commands to loose these people in the name of Jesus Christ.

The seventy passed the test.

The seventy had been with Jesus for quite awhile. They watched how He healed the sick and cast out demons. They were finishing their boot camp discipleship and now were being sent forth to try out their new authority and power. It was working!

Luke 10:17-20

Then the seventy returned with joy, saying, "Lord, even the demons are subject to us in Your name." And He said to them, "I saw Satan fall like lightning from heaven. Behold, I give you the *authority* to trample on serpents and scorpions, and over *all* the power of the enemy, and nothing shall by any means

271

hurt you. Nevertheless do not rejoice in this, that *the spirits are subject to you,* but rather rejoice because your names are written in heaven." NKJV

DWJD

- The seventy learned by doing. They practiced what Jesus had taught them. They discovered the awesome authority they had in the name of Jesus.
- We, too, can do what Jesus said we could do. We have to be bold and step out and exercise our authority in Christ. Though we may read about our authority, until we practice the authority we will never experience it.
- Demons are subject to us! Demons bow to the name of Jesus spoken from our mouths.
- We have nothing to fear. Jesus said we have authority over *all* the power of the enemy.
- We are to accept our commission to cast out demons without rejoicing about it. We are to get the job done in faith and then rejoice that our names are recorded in heaven. We can rejoice all the more when the people we set free live for Jesus and join us in heaven.

We need a personal revelation of this.

Luke 10:17-20 is what we refer to as one of the "heavy–revies" in Scripture. When we get the revelation that we are encouraged to personalize this passage as meaning "I have authority," it changes our perception as to how we approach the spirit world. Instead of fearing the subject, we embrace our responsibility to appropriate the authority given to us by Jesus Christ and become available to set others free. Some commentators interpret "serpents and scorpions" as referring to all categories of demonic spirits. It is very comforting to know as believers, we have *all* authority over all serpents, scorpions, and over all the power of our enemy, Satan. All demonic spirits are subject to us. This means they must obey our commands spoken in the name of Jesus. We are not to rejoice about all of this. We are to accept it, act on it, and use this authority and power whenever demonic spirits surface in people.

We must remain balanced as we rejoice.

It can be very easy to become enthralled with the whole subject of demons. Our destiny is not to be focused on the temporal conquering of the enemy and casting him out of people. Jesus said to focus on the destination of eternal salvation with Him. We are to rejoice that our names are written in heaven. Our destiny is to be in glory with the Lord of lords. Our *reason* for setting people free of spiritual bondages is to pave the way for them to also have a place in heaven. Then we both can rejoice!

It is all in the Name.

Regardless of whether you belong to a denomination or not, your authority and power to cast out demons are totally wrapped up in the name of Jesus Christ as we see in the following Scriptures:

> **Mark 9:38-41**   Luke 9:49-50
>
> Now John answered Him, saying, "Teacher, we saw someone who does not follow us casting out demons in Your name, and we forbade him because he does not follow us." But Jesus said, "Do not forbid him, for no one who works a miracle in My name can soon afterward speak evil of Me. For he who is not against us is on our side. For whoever gives you a cup of water to drink in My name, because you belong to Christ, assuredly, I say to you, he will by no means lose his reward." NKJV

DWJD

- Jesus confirms that His name is the final authority for the working of miracles. In this context, Jesus includes casting out demons along with serving others in any capacity as part of the "works" we are to do.

273

- If you witness other ministers of another church or denomination who are casting out demons successfully in the name of Jesus, do not criticize them.
- We must not become proud or promote an air of exclusiveness about how we set people free. Ministry styles and methods we may use are secondary to the goal of successfully setting people free from spiritual bondages.
- Always examine the fruit. Are lives being redeemed from bondages of addictions and habitual sin? Are the deliverance teams truly effective? Are people staying free? Are lives being dramatically changed? Is Jesus receiving all the glory?

Training starts by experiencing it.

During one of the weekend retreats for FGBMFI in the mid-1970s, I (John) witnessed some businessmen trying to set a man free of demonic spirits. I was passing through a lounge area where I witnessed what seemed to be an argument brewing between three men. Two men were quoting Scriptures to a third man who was not buying what they were selling. It stemmed from a disagreement about the Holy Spirit. As a fairly new Christian, I sat down to listen to see what I could learn. Suddenly the third man (who I will call Joe) turned on the other two, hunched over, and with a frightening growl, screamed, "You will never convince me. I hate all of you!" With that, the others immediately fired back, "We bind you, you foul demon. We command you to loose this man and come out of him!" I quickly got behind the two guys doing the commanding and watched what happened next.

Joe dropped to the floor in a crouched position and dared the other two to take him on. Joe said, "You are lying. I have power over you! Don't come any closer." By this time, other men gathered around the commotion. The guys on my side yelled, "Satan, you are the liar. We bind you, and command you to release this man, in the name of Jesus!"

The men grabbed him by the arms in an effort to subdue him and put him in a chair. With amazing superhuman strength, Joe quickly threw both men into a pile on the floor. This was remarkable because Joe looked to be no more than 150 pounds. The other two were big men.

Joe snarled.

Joe snarled at the rest of us, daring anyone to take him on. We all backed away not knowing what to do. The other two guys got up a little confused, wanting to re-engage but seemed reluctant. Joe quickly turned towards the door, left the building, got in his car, and left the retreat. We were all shaking our heads, discussing what went wrong, and why Joe was not delivered of the demon.

We later found out that he had come to the retreat under protest because of the insistence of a Christian co-worker. He was deep into satanic rituals and the martial arts and liked the powers that Satan was granting him. He did not want to be "delivered." He liked the demonic powers that allowed him to control others. This early episode again convinced me that the demonic realm was real and that I needed better training to properly deal with spirits should I happen to encounter them.

Who Are You Going to Call?

When I (John) was the area director for the regional 700 Club Crisis Counseling Center in the Seattle area, I trained over one hundred telephone counselors to competently handle everything from salvation to suicide. It was a wonderfully productive time of training and ministry. Early on, it became apparent that I needed a way to train the counselors how to discern and deal with demonic activity. Many of the counselors had family members and friends that they suspected were demonized and there was no place to take them for ministry. The churches in our area were ill prepared to handle people with serious spiritual bondages. After researching the subject, I decided to use the late Dr. Lester Sumrall's video course, "Demonology and Deliverance." After I had thoroughly trained a dozen people, I organized them into three teams. I then developed an extensive interview process for those people seeking deliverance. It worked very well.

Here are some of the things we learned:

- Only about half of the people who were interviewed truly needed deliverance. Most needed to repent of common habitual sins that held them captive.
- The half that truly needed deliverance received ministry and were, almost without exception, set free. One exception was a professional man who was set free of several spirits, but refused to complete the deliverance by forgiving his wife and reconciling with her. His spiritual condition today is as bad or worse than before.
- Many of the spiritual conditions were a result of unconfessed sin, unforgiveness, and just plain ignorance of biblical principles.
- Physiological conditions can produce behaviors that are *exactly* like demonic manifestations. It is crucial that the ministers of deliverance operate in the supernatural gifts of discerning of spirits, and/or words of knowledge and wisdom. Otherwise, they will be in danger of trying to exorcise demons that do not exist. Well-meaning, but misinformed ministers have afflicted much damage upon precious people by trying to cast out demons where there were none.
- We attempt to eliminate the possibility that a person's condition is physiological. We strongly advise a complete medical examination before inquiring into possible spiritual problems.
- Take time to properly arrange for an appointment to meet in a comfortable room away from the hearing of other people. Though we advise not allowing spirits to shriek or shout, they can surprise us at times.
- Always conduct deliverance with a team of trusted Christians that are mature and operate in the revelation gifts.

Desperate parents need help.

Today's youth are subjecting themselves to demonic spirits found in drugs, alcohol, witchcraft, promiscuous sex, and rebellion against any kind of authority. The woman from Canaan had a daughter who was subjected to these kinds of demonic spirits. Jesus shows us what to do in this next passage of Scripture:

Matthew 15:21-28 Mark 7:24-30

Matthew 15:21-28: Then Jesus went out from there and departed to the region of Tyre and Sidon. (Mark 7:24: . . . And He entered a house and wanted no one to know it, but He could not be hidden.) And behold, a woman of Canaan came from that region (Mark 7:25: . . . whose young daughter had an unclean spirit heard about Him, and she came and fell at His feet.) and cried out to Him, saying, "Have mercy on me, O Lord, Son of David! My daughter is severely demon-possessed." (Mark 7:26: . . . and she kept asking Him to cast the demon out of her daughter.)

But He answered her not a word. And His disciples came and urged Him, saying, "Send her away, for she cries out after us." But He answered and said, "I was not sent except to the lost sheep of the house of Israel." Then she came and worshiped Him, saying, "Lord, help me!" But He answered and said, "It is not good to take the children's bread and throw it to the little dogs." And she said, "Yes, Lord, yet even the little dogs eat the crumbs which fall from their masters' table." Then Jesus answered and said to her, "O woman, great is your faith!" (Mark 7:29: . . . "For this saying go your way; the demon has gone out of your daughter.") "Let it be to you as you desire." (Mark 7:30: And when she had come to her house, she found the demon gone out, and her daughter lying on the bed.) And her daughter was healed from that very hour. NKJV

DWJD

- When people from other churches discover a team of reputable Christians that are having success in deliverance they will go to great lengths to find them.
- When people are willing to submit to Jesus Christ, His Word, and the leading of the Holy Spirit, they are eligible to be set free and receive the blessings of God.
- When all the conditions of the Holy Spirit are met, and the ministry is complete, we proclaim the same words Jesus used: "Go your way, the demon is gone!" The demons leave because of the authority and power granted by Jesus Christ.

They came on a Thursday.

After training three teams to conduct deliverances at The 700 Club, we set up appointments for the friends and acquaintances of the team members. Around The 700 Club offices, Thursday became known as "demon day." We would only take one appointment in the morning and one in the afternoon. We gathered behind closed doors and began the interview process. Those who had completed the Sumrall video course were allowed to join in the appointments as part of their training. We would take up to two hours to thoroughly discuss any and all possible "entrance points" where an entity might have gained entrance into the person's soul nature.

The questions were so probing and specific that if the person did have a demon oppressing them it would manifest during the interview process. When it was determined the person truly had a demonic entity troubling them, we would make additional appointments until they were completely free. It would normally take a second, two-hour session to cast out whatever spirits the Holy Spirit identified. Deliverances were always done in a very professional and closely monitored fashion. The team members have since gone on to very productive ministries on their own.

The woman in a wheelchair.

We were surprised by a demon during one of our Thursday deliverance appointments at The 700 Club offices. We were ministering to a precious Christian lady who was confined to a wheelchair because of a spinal birth defect. She seemed normal in most respects though she was slow of speech. She had to rely on others to help her with daily routines of living. During the interview process, we discovered an unclean spirit had tormented her since puberty. She began to weep uncontrollably as she tried to tell the deliverance team of a horrific experience with a young man who had raped her repeatedly during those early years. The Holy Spirit revealed that we were faced with an unclean spirit of lustful perversion that had a stronghold in her mind and body. When we addressed this spirit to come out of her, the demon screamed so loud that the offices above and below could hear it. It was the most bloodcurdling scream I had ever heard. We immediately took authority over the spirit and commanded it to be quiet while we ministered to her. It took one other appointment to set her free. The lesson we learned from this event was to immediately do what Jesus did. He said, "*Be quiet* and come out of her." We know why He said that.

Victory was achieved.

During that year and a half, I gained several insights regarding how spirits attach themselves to those vulnerable to Satan's deceptions. These became evident during my oversight of the Thursday deliverance sessions. The experiences both Sonja and I have had are invaluable to what we are teaching about the subject today. We have absolutely no fear of demons. The Holy Spirit has always been gracious to lead us into total victory when we came face to face with powerful demonic forces. Here are some of the more valuable lessons we learned:

- Focus on Christians that are having severe spiritual problems.

- Pre-Christians need to repent and accept Jesus Christ as Lord before anything can be done for them.
- The person needing deliverance should be the one to call for help. If they are personally unwilling to come in for an interview, go no further.
- Never allow the friends of the person to rush you into it. Take sufficient time to interview and probe for what may have caused the person's condition.
- Get all the facts surrounding the person's history before committing to an appointment for deliverance.
- If possible, talk to their parents, siblings, close friends, and any Christian that really knows the person. The person should be informed that you are talking to these people. A phone call is all that is needed.
- Use terminology such as "personal prayer" instead of "deliverance" to the family or friends of the person receiving ministry.
- Completely rule out physiological or medical problems, such as a bipolar condition, by insisting on a thorough medical examination before going any further.
- Deliverance should never be viewed as a "quick fix" to a person's spiritual instability. Deliverance should be considered the first step, allowing a person to fully grasp dependence on the Lord Jesus Christ.
- Successful deliverance requires follow-up. Long-term, personal accountability will be needed for the person to stay free. They need resolve to not revisit the same people or situations that caused the problem in the first place.
- We suggest a Spirit-filled and very mature prayer partner to meet with the person regularly for about a year or more.

Monkey Temple experience.
Here in America we are seeing a rise of demonic worship, and it produces fear-based results. I (Sonja) had a recent conversation with a Spirit-filled Christian who attends our church here in Bend, Oregon. She had been a New Age devotee before coming to Christ. She related how she would visit a

Monkey Temple in the Southwest USA. The reason for going was to seek further enlightenment about the supernatural realm. Her little daughter would begin crying uncontrollably the moment they would enter the temple. Finally, this mother was able to find out why her little one was so terrified. She said, "Mommy, can't you see those ugly things flying through the air around the monkey? They hate us and want to kill us." Apparently this child had a perception into the spirit world, and the Lord used this to put a stop to the visits into that demon-infested temple.

Stay out of those temples!
Uninformed Christians are an easy target when their curiosity leads them to visit satanic, Buddhist, Hindu, or Islamic temples. As mentioned before, we cannot stress enough how dangerous it is to visit such places of concentrated demonic activity. One time, I (Sonja) had a young mother of twins come to me and explain that she had some extremely tormenting and scary spiritual activity going on in her life. I asked her if she could recall when it began. She immediately responded by telling me that it began the very night after a visit to the Church of Satan while she was attending university in San Francisco. She and her girlfriends had decided to go as a lark—they were not seeking spirituality, they just did it out of curiosity and boredom. What a tragic mistake! Apparently, some spiritual entity (demonic spirit) attached itself to her. She was constantly tormented with fear and horrible nightmares.

I know who you are, and I hate you!
I discerned the presence of spirits and asked her if she truly wanted to be set free. She responded with, "Yes, more than anything! When?" I set up an appointment for the following week. There were three pastors, one of their wives, and myself as a ministry team. We went into a prayer room, sat in a circle, and began to pray. This woman immediately lost consciousness and slowly slipped to the floor. She was out like a light. We began to address the spirits, and the most horrible man's voice began to speak through her even though she was

not conscious. "I know who you are, and I hate you!" the demon hissed. We commanded it to be quiet, and it then began to violently throw the woman around on the floor. It took all three pastors, who were big men, to restrain her.

After about ten minutes, the spirits were gone. We then called her by name, and she began to regain consciousness. She did not remember a thing, but she knew something wonderful had happened. Her black, naturally curly hair was wet with perspiration and she was exhausted. We led her into a complete understanding of repentance and salvation in the Lord Jesus Christ and the power in His blood that was shed on the cross. She was completely set free that day. Praise God for the power over Satan's minions!

The Exorcist.
When John was the area director for The 700 Club Crisis Counseling Center in Bellevue, Washington, he had a young family man who was in such a place financially that he could volunteer forty hours a week at the center. He was well educated, a pilot, and a faithful, Spirit-filled Christian. His family attended Eastside Foursquare Church with us. As we got to know them better, he shared a bizarre story with us.

When he was younger, he loved to attend horror movies. He loved the adrenaline rush and the gorier, the better. However, something happened that radically changed his life forever when he attended the movie, "The Exorcist." During the movie, he experienced something that literally scared him to within an inch of his life. He could feel a real presence pressing on his chest. As he tried to shake it off and could not, an ominous fear gripped him and left him literally terrified! He was sure it would leave him as soon as he left the movie theatre, but it did not.

The fear would almost suffocate him.
Every night when he would turn out the lights to go to sleep, this demonic presence would press in on him. The fear would almost suffocate him, and he would scream out and turn the lights on. He thought he was losing his mind, and he began crying out for understanding. God revealed Himself to him through a series of situations, and he accepted the Lord and was eventually set free from the spirit of fear. We share this story as a warning to those innocent people who attend movies like "The Exorcist."

"Psycho" caught me off guard.
I (Sonja) remember attending a movie when I was in high school called "Psycho," featuring Anthony Perkins. I had no idea what it was about, and was completely caught off guard and emotionally unprepared for the shower scene where Vivian Leigh was stabbed to death. This impacted my psyche so badly that for years I would not take a shower when I was home alone at night. Now I know that is stupid, but it shows how something like that can imprint upon our emotions for our entire life. I am concerned about the long-term negative effects of some of the movies and TV episodes that children watch. Let us be wise to the ways of the enemy!

Spirits Visit Our Churches

Precious people who attend our churches may carry entities of "shadows from their past" that still plague them. They have learned to suppress the stronghold because they feel there is no way to get rid of it. They have learned to "gut it out" and cope with the feelings it produces. As leaders, we must realize that these precious people need help but they do not know where to get it. The best they know what to do is attend church in hopes that God will somehow intervene. When the awesome presence of the Holy Spirit manifests during worship or anointed preaching, it may cause these spirits to come to the surface. We should have a plan in place to deal with the inevitability of such an event.

They manifest at very inconvenient times.

Demonic spirits always seem to manifest at very inconvenient times. Their mission is to cause confusion and interrupt what the Holy Spirit is doing. They can manifest in classrooms, home meetings, and church services. They appear in the USA and in every country where we minister. People used to think "all the demons are in Africa," but we know they can be found anyplace where there are human beings! The following story should give us some insight about how to deal with demons when they manifest in our church services.

Mark 1:23-27 Luke 4:33-35

Mark 1:23-27: Now there was a man in their synagogue with an unclean spirit. And he cried out, saying, "Let us alone! What have we to do with You, Jesus of Nazareth? Did You come to destroy us? I know who You are—the Holy One of God!" But Jesus rebuked him, saying, "Be quiet, and come out of him!" And when the unclean spirit had convulsed him and cried out with a loud voice, he came out of him. (Luke 4:35: . . . And when the demon had thrown him in their midst, it came out of him and did not hurt him.) Then they were all amazed, so that they questioned among themselves, saying, "What is this? What new doctrine is this? For with authority He commands even the unclean spirits, and they obey Him." NKJV

DWJD

It is interesting that the person with an unclean spirit was in church (synagogue). Though extremely rare in North America, we may have to contend with demonized guests who may visit our services. Jesus teaches us how to confront the spirit that is attempting to disrupt a church service. Like Jesus, the person in charge of the service needs to do the following:

- Quickly and firmly rebuke the spirit that is talking through the person by saying, "Sir/Madame, I forbid you to speak!" This will normally "bind" the person from causing any more disruption.
- Do not engage in any conversation with the person whatsoever.
- Instruct the ushers to tactfully escort the person from the sanctuary and take them to a room with closed doors.
- Begin the deliverance with an experienced team. This is when they would say, "Come out of him/her."
- Be aware that demonic spirits want to distract worshipers and to turn their attention to them and away from Jesus. They may manifest in a *loud* challenge any time the presence of the Holy Spirit is manifesting.
- Remain calm and operate in the firm confidence and authority of Jesus Christ.
- Deal with the person, telling them to be quiet rather than allowing a worse commotion by having the ushers drag the person screaming from the sanctuary. A very firm, "Be quiet in Jesus' name," is usually all that is needed.

It happened in our classroom.

One time John was teaching our Ministry Training Centers class at Eastside Foursquare Church in Bothell, Washington. This particular lesson was in our advanced curriculum and was dealing with breaking spiritual bondages. The Holy Spirit gave him a word of knowledge about someone in the class being oppressed by a spirit of fear. He no sooner got the word out of his mouth than a woman in the class began shrieking and crying. The spirit then went into full manifestation. John immediately went to the woman, and still in an instructor's mode, took authority over the spirit, and cast it out of the woman. It was beautiful how the women sitting around this precious soul ministered to her after she was set free. It so happened that we were video taping all of our classes at that time, so the entire incident was caught on film!

She was a Christian.
The Lord has been gracious over the years to illustrate what we are teaching by real-life examples. We are humbled by His graciousness to our students and us by being faithful to demonstrate His power with signs and wonders following the teaching of the Word. The above incident clearly illustrates how Christians can be oppressed of the devil and need deliverance. This woman had been in our class for over six months. She was saved and had been filled with the Holy Spirit. We knew she had some deep hurts from devastating life experiences, but we had not discerned the spirit that was ruling a big part of her life. It was through the supernatural gift of a word of knowledge that the Lord directed her deliverance from this tormenting spirit of fear that had been in her life for years. How gracious is our God!

Spirits want to return.
Once a person is set free, we must help them stay free. Jesus encourages us to fill the house totally (body, soul, and spirit) with the Spirit of God. They must daily renew their minds with the Word of God and pray in their spiritual languages at every opportunity. They also need to fellowship weekly with healthy, Spirit-filled Christians. Jesus illustrates this in the following Scriptures:

> **Matthew 12:43-45** Luke 11:24-26
> "When an unclean spirit goes out of a man, he goes through dry places, seeking rest, and finds none. Then he says, 'I will return to my house from which I came.' And when he comes, he finds it empty, swept, and put in order. Then he goes and takes with him seven other spirits more wicked than himself, and they enter and dwell there; and the last state of that man is worse than the first. So shall it also be with this wicked generation." NKJV

- Dry, waterless places are very difficult to define. Scholars shed very little understanding of what "arid or dry places" mean. There seems to be a consensus that it may mean a totally uninhabitable desert-like place that is desolate and without animal or human habitation. Such a description is given to the fallen city of Babylon as a dwelling place for demons in Revelation 18:2.
- Confirming a person's salvation and leading them into the Holy Spirit baptism will ensure they are full of the Holy Spirit.
- If we neglect to do this, the person is extremely vulnerable to the same entities that held them in bondage. Demons try to return and bring even more spirits with them.

He began to growl.
One Tuesday evening during our home group meeting, we were teaching about the Holy Spirit baptism. Several attendees had indicated interest the previous week, and had asked us to lead them into the experience. After we had thoroughly taught on the subject, we asked those who wanted to receive the gift of the Holy Spirit and their spiritual language to come over to the dining room area. Four women and a man responded. As we began to lay hands on them and pray, the man began growling in an ugly guttural voice. He doubled over as the spirit manifested. I (Sonja) was standing next to him, so I was the first to see what was happening.

Whoops, there is a spirit here.
John was on the other side of the room, so I quickly went to him and whispered, "We have a spirit manifesting over there." He went to the man and quickly discerned it was a lying spirit. It was telling him he was not worthy to receive this gift, and as he tried to respond to our teaching, the spirit showed itself. John dealt with the spirit in the mighty name of Jesus Christ, and it left. It was a great teaching time for our group,

most of whom had never witnessed a spirit acting out in a person's life.

I am scared of that "demon stuff."

The humorous thing about this evening was a woman had said to her husband on the way to the meeting that night, "Honey, I hope I am never around when that 'demon stuff' happens. I think it would scare me to death." However, afterwards she relayed how she was so grateful that she was able to observe the whole incident because it dispelled her fears. She said it was the most natural thing she could ever imagine. The evil spirit manifested in an ugly way, but the power of the name of Jesus Christ simply took authority over it and it left. Easy as that! She was amazed.

Leadership couple seeks deliverance.

While ministering to leaders in a central California church, we opened a discussion on how unclean spirits can gain a foothold in our lives. We mentioned how they have a lifetime to play hide-and-seek until they have established a firm stronghold, causing people to lie and deceive. To our amazement, a leadership couple came to John after the service. He told John he had experienced exactly what we had described, and how he had begun lying to his wife about the sinful behavior. His dear wife was at her wit's end. John got one of the pastors to minister with him, and they set this young man free from the perverse and lying spirits in the name of Jesus Christ. Then they established accountability in the young man's life; and the last we checked, he was doing great.

As is often the case, John learned that an uncle had molested him when he was younger and had always had a leaning toward pornography, but the total enslavement came when he kept indulging the impulse via the Internet. Then one day he discovered he could not stop, even when he understood the horrific ramifications of living in willful sin and possibly losing his precious wife.

Willful sin is dangerous.

This life story demonstrates what happens in demonic bondage. It can be alcohol, drugs, shoplifting, lying, gossiping, and similar destructive behaviors. It is extremely dangerous for a Christian to continue in willful sin. It has been said of sin that it always takes you further than you wanted to go, keeps you longer than you wanted to stay, costs you more than you wanted to pay, and damages you more than you ever imagined. It can have eternal consequences.

If you are reading this and you feel what we have described has happened to you, please seek help immediately from a pastor who understands this spiritual dimension and how to exercise God-given authority so that you may be set free. The minister needs to have the supernatural revelation gifts of the Holy Spirit operating in his life if he is to be effective in this type of ministry.

Obscene Phone Calls and Mental Hospitals

One day a dear friend called me (Sonja) and related a heartbreaking story. His father had been fired from a job he loved, and, as a consequence, had lost a large part of his retirement benefits. My friend lived in another state and asked me if I would visit his devastated parents who lived in my city. It was a difficult thing for me to do. I had known this couple since I was in high school and had always had great respect for them.

After greeting this older couple with hugs and tears, the most pitiful story unfolded. It was painful for them and me as he answered my respectful, but probing questions. He had indulged in pornographic material for years, but something had happened the previous year that changed his life forever. He had begun to make filthy telephone calls to women. Before too long, the police had traced the calls to him at his workplace. No one wanted to press charges because he was so well liked and respected at this place of employment. He was simply given a verbal warning.

Within a matter of days he made more calls. Of course, he was caught red-handed and given a written warning that if this happened again they would terminate his employment. They explained all of the ramifications of vesting in retirement plans, health insurance, etc. They offered to send him to a psychiatrist. He refused the offer for help. They told him his telephone was under surveillance; but to my utter amazement, he said he went ahead and made more obscene telephone calls. By this time, his precious little wife was weeping uncontrollably, and I was having trouble believing this incredible story.

He continued his story. The police came to his place of employment and arrested him on the spot in front of his coworkers. He was immediately terminated with the resultant financial loss. There was an article in the local newspaper, and the humiliation and shame were almost more than they could bear.

He said he was "under its spell."

When I asked him why in the world he went ahead and made those final calls even knowing that his telephone was being monitored, he said a very revealing thing:

> "I knew in my mind that this would ruin my life, my marriage, my retirement. I also realized it would bring shame on my children, but I could not resist the compulsion to make the calls. It was as if something came upon me at those times, and I was under its spell and I was powerless to resist."

That describes the state of a person under demonic influence. The poor man was not ready to hear the Good News of salvation and deliverance through Jesus Christ, but his little wife was, and she re-dedicated herself to the Lord that night. Sad to say, he lived many more years under the torment of that evil spirit and did not truly repent and accept the Lord until he was on his deathbed. What a waste! Living all of those years under Satan's power. Yet, God's unbelievable love and mercy are extended "to such a wretch as I!"

Generational spirits.
We have all heard the expression: "He has a horrible temper, just like his father." All families pass on habits, characteristics and behaviors, but familiar spirits can also pass from one generation to another if they go undetected.

In the case I just described, this unclean spirit was most likely passed along to his son, our friend. Even though he was a Spirit-filled Christian, he had never dealt with this fascination he had with pornography, primarily magazines and videos. But, because he continued in willful disobedience to God, the very same thing happened to him! He was arrested for making obscene telephone calls and fired from his job. Unbelievable as it seems, knowing what happened to his father, he did the same thing. This soon followed his addiction to Internet porn.

I said they should immediately come to our home.
After his arrest, his wife called me (Sonja) and I said they should immediately come to our home (we live in another state). They responded to our invitation and arrived within hours of our phone call. The man was a highly respected person in their community, and this was a devastating blow to him, his wife, family, work associates, and friends. He appeared to be in an emotional meltdown when he arrived. His wife was in a state of shock and trying to make her decision of whether to initiate divorce proceedings.

We called our associate minister and, after determining that our friend's repentance was deep and genuine, John and our associate led him through a complete and thorough deliverance. It was an amazing transformation before our very eyes.

We earnestly prayed for wisdom from on high.
All the while, I (Sonja) was with the wife, helping her process the unbelievable pain she was experiencing. She told me of

losing respect for her mother-in-law when she did not leave her husband when he was arrested and fired for his out-of-control behavior. And now she was facing the very same circumstances! We talked about how deliverance works and that restoration was possible. She wanted to believe, but it was difficult to imagine how such a horrific breach could be healed. We earnestly prayed for wisdom from on high.

Totally free.
The deliverance was complete and total. They did everything we recommended, including getting into a good Spirit-filled church. Now, a couple of years later, they are totally and completely free and healed. Their marriage is the best it has ever been. They are serving God with everything they have. What a victory! What a joy! Only our God could perform such a miracle!

Our friend ended up in the mental ward.
A friend of ours has a bipolar condition, and if he does not take his medication, he becomes delusional. One such time, he ended up in the psychiatric ward of a local hospital. His family called and asked us to go see him. They told us of the delusions he was having about the FBI following him, watching his every move, and getting ready to arrest him. He was paranoid to the point that he was afraid to go to work.

He was glad to see us, but was still suffering from the paranoia. We began talking with him about what he was experiencing. We looked him right in the eyes and told him we knew these things were absolutely real *to him*, that he would likely pass a lie detector test if he took one, but *nonetheless* they were not so. We did not discern any spirits, but sensed it was truly a physical problem that produced the abnormal mental behaviors.

There were no FBI agents chasing him.
This man loved and trusted us, but it was so hard for him to believe that *his reality* was not so. We reinforced what the doctors and his family were telling him, that the medication

would put him back in touch with the reality we all were experiencing—there were no FBI agents chasing him. After a few weeks on the medication, he was fine again. He is a brilliant man and does not like the medication because it seems to slow down some of his mental functions. We think that is why people with this and similar conditions quit taking their prescriptions. The appropriate response at this juncture is to pray for healing, which we are doing for our friend. It seems that spirits do not respond to medication, but physical problems do.

The movie, "A Beautiful Mind," released in 2002, is a wonderful true story about John Nash, the brilliant mathematician. It portrays how he coped with his condition and was awarded the Nobel Prize. We pray this insightful film will raise our nation's consciousness and understanding of the precious people who suffer with these conditions.

A Baptist Girl Learns About Demons

After I (Sonja) was baptized in the Holy Spirit in 1965, I immediately became a serious student of the Bible. It had become alive and totally relevant. One unlikely subject for a Baptist girl to study was demonization, yet I was fascinated by the New Testament accounts of this supernatural activity. I read everything I could find that related to this other-dimension realm. They were mostly accounts by missionaries in Third World countries.

They told me I should leave all of that weird stuff alone.
One time my pastors stopped by for a quick visit, and they noticed the stack of books I was reading. After glancing at the titles, they told me I should leave all of that weird stuff alone. No good would come of it. I was surprised at their adamant and adverse reaction to the subject of the supernatural, so I thought I had better listen to them. I put the books aside for a couple of weeks and asked the Lord to lead me in the matter.

The Holy Spirit as "The Teacher" was leading me.
Not only did the interest remain, it dramatically increased. Looking back, I was being led by the Holy Spirit as "The Teacher." It was good that I had listened to the cautions of my pastors because I became extremely critical of everything I read. Could I find biblical-based correlations in the Bible? If not, I was very suspect of the accounts. By this time I had read the Bible through several times, and had learned to utilize good study aids, including an interlinear Greek–English New Testament. If anything, I always erred on the more conservative side of theology, and I felt comfortable there.

I was being prepared for a very special assignment.
Little did I know that I was being prepared for a very special assignment—one I would not have dreamed of in a million years! My precious Grammy Hatcher was thrilled at my spiritual growth since I had been baptized in the Holy Spirit. She was my biggest fan and was amazed how easily I was leading people into the Holy Spirit baptism.

One day, Grammy called me and asked if I would be willing to meet with her good friend's son who had just returned to Richland, Washington after a drug-filled lifestyle in the Seattle area. I could not imagine what I could say to a young man addicted to drugs—I was as straight as could be!

I asked her why she thought I should do this, and she explained that the young man had been walking in downtown Seattle, and he was literally struck down on the sidewalk and could not move. He said he knew it was God telling him he was soon going to be dead if he did not get right with Him. He had immediately returned home to a praying mother who arranged for him to meet with her Pentecostal pastor. Apparently it was not a good experience for either of them, and his mother was desperate for someone to help her son. Thus, the call came from my Grammy.

The body art on his arms really caught my eye!

I reluctantly agreed to meet with the young man the next Saturday afternoon. My Grammy, his mother, and my Saturday morning prayer group were interceding for this most unusual appointment. At the appointed time the doorbell rang, and I opened the door to a most unusual sight. The young man that stood towering over me was in his early twenties, six-feet tall, long blond hair, and the most beautiful, big blue *empty* eyes I had ever seen. The fluorescent pink body art on his arms really caught my eye! I am sure he was also sizing me up and thinking what in the world would this obviously super-straight little woman have to say that would be relevant to his life.

The Holy Spirit came upon me in a most unusual way.

I asked him to have a seat and tell me what was happening in his life. He was understandably nervous and began to relate the sidewalk encounter with God. While he was speaking, the Holy Spirit came upon me in a most unusual way. I was totally immersed in God's agape love for this young man. My heart cried out, "Dear Lord, how many of these lost young people are out there? They are on their way to hell and without hope in a hostile world. No wonder they are medicating themselves with drugs, sex, or who knows what else!"

Somehow, through God's extravagant grace, we connected. I felt his fear and confusion, and he felt God's love emanating from me. All of a sudden he jumped up, startling me, and he said, "Lady, you put out the most far-out vibes I have ever felt! May I come back and bring a couple of friends?" "Well, uh, sure," I muttered in complete dismay.

I later learned that they were big drug dealers.

He did return with two friends that I later learned were big drug dealers in our area. Within a couple of weeks the group had grown to around thirty, and it was an unbelievable sight. They were having genuine encounters with the living Christ by truly repenting, turning their back on drugs, and seeking to please their new Lord. One night, I looked around my living and dining rooms that were full of hippie-type kids sitting on every available space of carpet. They all had their Bibles out and were discussing what Jesus meant by a certain passage. I had to laugh, because the house was full of smoke. Many churchgoing folks would have thrown up their hands in disgust if they had walked in at that moment. What they would not have realized is just how far these kids had come in a matter of weeks. Smoking cigarettes was a pretty minor thing at this point.

My house was staked out!
A few weeks after that, one of the former drug dealers came to me during one of our smoke-filled gatherings and asked me if I knew that the police had staked out my house. "What! Why would they do that?" I asked. He told me to just think about it for a moment. All of a sudden the biggest drug dealers and users in the area are carrying around big black Bibles and congregating in a certain home several times a week. Would you not find that of interest if you were the police? I smacked my forehead with my palm, and marveled at how naive I was. I had been thrust into an entirely new culture.

I have already run narcs into your group.
I called the parents of one of the kids and asked if they would go with me if I got an appointment with the chief of police. They indicated they would, and I called for the appointment. Surprisingly, we were given an appointment the next afternoon. I had never personally met the chief of police. All I knew was that he had a good reputation in our town. As his secretary showed us into his office, we were shocked as he stood up, walked around his desk, and put out his hand. "Before you say anything," he began, "I want you to know I am a born-again Christian, and I believe what is happening at your home is the only hope for the youth of our community! I know this because I have already run narcs into your group, and the reports are most positive. They don't understand all the religious stuff, but they said it is wholesome." I stood there shaking this wonderful man's hand with my

mouth hanging open. When our group became too large to meet in homes, the Police Department gave us four hundred dollars to pay the rent on our first meeting place. What an amazing thing!

My special assignment.

Now, for the aspects of my special assignment for which I had been training without even knowing it. Most of these kids were from middle-to-upper class homes. They had attended church at some point in their lives, but it was not relevant. Being disillusioned with life in general, they were easy prey for experimenting with drugs and the associated breakdown of all morals. Stealing to support their ever-increasing drug habits became the norm. The ones who had used the hallucinogenic drugs were in a pitiful state.

As they came to fully trust me, they began to relate the horrific experiences they had while "tripping." Most of them were still having flashbacks, and they came without warning. To my amazement, they were describing demonic encounters just like the ones described by the missionaries. I shared what I had learned in the previous months of study. As they read the New Testament accounts of Jesus taking authority over the evil spirits, they believed that they, too, could be set free, and they were. It was pretty amazing. The first ones set free were setting the others free in a matter of weeks. They simply used the books to show examples of how demons work and then showed them in the Bible that Jesus set people free. Amazing stuff!

Talk about power-encounters!

I know these supernatural deliverances were what made this New Testament-type Christianity relevant to them. They had experienced dead religion and wanted no part of it. Talk about power-encounters! They needed them, and they received them! Yes, the Holy Spirit knew exactly what He was doing when He led me to "study to show myself approved" (see 2 Timothy 2:15).

About this time an evangelistic couple from Canada came to our area. Several of the young men went to hear them. They came back quite excited because they were dealing with demons and people were getting healed. Now my sweet parents were in the middle of all this with me, so I drug them over to the tent meeting. Sure enough, they were preaching a Full Gospel message with signs and wonders following.

Some were barefoot.

We met with them after the service and explained what was happening in our midst. I asked them if they would consider doing some teaching. By this time I was feeling overwhelmed. None of the churches in our area wanted these turned-on hippies to influence their young people. I guess I can understand their feelings. Like the time I took a group to visit my evangelical church. Some of them were barefoot. One had on overalls, no shirt, no shoes, and a brown Derby hat that he did not remove during the service. Now I was so thrilled with what was happening in their lives, I was past the outward appearance thing. But unfortunately, the straight-laced members of my church just did not have that kind of grace. Yes, they were happy that they were getting saved, but they just wanted them to be someplace else.

Jesus People.

The Canadian couple had a few more commitments in the Northwest, and then they agreed to return. What a godsend they were! We became a church with about four hundred attendees (Grammy and my parents were right in the middle of it all). Our worship was fantastic, and the new leaders brought wonderful pastor-teacher friends to minister to these Jesus People, as they became known. History shows us that we were a part of a sovereign move of God that began on the West Coast of America among hippie drug users. It is heartening now after more than thirty years to hear from some of the original young people in the group. They are pastors, evangelists, and missionaries. Yes, it really did take and they have been doing what Jesus did all these years!

Jesus is our hero and supreme example.

Yes, setting people free from spiritual bondages is not an easy thing. It can be a confusing, messy ministry. We certainly do not seek it out; however, we deal with it when it becomes necessary in fulfilling the assignments the Lord gives us. Most often in Jesus' ministry, He was walking along to some place when He was interrupted by the need, met it, and went on His way. He is our hero and supreme example!

Only Christians can do it.

It is very interesting that only in the Christian belief system dwells the power and authority that cause spirits to obey spoken commands. All other beliefs either worship and appease them or deny their existence. When confronted with spirits, their attempt to deal with the situation results in confusion, fear, and frustration. An example of this is in the following Scripture:

Acts 19:13-16

Then some of the itinerant Jewish exorcists took it upon themselves to call the name of the Lord Jesus over those who had evil spirits, saying, "We exorcise you by the Jesus whom Paul preaches." Also there were seven sons of Sceva, a Jewish chief priest, who did so. And the evil spirit answered and said, "Jesus I know, and Paul I know; but who are you?" Then the man in whom the evil spirit was leaped on them, overpowered them, and prevailed against them, so that they fled out of that house naked and wounded. NKJV

DWJD

- Only Spirit-filled Christians are authorized and empowered by Jesus Christ to successfully cast out demons. The demons know who has the authority and who does not. They will challenge us to find out if we know what we are doing.

- Demons give superhuman power to those they possess. We have nothing to fear when we engage them in the name of Jesus Christ and under the leading of the Holy Spirit.
- Superhuman power is reduced to nothing when the Christian boldly stands in the power of the blood of Christ and commands the spirit to obey in the name of Jesus Christ.

Intercessors are imperative.

If you are doing this type of ministry or desiring to, we urge you to ask God to give you believers who will cover you in prayer. We have over one hundred faithful intercessors that receive our monthly "Prayer Alert" and intercede on our behalf. Their prayers are so powerful that we can actually feel the effects—especially when we are in foreign countries where the spiritual battles are intense. Jesus Christ wants us to function as a body with everyone contributing according to their giftedness. Thank You, Lord, for our intercessors!

It Is Our Responsibility

Many Christians refer to the above "seven sons of Sceva" episode as a personal warning to never get involved with demons or deliverance. With a chuckle, they shrug their shoulders, and refer to this as what would happen if they got involved. Not so! This Scripture is a warning to pre-Christians. For Christians who know their authority and power, it is an invitation to exercise this authority and set people free!

The people who do not have a relationship with Jesus Christ have an ever-increasing dilemma. They are unknowingly being prevailed upon and seduced by demonic influences. Demons are literally leaping upon them, overpowering them, and causing some to run out of houses naked. Their minds are becoming so poisoned and twisted by drugs, lies, and hopelessness that the demons are causing them to commit suicide. The evening news is replete with children being kidnapped, sexually assaulted, and murdered. Our senses are being barraged with reports of murders, rapes, and evil violence. Every community and strata of society are being bombarded with horrific images of our youth being swallowed up by demonic powers beyond their control.

Their hope is Christ in us, the hope of glory!
Christian, we are the only hope for this lost and dying world. If we do not answer our Lord's call to go into our part of the world and set people free and do what He said we could do, then who will? We have the answer! It is Christ in us, the hope of glory. Jesus has given us His name, His authority, and His power to take up where He left off. Our only response is what Isaiah said, "Here am I, send me!"

Let's Practice
- James 1:22 says to *DO* what we have heard (read).
- Consider doing what is recommended in this chapter by referring to the "Let's Practice" in Appendix B, page 329-330.
- Do the Ministry Skill Assignment entitled, "Dealing with Demons."

Chapter Seven

WHERE DO WE GO FROM HERE?

Once we have discovered all that Jesus Christ has done for us, we are commanded to go tell others and teach them to observe everything He commanded.

Matthew 28:18-20
". . . All authority has been given to Me in heaven and on earth. *Go* therefore and make disciples of all the nations, baptizing them in the name of the Father and of the Son and of the Holy Spirit, teaching them to observe all things that I have commanded you; and lo, I am with you always, even to the end of the age." Amen. NKJV

Luke 9:2
He sent them to preach the kingdom of God and to heal the sick. NKJV

Matthew 10:7-8
". . . *go,* preach, saying, 'The kingdom of heaven is at hand.' Heal the sick, cleanse the lepers, raise the dead, and cast out demons. Freely you have received, freely give." NKJV

Go!

We can do it.
With a change of thinking and some training we can do what Jesus did. Jesus has empowered, authorized, and commanded us to go do what He did. It is more than going to church. It is more than going to a Bible study or prayer meeting. It means going into our part of the world and touching people

with the Gospel of salvation, empowerment of the Holy Spirit, physical healing, and setting them free from demonic bondages.

True miracles are needed.

We totally understand why Christians have been reluctant to answer the Lord's commands to "Go." Few know they should be doing it, and even less have been taught how. It takes a radical change in thinking and high-impact, hands-on training to change people's lives. Our point is this:

There are many around the world that will not be drawn to Jesus Christ unless they experience an authentic manifestation of God's glory.

John 14:11

"Believe me when I say that I am in the Father and the Father is in me; or at least believe on the evidence of the miracles themselves." NIV

DWJD

- Miracles may be necessary to authenticate our message as being from God.
- The messenger who preaches the Gospel of the Lord Jesus Christ, allowing for and expecting signs and wonders to follow, demonstrates that the message is from a life-changing God who is alive and real.

Where Do We Begin?

In the previous chapters, we have carefully documented how we came to not only believe in miracles but to expect God to do them through us. It took thirty years to get to where we are today, but it does not have to take that long for others to get there. We believe it can take about a year, perhaps two at the most. It all depends on how serious a believer is about pursuing God.

We believe the road to doing what Jesus did is very straight and simple. For some it will be easy. For others it requires a change of thinking. It seems that the more sophisticated and highly educated we are, the more difficult the journey. But it does not have to be that way. Jesus advocates becoming like a trusting child in how we believe and apply the Gospel to our personal lives.

To begin doing what Jesus did may require setting aside rigid mind-sets that have impaired our vision of who Jesus has made us to be. It does not matter how long one has been a Christian. The challenge is how long it takes to get equipped so we can set others free in the name of Jesus. It may seem difficult, but it can be done.

Training should be through the local church.
Where is the logical place for believers to be trained to do what Jesus did? We believe it should be through a believer's local church, not by running off to every conference and "revival" they hear about. It is the deep longing for the reality of the supernatural that causes people to be constantly on the search for that "something" they know they are lacking.

Systematic teaching and hands-on experience in a classroom environment is the best way to meet this need. We know from firsthand experience that this model works extremely well. The following Appendix A outlines exactly how pastors are using the *Ambassador Series* and *The Ministry Skill Series* curriculum in Ministry Training Centers in their local churches.

All training must have a hands-on practicum element.
In our opinion, whatever training you decide to use, it must have a hands-on practicum element that allows the students to be exposed to the supernatural in a safe environment.

By laying a strong scriptural foundation concurrent with the practicum sessions, we avoid non-biblical experiences and excesses. We do this by basing our experiences on the Word.

When hungry Christians go to conferences or revivals in other locations, they can easily get caught up in the emotional fervor and fall into copycat behavior based in the soul realm rather than authentic, Holy Spirit manifestations.

The power of God.
We are contending for the powerful expressions of the Holy Spirit as demonstrated by our Lord Jesus Christ. As we have stated, there are ample Scripture references for us to follow in all of these things. We sometimes see the power of God come upon people in such a mighty way that they cannot stand under the weight of it. That is authentic. But to get into a copycat behavior where everyone lines up so they can fall down smacks of manipulation and contrived behavior. We do not think the Holy Spirit needs our assistance. It is sad when Christians develop the attitude that nothing of value is happening unless they are on the floor. Show us that in Scripture.

Here is How it Could Work

We are not advocating that this type of ministry training would replace or alter a church's weekend services. Rather, it would evolve something like the following:

- The senior pastor determines that training his congregation to do what Jesus did is something the Lord is leading him to do.
- Training classes with practicum are offered on a once-a-week basis.
- Those completing the classes become or enhance the organized prayer ministry in the church (after-service prayer, hospital visitations, emergency counseling, etc.)
- Those students with identified gifts of discerning of spirits, words of knowledge and wisdom, and faith can be trained and formed in teams to set people free from demonic bondages. This, of course, is under pastoral oversight. Through a structured interview process, this can be a wonderful ministry to church members. Again, this

should be done in the context of the local church where proper accountability and follow-up exist.

- The students who complete the training will have become effective marketplace ministers. They will be doing what Jesus did, and will they be excited!

Weekend services can be "visitor sensitive."

The classroom instruction is at the church, and the trained believers can relieve the pastoral staff of much prayer and personal ministry, but the actual weekend church services are altered very little. We feel they should be "visitor sensitive" in the sense that all members and attendees can feel safe to invite their friends, neighbors, relatives and co-workers. By "feel safe" we mean members will not have to worry about something happening that they cannot explain. People will not risk looking foolish. However, the trained prayer team should always be available for after-service prayer ministry, including prayer for healing, etc.

Mid-week believers' meeting.

Mid-week services can be structured as a believers' meeting with the release of the gifts of the Holy Spirit. Leadership should inform those in attendance that the focus is definitely for believers. These meetings can be powerful and life changing. Prolonged worship allows people to truly enter into the presence of the Lord. Corporate singing in tongues is a tremendously edifying spiritual experience. The key to successful believers' meetings is to have strong platform leadership that is sensitive to the Holy Spirit's leading and will not allow a bunch of nonsense. When the Holy Spirit is directing, everything will be done decently and in order by edifying, exhorting, and comforting the worshipers. The end result is that the Lord Jesus Christ will be exalted.

Small group growth.

Small group leaders who have been given ministry training can encourage the release of the supernatural gifts and ministry to those in attendance at their meetings. From years of personal experience, we know it adds the dynamic that causes growth and excitement in the lives of those involved.

Strategy for the end-time harvest.

Our burning desire is to see believers trained to be effective marketplace ministers just like Jesus was. He wants us to lead people into salvation, baptism in the Holy Spirit, healing, revelation knowledge, and set them free from spiritual bondages. Then He wants us to bring them to church and disciple them so they can do the same. That is how the world will be won. That is a fine strategy for the end-time harvest. If you are not already engaged in this awesome and eternal activity, please join us!

So, there you have it! It is really pretty simple—properly train believers and show them how to do what Jesus did, and they will!

Appendix A

How to Establish a Ministry Training Center

Every Church is a Training Center

The local church is the logical place to begin training Christians to become effective "marketplace ministers." That is, effective disciples that know how to share their Christian testimony, lead people to Christ, pray for them to be baptized in the Holy Spirit, and pray for the sick. Advanced training would include how to hear from God, the discerning of spirits, and setting people free from spiritual bondages. Over the last twenty years, we have proven this can be done without disciples becoming weird. Ministry Training Centers (MTC) is producing biblically based lay ministers who can relieve the salaried staff by assuming most of the prayer ministry, hospital visitations, and other time-consuming areas of ministry.

We learn by doing.

It is a major decision for pastors to begin training members to operate in the supernatural. Many pastors want to avoid the recent "excesses" reminiscent of the Methodist camp meetings at Cane Ridge, Kentucky in 1801.[1] The excesses can be avoided when the training is biblical, well thought out, high quality, practical, and totally reproducible. To be effective, the training must include a balance of sound theology, while giving multiple opportunities for every student to experience hands-on ministry. Everything should be done under the watchful eyes of mature trainers, who can

---

[1] Vinson Synan, *The Holiness Pentecostal Tradition,* (Grand Rapids MI, 1997), page 12. "Their 'Godly hysteria' included such phenomena as falling, jerking, barking like dogs, falling into trances, the 'holy laugh' and 'such wild dances as David performed before the Ark of the Lord.'"

discern the difference between authentic manifestations of the Holy Spirit and weirdness. Using *Doing What Jesus Did* and *The Ambassador Series* as the curriculum, trainers have everything they need to produce effective, reproducing disciples of Jesus Christ.

The Ambassador Series

Using the author's six-volume *Ambassador Series* and this book, local churches can establish a Ministry Training Center in any part of the world. It is remarkable that the curriculum works for a meeting place in Third World countries, as well as mega-churches in America and everything in between. We attribute this to the Holy Spirit's influence and anointing that accompany the teaching and hands-on practicum training sessions.

First, select an equipper.

We recommend that the senior pastor not be the one who runs the Ministry Training Center, especially in larger churches. He or she is already too busy. We do recommend that the senior pastor be a part of the MTC teaching team. The person in charge must have a vision for training people to do what Jesus did. Obviously, the instructors must have experience operating in the supernatural if they are going to successfully teach others how to do it. You cannot show someone how to work with the Holy Spirit unless you have done it.

Teachers with experience and a hunger for operating in supernatural ministry obviously make the best trainers. Though hard to find, they exist throughout the Body of Christ. Retired or returning missionaries can be a terrific resource. Being trained by leaders in the local church who are operating in the supernatural of God is the quickest and best way to transfer the same anointing to those being trained. This is how we train MTC trainers. The students start doing what their trainers have been doing.

This is how Jesus trained the first disciples. This is how it can be done today. First, they watched Jesus do it. Then, they helped Jesus do it. Next, Jesus watched as they did it. Finally, they did it when Jesus was no longer with them. Today, we call this mentoring.

Second, train the trainers.
Leaders with a calling to disciple Christians are encouraged to attend a two-day, DWJD Seminar. The train-the-trainer seminar is designed for pastors, teachers, and leaders. In a Friday night and Saturday, leaders are shown how to teach *The Ambassador Series* and conduct the six ministry skills from *Doing What Jesus Did*. The leaders are then authorized to order and teach the curriculum. Audio and videotapes of the six-volume *Ambassador Series* are available as teaching aids for leaders. The tapes are reviewed prior to teaching the lessons and are full of teaching tips and ideas to make the curriculum come alive.

Administrative and practicum guides are made available to leaders so they can put together a successful ministry institute. Any leader, pastor, or teacher who has attended a DWJD Seminar will be fully equipped to oversee or conduct an enduring Ministry Training Center.

Third, plan for a nine-month institute.
We recommend a nine-month schedule for an MTC institute. In the USA, it should be offered concurrent with the school year (September-June) with a graduation immediately following. The three-hour, once-a-week class is offered in an evening format. Leaders wonder if people are willing to make such a long commitment. We have addressed this issue by having them commit to twelve weeks at a time. By the time they have finished the first twelve weeks, you cannot keep them away! We have very little attrition because of the exciting hands-on ministry skill sessions. The graduation is a special time where they receive a formal diploma in practical ministry along with the laying on of hands and being commissioned as ambassadors for Christ.

MTC is a proven concept.

The MTC institutes worldwide are doing what Jesus did. The classes are structured for maximum effectiveness. MTC trains the trainers how to train others. Effective discipleship must be more than a teacher conducting classes where students take notes. True discipleship is personally working with disciples until they know what the mentor knows and can do what the mentor can do. That is how Jesus did it. MTC functions the same way.

A Typical Class Session

Worship and teaching.

First, strong worship of the Lord helps put everyone into the right frame of mind. Second, the trainers teach two lessons on the many facets of living the abundant life in Christ, obeying God's Word, and doing marketplace ministry. Every student receives a comprehensive teacher's manual where they record personal illustrations so they can re-teach the lesson in the future.

Divide into practicum groups.

Between lessons, the entire class is divided into groups of twelve or less where every student practices the ministry skill from *Doing What Jesus Did*. Every student is scheduled to demonstrate the ministry skills in conjunction with the teaching of *The Ambassador Series*. This is done until every disciple feels confident to attempt the skills in the marketplace. Over the nine months, all six ministry skills are practiced until mastered: leading people to Christ, the Holy Spirit baptism, healing the sick, hearing from God, healing the sick by revelation, and dealing with demons. An optional preaching practicum is offered for those preparing for public ministry.

Everyone receives ministry.

The highlight of the weekly gathering is each student knowing they will both give and receive one-on-one prayer ministry whenever there is a need. When it is time for a student to demonstrate the assigned ministry skill, it is done within a group of twelve or less with a trained leader. Afterward, they can request personal ministry for current needs. The others are encouraged to respond and pray over the person. The Holy Spirit will often manifest in profound ways, using another student through whom revelation or healing will take place. Everyone gets to minister and receive ministry. Everyone goes home praising God for what they have personally experienced each week. The love quotient and bonding produced in these classes are amazing. It produces true, biblical *koinonia*.

Graduation comes after doing it for real.

In order to graduate and receive a diploma in Practical Ministry, every student minister must demonstrate that they can do all six ministry skills. The final "exam" requires each student minister to take what he or she has learned and "do it for real" in the marketplace. They must make two attempts to lead someone to Christ, two attempts to lead believers into the Holy Spirit baptism, and two attempts to heal the sick. All of the attempts must be done outside of the classroom, in the marketplace.

Confidence is catching.

During the last month of training, the testimonies of doing what Jesus did "for real" start coming in. Student after student gives spontaneous reports of healings, deliverances, and various miracles as they "attempted" to fulfill the marketplace assignments. It always brings a smile to the instructors when they hear exciting testimonies of how the Holy Spirit "took over" the attempt and turned it into a genuine "doing what Jesus did" success story.

Months before, these Christian "laymen" were ineffective and even fearful of reaching out in the name of Christ. By this time, they are going into their part of the world and doing greater things for God than they ever dreamed possible.

Here is How to Get Started

Trainers must experience the MTC mentoring dynamic. The hands-on practicum is the heart of the training and cannot be learned by reading a book. We have developed the fast-paced DWJD Seminars so pastors and leaders can experience how to conduct the ministry skill sessions. Teacher aids are also available for teachers to start an exciting MTC in their church.

Seminars

We cannot improve on Jesus' strategy for training believers. He put His life into a small group of "trainers" who turned the world upside down. Here is how it is done:

- MTC will "train the trainers" in regional DWJD Seminars. These are open to any active leader involved in pastoring, teaching, evangelizing or missionary work.
- The pastor of an established church must initiate the inquiry for hosting a seminar.
- Tentative dates, seminar location, and costs for hosting a regional DWJD Seminar are negotiated and agreed upon with the host church.
- Other pastors in the region with a vision for ministry training are contacted and invited to participate.
- Once a final estimate of participating churches and attendees is confirmed, a firm date, and seminar location are established.
- Seminar fees, updates, and other details are available through the website: **www.dwjd.info**

DWJD Seminar content:
- The seminars are conducted on a Friday night and all day Saturday.
- **Leaders learn how to:**
  - Teach *The Ambassador Series* and learn how to minister and teach the six DWJD ministry skills.

313

- Prepare for and conduct a nine-month, church-based MTC institute.
- Implement the administrative tasks, including ordering materials, and conducting an MTC graduation.

The word is spreading fast.

After starting our first Ministry Training Center in our home church in the fall of 1996, by the end of six years there are over one hundred training locations functioning in seventeen countries. The need is overwhelming! Christian leaders all over the world are hungering for a way to introduce the supernatural of God into their churches in a sane and biblical way. Pastors who lacked confidence in doing this kind of ministry are now rejoicing. They are confidently leading their people into the Holy Spirit baptism, acting on a word of knowledge for healing, and teaching others how to do the same. Genuine excitement has returned to the church as they are doing what Jesus did.

The Curriculum

Doing What Jesus Did

You are holding the key to a successful Ministry Training Center. This book should be required reading for everyone enrolled in an MTC institute. Each chapter is dedicated to showing how we can minister in the revelation and power of the Holy Spirit. It will become the handbook for doing the things Jesus said we could do.

The Ambassador Series

The Ambassador Series is a three-level, seventy-two lesson discipleship training course authored by John and Sonja Decker and is being used in churches worldwide. These lessons are the academic segment of the curriculum used in all MTC institutes. There are a total of six volumes.

The Ambassador Series is composed of Discipleship One, Two, and Three, each of which uses two volumes of the series. Each level consists of twenty-four lessons in two volumes, taught in twelve weeks. Six weeks are dedicated to learning each one of the ministry skills. The content of each lesson can be reviewed by visiting our website:

www.ministrytraining.org

Discipleship One:
Foundations for Discovery and *Disciplines of the Disciple.*
The ministry skills: Leading People to Christ and Leading Christians into the Holy Spirit Baptism.

Discipleship Two:
Bible Basics and *The Christian Life.*
The ministry skills: Learning How to Heal the Sick and Hearing from God.

Discipleship Three:
Kingdom Living and *Equipped for Leadership.*
The ministry skills: Healing the Sick by Revelation, Dealing with Demons, and Preaching the Full Gospel (optional).

The MTC Institute

Discipleship One, Two, and Three can be completed in a nine-month time frame, allowing three hours per week for the ministry training. Two forty-five minute lessons and a forty-five minute practicum session are conducted each week.

Graduation
Both *The Ambassador Series* and the six ministry skills are designed to equip believers to eventually go into their part of the world and make disciples by doing what Jesus did. The course combines the teaching of orthodox and very practical theology with at least one-third of the time dedicated to learning the six ministry skills. The course equips disciples with the tools necessary for effective evangelism. Jesus preached, taught, and healed the sick. Graduates of MTC can do what He did.

A Personal Invitation

If you have read this far, you undoubtedly know that our (John and Sonja's) passion is to see the Body of Christ equipped to do what Jesus did. We are assisting pastors in establishing Ministry Training Centers in local churches around the globe. Please contact the MTC offices if you are interested in learning how to start a Ministry Training Center by attending a DWJD Seminar. We schedule seminars by direct invitation from senior pastors. If you are a pastor that has read this book and are interested in pursuing ministry training, you are invited to contact the MTC offices. Planning will then begin for a seminar in your region. We would consider it a privilege and an honor to serve pastors of local churches anywhere in the world!

To contact John and Sonja Decker:

- E-mail: mail@ministrytraining.org

- Regular mail: P.O. Box 3631, Bend, OR 97707

For more information regarding:

- *The Ambassador Series* curriculum.
  www.ministrytraining.org

- DWJD Seminar dates, locations, and costs.
  www.dwjd.info

To order additional copies of *Doing What Jesus Did:*

- Toll Free: 1-877-866-9406

- On Line: www.ministrytraining.org

Appendix B

Let's Practice
Doing What Jesus Did

We encourage those who are followers of Christ to begin putting into practice what He said they could do. The purpose of this book is to help equip believers in Jesus Christ to do what He did. Each chapter presents a different ministry skill that takes some effort to master. When all six ministry skills are mastered, the Christian would become a very powerful and effective marketplace minister. We strongly recommend completing the assignments in this final section of *Doing What Jesus Did.*

James 1:22 says, *"Do not merely listen to the word, and so deceive yourselves. Do what it says."* NIV

First Step: *DECIDE*
- To learn the skills *as an individual,* working with another Christian or
- Learn the skills in *a group* study.

Second Step: *DO IT!*

DWJD as individuals:

- Find another person to read and discuss this book with you. Agree to meet on a regular basis with the goal of practicing what is presented in each chapter.
- Attempt to complete the ministry skill assignments for each chapter.
- When the assignment refers to a "group," apply it to the two of you.

317

- If there is a portion of the chapter you find difficult, be honest and admit your feelings. Study the supporting Scriptures to see if you can really believe what it is telling you to do.
- Keep reading, praying for the Lord's help, and attempting to practice what is recommended.
- Finally, attempt to exercise the ministry skills in the marketplace.

as a group study:

- Pray for a group leader to assume the responsibility for a *weekly* study group.
- Plan on spending two months or more discussing this book, allowing a minimum of one or more weeks in each chapter.
- Each person should obtain a copy of this book and prepare to do the weekly assignment for each chapter in Appendix B.
- One or two people should prepare to fulfill the ministry skill assignment each week.
- The others should critique how well they shared or demonstrated the ministry skills by offering constructive comments and positive feedback.
- Make time for personal prayer at the end of the meeting for those needing prayer. This is especially important during the study of chapters 4, 5, and 6.
- Always end the study by thanking and praising God for what happened.
- Finally, each person should attempt to exercise the ministry skills in the marketplace and report to the group what happened.

INTRODUCTION

SHARE WHAT YOU BELIEVE ABOUT MIRACLES

The purpose of this assignment is to prepare believers to share what they believe the Bible says about miracles. This exercise will give an opportunity for Christians who have never shared with others to do so. There is great joy that comes with being able to share your beliefs about Christ and what He has done for us. Even though talking about miracles may seem difficult at first, it will become easier once we have done it with other Christians. The Holy Spirit is always with us to help us share our beliefs. This introductory assignment will better prepare Christians to gain the confidence to complete the remaining assignments.

How to share what you believe about miracles:

- Read the introduction of this book.
- Take time to put in writing your beliefs and conclusions from the pages of the introduction of this book. Especially make notes regarding what the Scripture references mean to you personally.
- Prepare and share a three-to-five minute talk on what you believe about miracles and what the Bible says about miracles happening today.
- Share about any miracles you have witnessed or experienced. Share how they affected your life.
- Ask for feedback and constructive comments that may help you regarding how and what you shared and how you may say it better in the future.

Preparation:

- Make a short outline of what you want to share.
- Organize it according to the points in the introduction of this book.
- Practice your talk and time yourself.
- Avoid rambling and providing too much detail. Five minutes goes very fast, so keep an eye on your watch.
- Remember, others will have to do this assignment also.
- Have fun. Use humor if it applies.
- Relax!

CHAPTER ONE
MINISTRY SKILL ASSIGNMENT ONE

LEADING PEOPLE TO CHRIST

Sharing your story of how you came to Christ

Read chapter 1 and prepare a five-minute story of how you came to personally know Jesus Christ. Use the recommendations in this chapter to help you prepare by using the five discussion points below. Practice your story at home before sharing with the group. Remember to keep it simple by just telling what happened as outlined below:

- Tell who you were and the circumstances in your life prior to coming to Christ.
- What caused you to look to God?
- What happened when you surrendered?
- Now what is happening?
- End your story with a simple (role-play) invitation for those listening to receive Jesus Christ into their life. Say something similar to:

"He did all this for me, and He will do it for you, too. Would you like to ask Jesus Christ into your life now? I'll help you do it."

When anyone responds, then simply ask him or her to pray the following prayer with you:

"Jesus Christ, come into my life. I repent of all my sin. Forgive me for what I've said and done that were wrong. I receive You as my Savior and Lord. Thank You for forgiving me. Amen."

After you gain confidence by practicing sharing your story with fellow believers, pray for opportunities to share your story with pre-Christians. The Lord will give you many opportunities.

CHAPTER TWO
MINISTRY SKILL ASSIGNMENT TWO

LEADING CHRISTIANS INTO THE HOLY SPIRIT BAPTISM

Sharing what the experience means to you

The purpose of this assignment is to prepare believers to share how God is using them since they were baptized in the Holy Spirit. This assignment will also open opportunities to lead other believers into the *Holy Spirit baptism*. At the end of sharing, give an invitation (role-play) for those listening to allow you to pray with them to receive the Holy Spirit baptism.

Read chapter 2 and prepare to share your experiences with the Holy Spirit.

* **Prepare** a short outline so you can share a five-minute talk on how God is using you since you were baptized in the Holy Spirit.
* **Start** by sharing the events leading up to *when* you were baptized in the Holy Spirit and how it has made a difference in serving the Lord and ministering to others. Did it help your prayer life? In witnessing to others?
* **Continue** by giving some personal examples of how God has used you to demonstrate His power and how you have helped others since being baptized in the Holy Spirit.
* **Finish** your talk by encouraging those believers who are listening to receive the gift of the Holy Spirit. Say:

"The Holy Spirit desires to empower all of us to be better witnesses. I would like to pray with anyone desiring to be baptized in the Holy Spirit. If you want this gift now, I would love to pray with you."

- **Pray** with those responding:

  "Jesus, baptize me in the Holy Spirit. Fill me with Your power so I can be a better witness for You. Thank You, Lord. I have received. Help me now to release my spiritual language. Amen."

- **Continue** to minister until everyone releases their spiritual language (role-play).

Hints:

- Share what happened the moment you knew for sure the Lord had baptized you in the Holy Spirit. Share when you released your spiritual language. Share what has happened since you were empowered by the Holy Spirit.
- Practice your talk and time yourself. The time goes very fast, so keep an eye on your watch.
- Have fun! Remember, others in your group have to do this assignment, too. So relax!

CHAPTER THREE
MINISTRY SKILL ASSIGNMENT THREE

LEARNING HOW TO HEAL THE SICK

Sharing what you believe about divine healing and offering to pray for the sick

Read chapter 3 and prepare to deliver a five-minute message responding to the following statements:

- What the Bible says about divine healing.
- What I believe about divine healing.
- Today, may I pray for anyone who needs healing?

Prepare to share your response to these statements with the people in your group using the following suggestions:

- Refer to a concordance and select up to five Scriptures that promise healing and include them in a short outline.
- Include key phrases in your outline about what you believe about healing with any *testimonies* you may have about healing in your own life.
- End your story with an invitation for anyone listening that needs healing to be prayed for at the end of the sharing time. Be prepared to *pray for those needing healing.*

Praying for the sick: It is highly recommended that prayer for the sick be offered to anyone not feeling well *at the end* of each meeting, just after the sharing time. Those who shared should be the ones to pray for the sick.

Reason for this assignment: Jesus said believers in Him would be able to do the things that He did, including healing the sick. This assignment gives new ministers opportunities to not only express what they believe, but to pray for those who need healing. Mark 16:20 says the Lord will work with us confirming the Word we preach with signs following. Let us give the Lord the opportunity to do that.

CHAPTER FOUR
MINISTRY SKILL ASSIGNMENT FOUR

HEARING FROM GOD

Do what He says

Read chapter 4 and prayerfully prepare your mind and heart prior to meeting together.

- The day prior to the weekly meeting, each person should read and meditate in three to five chapters from the New Testament with pen and paper in hand.
- Ask the Holy Spirit, *"Lord, please cause me to see, understand, and record the fresh insights You want me to know from Your Word today."*
- Each person prays in his or her spiritual language as they meditate in the Bible.
- Each person should record anything and everything they are inspired to write during this time with the Lord. It is recommended that they spend from thirty minutes to an hour each day for this devotional exercise.
- Each person brings his or her notes to the next meeting.

Meet together:

- Open in prayer, relinquishing control of the meeting to the Holy Spirit.

- **First part of meeting:**
  Spend this time sharing what the Holy Spirit revealed during each person's quiet time the past week. Each person should comment regarding his or her experience. Did they hear from the Holy Spirit?

- **Second part of meeting:**
  Spend this time praying for persons with the *most critical needs* in their lives:

  - Place the persons, one at a time, in a chair in the middle of the people gathered.
  - Have the person in the chair share their critical need, *very briefly*. Have the person refrain from going into detail.
  - Begin praying over the person by everyone laying a hand on his or her shoulder and praying in their spiritual language for a few minutes.
  - Encourage each person to participate, allowing the Holy Spirit to spontaneously give answers to the critical need as they pray.
  - Limit the number of people with critical prayer needs to not more than two each week. This exercise normally takes a lot of time.
  - Conclude in thanksgiving and praise for what God did.
  - End on time.

> # CHAPTER FIVE
> # MINISTRY SKILL ASSIGNMENT FIVE

HEALING THE SICK BY REVELATION

Read chapter 5 and prepare to meet together.

- *Continue* the weekly quiet time assignment from chapter 4 by having each person read and meditate in several chapters from the New Testament during their daily quiet time with pen and paper in hand.
- Ask the Holy Spirit, *"Lord, please cause me to see, understand, and record the fresh insights You want me to know from Your Word today."*
- Each person prays in his or her spiritual language as they meditate in the Bible, recording anything and everything they are inspired to write during this time.
- Each person should attempt to increase the time to an hour each day for this exercise. Each person brings his or her notes to the next meeting.
- Each person should ask the Holy Spirit to lead them to *a friend who is in pain or is not feeling well, and invite them to come to the next meeting.*

Meet together:

- Open in prayer, relinquishing control of the meeting to the Holy Spirit.

- **First part of meeting:**
  Spend this time sharing what the Holy Spirit revealed during each person's quiet time the past week. Each person should comment regarding his or her experience with the Holy Spirit.

- **Second part of meeting:**

  - Spend this time praying for those that are not feeling well or in pain, allowing the Holy Spirit to reveal how He wants to heal them.
  - Have the person sit in a chair in the middle of the gathering. The others should come and lay hands on them. Everyone should start by praying softly in his or her spiritual language, *asking the Holy Spirit to reveal how best to pray.*
  - Have each person attempt to hear from the Holy Spirit and pray accordingly.
  - Ask the person after all prayer is complete, "Tell us what is happening?" Allow the person to be honest and give testimony of what happened.
  - Invite the next person needing healing to sit in the "hot seat" and continue as before.
  - Encourage those who heard from the Holy Spirit to give a short testimony to how it influenced the way they prayed.
  - End the meeting in prayer, thanking and praising God for what happened.

CHAPTER SIX
MINISTRY SKILL ASSIGNMENT SIX

DEALING WITH DEMONS

Read chapter 6 and prepare for the weekly meeting.

- The group leader should *notify the senior pastor's office* of the church he or she attends regarding what the purpose is for the weekly meetings.
- *Continue* the same weekly quiet time assignments outlined for chapters 4 and 5.
- Each person reads and meditates in a series of chapters during their daily quiet time from the New Testament with pen and paper in hand as they pray in tongues.
- Each person prays asking the Lord to reveal insights from the Word and then record their thoughts. Each person brings his or her notes to the next meeting.
- Each person should *ask the Lord to lead them to a Christian friend who is experiencing severe bondage, spiritual confusion, or attacks from the enemy.*
- Interview the friend thoroughly to make sure they have repented of all sin that may have caused the problem. (This assumes they want to be set free.)
- Call the group leader and schedule the person for the next available meeting. Do not schedule more than *two people* for each meeting.
- The group leader should *notify the senior pastor's office* of the church where the friend attends explaining how the group intends to minister and offer to report the results of the ministry. The group leader should also *keep his or her pastor aware of what is happening* in the weekly meetings.

Meet together:
- Open in prayer, relinquishing control of the meeting to the Holy Spirit.

- **First part of meeting:**

  Spend this time sharing what the Holy Spirit revealed during each person's quiet time the past week.

- **Second part of meeting:**

  - Spend this time ministering to the one or two guests that are experiencing spiritual difficulties, allowing the Holy Spirit to reveal *IF spirits are involved.*

  - Have the person sit in a chair in the middle of the gathering, while the others lay hands on them. Everyone should start by praying softly in his or her spiritual language, asking the Holy Spirit to reveal the source of the person's problem.

  - Explain that the *goal is to discern the presence of spirits.* If there is *no confirming evidence* that spirits are the source of the problem, the group leader should not allow the manufacturing of something that is not revealed by the Holy Spirit.

  - Minister according to the recommendations in all the *DWJD* boxes in chapter 6 *if spirits* are the source of the problem.

  - Ask the person after all prayer is complete, "What did the Lord do for you tonight?" Allow the person to be honest and give testimony of what happened.

  - Invite the next person needing ministry to sit in the "hot seat" for ministry.

  - Encourage those who prayed and truly discerned the source of the problem to give a short testimony to how the discernment manifested and how it helped him or her to minister.

  - End the meeting in prayer, thanking and praising God for what happened.

  - Notify the senior pastor's office of each guest's home church of what happened.

To Order Additional Copies

On Line: www.ministrytraining.org

or

Call Toll Free: 1-877-866-9406